BARTY PHILLIPS

THE COUNTRY HOUSE BOOK

Salem House Publishers
Topsfield, Massachusetts

First published in the United States by
Salem House Publishers, 1988
462 Boston Street, Topsfield, MA01983.

Library of Congress Cataloging in Publication Data:

Phillips, Barty.
  The country house book.

Includes index.

  1. Interior decoration.   2. Decoration and ornament,
Rustic.   I. Title
NK1986.R8P45 1988   728.3'7'091734   87-20502
ISBN: 0-88162-316-4

Filmset by Advanced Filmsetters (Glasgow) Ltd
Colour reproductions by Swains (London) Ltd
Printed and bound in Italy
by New Interlitho S.p.a., Milan

CONTRIBUTORS

Country House Architecture	Gillian Darley
Cottage Style	Sarah Graham
Farmhouse Style	Linda Sonntag
Manor House Style	Jane Newdick
Colonial Style	Sarah Graham
French Provincial Style	Linda Sonntag
Mediterranean Style	Jane Newdick
Country Gardens	Susan Conder
Special Features	Sarah Graham

Senior Editor	Fiona MacIntyre
Editor	Alison Wormleighton

Art Director	Frank Phillips
Designer	John Meek

Picture Research	Jan Croot, Jane Lewis, Philippa Lewis

All available information about the
photographs is given on page 304.
The publishers cannot provide further details.

CONTENTS

INTRODUCTION

COUNTRY HOMES and the ideal of a country life have always held great appeal. Today, in a world becoming more technology-oriented, country house style epitomizes something we feel we are losing: a way of life based on the earth and the things that grow in it and live off it. We are enchanted by the seeming simplicity and prettiness of country house style. But what really delights is more basic —its sense of place and season and its general capacity to make sense of its surroundings. It is a look based on practicality, not sentimentality.

Country house architecture originally reflected the nature of the local countryside: the weather conditions and the materials available. Similarly, crops were grown and animals raised which suited the local soil and the available fodder; food was eaten, prepared and preserved in the manner most convenient for the area. Thus you get, in many parts of France, the great attics for drying plums to make prunes; in the wooded areas of colonial outposts you find clapboarding, which was the cheapest form of insulation; and in hot countries like Australia, there are cast iron balconies running right round the house.

Traditional country skills, such as preserving, bottling, crochet and patchwork, are still very popular. Though they originated in the days when life was lived at the pace of a horse and cart rather than an estate car, they are perfectly in context within a modern lifestyle. Wood, though expensive, is being turned into excellent modern versions of country furniture, and old furniture is still available which is very much in keeping today. Collections of smaller items reflecting classic country crafts and pursuits—whether actually in use or simply on display—fit in equally well, as do traditional decorative schemes.

The country house is presented here in many of its forms: the well-proportioned austerity of the French provincial farmhouse; the dark, cave-like interior of a Mediterranean fisherman's home; the imported grandeur of the medieval manor house; the simple furnishings and folk art of the colonial home; the comfortable practicality of the farmhouse; and the roses-round-the-door charm of the English country cottage.

For each style of country house, an analysis of how the look can be achieved, in terms of wall, floor and window treatments, furniture and accessories, is followed by a detailed look at each room in turn. Also featured are country collections—items often associated with that particular style. Separate sections cover major aspects of country house architecture and the principal types of country garden.

Gardens, of course, have always been an integral part of country houses and country style. The Mediterranean garden is a splendid clash of reds and puces in banks of terracotta pots, or painted cans marching down a white staircase. In more temperate zones the sitting-out area will be a lush shelter of foliage and herbaceous plants, while in warmer climates it may be shaded by vines. The manor house garden, with its staff of full-time gardeners to plan it, plant it, weed it and water it, has taken many forms, depending upon what was fashionable at the time.

Above all, the garden has related to the house. Most country homes have porches, verandas, patios, conservatories, French windows, stable doors or similar devices linking them to the garden beyond.

Primarily a celebration of the countryside, country house style is based on certain fundamental components: natural materials and colours, functional design, good workmanship, home skills—and the relationship of indoors to outdoors, which is all too easy to forget in modern cosmopolitan life.

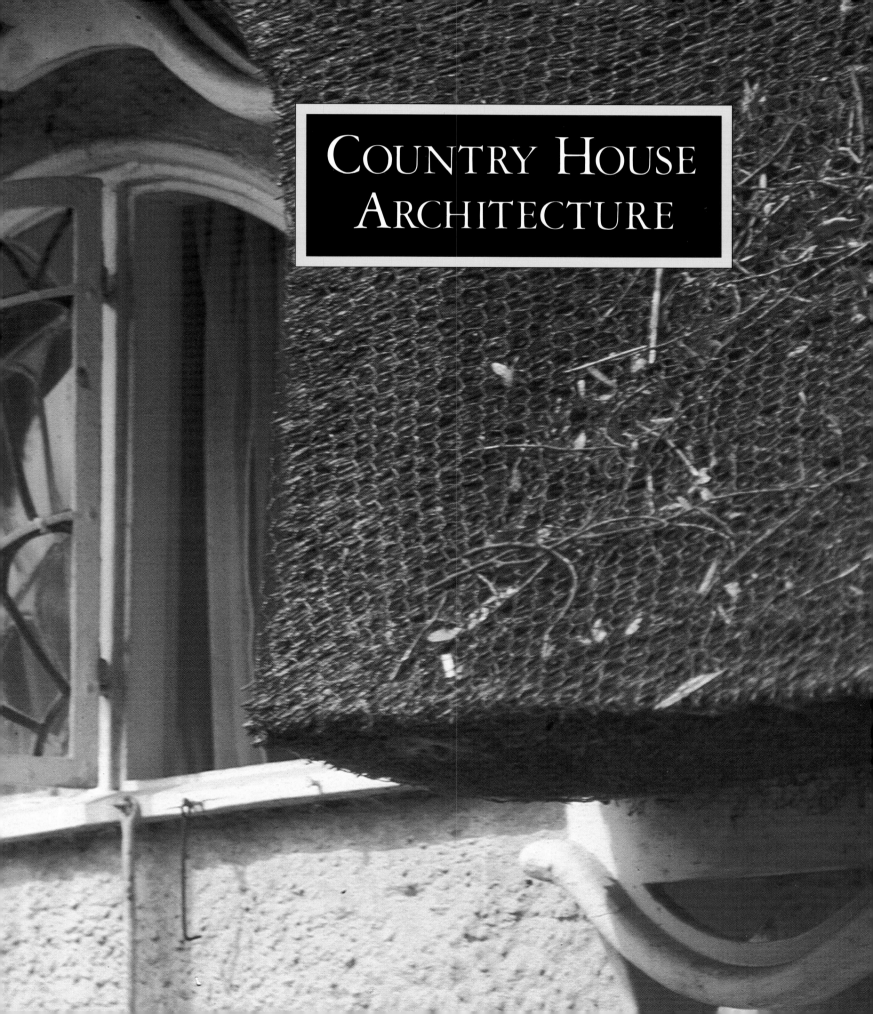

COUNTRY HOUSE
ARCHITECTURE

It is hard to imagine, looking at houses today, that in the past each small area of a country had an utterly distinct style of architecture. Traditional buildings were designed for the local weather, extremes of temperature, even the light, and the builder used whatever materials were to hand. In Europe these commonsense ideas determined the way farmhouses, village houses and cottages, even manor houses, were designed, well into the 18th century. (In countries settled later by Europeans, the traces of the old traditions lingered on even longer, as people hung on to the familiar trademarks of their domestic architecture.) But the Industrial Revolution eventually changed everything, and now, in the 20th century, houses are built more or less in the same fashion all over the developed world. The old understanding has gone so that we treasure all the more what remains of the traditional.

STYLE

The traditional architecture of Europe spread outwards across the world that Europeans settled. So, too, did the little touches of architectural fashion that came, often on the classical route from Renaissance Italy to 17th and 18th century northern Europe and then to the US. The details did not, on the whole, affect the choice of materials or the fact that houses had to be practical, but they did suggest the way to design, say, a grand window, a staircase or the mouldings in wood or plaster.

The classical style was widely used into the 19th century. It was sufficiently suited to domestic needs that the Georgian or colonial styles lingered on long after they had ceased to be fashionable in the big cities. Whether in Ireland or upstate New York, the results were remarkably similar, partly due to the exchange of ideas from pattern books.

In the countryside things always move more slowly. Nevertheless, in 18th century England the new, richer farmers became conscious that a medieval house was no longer quite the thing. Often they just attached a smart Georgian front to it.

The mansions led the way and the smaller houses followed. In most European countries you can see the ways that the architecture of the great houses moved down the social scale. In France, for example, the mansard roof, the oval window at attic level, even the sweep of outside steps became the hallmark of the professional man's house on the edge of country town or village. In the 'new world', where there was less social hierarchy, the comfortable farmhouse-type was the model for anybody moderately well-off. There the pattern tended to be taken from the architecture of the

An early, timber-framed house disguised by a Georgian brick addition. Many apparently 18th century houses are refronted Tudor farms and show how farmers managed to be both fashion-conscious and economical at the same time.

A medieval manor house has been added to in the 18th century, with a section slotted in between two wings. The plastered part, with sash windows, is Georgian; the gables to either side of this section are largely Tudor or earlier.

A 20th century manor house, designed by Sir Edwin Lutyens on the model of a 17th century manor.

An 18th century village house in New England shows the same attention to symmetry as its English counterpart.

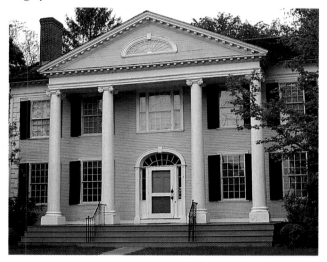

Another American style: here, a Federal house of 1817 from Connecticut. Houses like this were based on classical examples published in architectural pattern books, then copied and adapted on American soil.

country from which the immigrants had come. In Australia and New Zealand, where early settlers were mostly British, the influence of Scotland and its architecture can be seen. The process goes on world-wide.

Return to the traditional

The last important influence on the style of architecture in the country was, appropriately enough, those early tra-ditional ways of building. Around the turn of the 20th century, in both Britain and the US, the Arts and Crafts movement went back to the old skills and materials. There was a similar tendency in Scandinavia at about the same time. Industrialization had removed the regional distinc-tions between area and area, country and country, and prompted the reaction, which was very important in deter-mining the direction of modern domestic architecture.

A 19th century house, in Texas, perfectly designed for living in a near-tropical climate. With balconies and verandas tucked under deep eaves, it offers shade as well as the chance of a breeze.

This mid-19th century Texas house has a veranda which wraps all round the ground floor. Before the age of air conditioning, shutters offered extra protection against too much heat and light in a steamy climate.

The walls of this house in a Cornish fishing village are protected against the elements with an outer cladding of local slate. The builder put windows only into the side of the cottage that got the most light and the least wind and rain.

A Victorian stone villa combines fashion and practicality. The picturesque Swiss Gothic style has functional steep roofs to shed rain or snow, and bargeboards to deflect rain from the wooden eaves.

CLIMATE

Whatever the period of a house, the influence of climate on the design is apparent in many architectural features.

In hot countries it is necessary to have plenty of openings, so that currents of air will pass through. Verandas, balconies, rooftop terraces, courtyards (often around a fountain, just to make people feel cooler), screens pierced with latticework, slatted blinds to cut out glare without restricting the flow of air, are obvious ways to do it. Sometimes rattan blinds replace walls altogether, secured by a series of posts or columns.

Wall thickness

When a climate has considerable extremes of temperature, solid-built houses with thick walls are best, as these retain the temperature. The interior will stay relatively cool during a hot summer and will keep in the warmth during a cold winter. In cold climates, the same applies. The stone houses of Wales and Scotland, which combine a cool or cold climate with heavy rainfall, are always heavily built, with enormous fireplaces to build up the temperature.

Another way of beating the cold, especially where winds

A latticed outer door, here in southern Portugal, is an attractive detail which also enables the inner, secure door to be opened to let in fresh air in the hottest months.

A very ornamental carved wood bargeboard. The bargeboard was there to deflect driving rain from the roof timbers, but it was also a way of casting pretty shadows on the walls when the sun was out.

This large medieval timber-framed house has a magnificent crop of brick chimneys. The fireplace was important for warmth, as well as for cooking and light. It is noticeable that these chimneys are built of brick, the most expensive and durable material at the time.

A window in an Algarve house has a fixed trellis screen so that when the windows are open, the occupants are still guaranteed their privacy from the street. There is a further set of shutters inside for night-time use.

or sudden frosts are the problem, is to give the house an extra skin—sometimes just on the side where the prevailing wind comes from. Cladding, which might be in the form of clay tiles, slate or weatherboard (clapboard), is added to the brickwork or timber beneath.

Roof design

Where there is a long season of snow, then it is the roof that takes the brunt. An enormous weight builds up, and so the roof pitch will be extra steep to ensure that the snow shifts down. The eaves, too, need protection and so bargeboards—heavy sheets of wood along the gable eaves—were developed. In Switzerland, Scandinavia and many northern states of the US, the houses are specially developed to deal with that. In other parts of Europe, such as upland Britain, where there is not a great deal of snow, it is rainfall that is the problem; again, a steep pitched roof, together with heavy gutters and downpipes, is the best way of getting rid of the water. Before the age of modern convenience, builders had to be, above all, practical.

A traditional Tuscan farmhouse, built of a mixture of rough stone, or rubble. Because the walls are of immensely thick stone, the house holds its warmth in winter but is refreshingly cool in summer. Tiny windows help by excluding the strong sunlight.

Thatch and timber framing were the typical materials of medieval English cottages. The chimneys, however, were often of brick (or stone) to be more fire-resistant. The timber framework is infilled with lathe and plaster.

When timber-framed buildings have brick panels, the technique is called 'nogging'. Often the brick is set in a herringbone or chevron pattern, as here, and becomes decorative in its own right.

The traditional curved clay pantiles on this Spanish house are elaborated by setting glazed tiles into patterns. Adding to the effect, a chequered design has been painted on to the plasterwork. Ceramic finials on the gables are another decorative touch.

MATERIALS

Often you can see from looking around an area what the available materials for the builder would have been. They are revealed in cliffs or outcrops, or in the fields or vegetation of the place. The other reason that traditional building was always so strongly localized was that craftsmen, because of the limitations of transport, would only work within a relatively small district all their lives. The special trademarks, the personal signatures of skilled masons, carpenters or ornamental plasterers might all be concentrated in a very small area.

Stone and brick

Surprisingly, many areas where stone might seem the obvious choice and where it has been used widely, were originally forested. In these areas early houses were not built of stone at all, and it only came into use when the forests had been cleared and good timber had become scarce. Stone in medieval times was reserved for grand buildings, cathedrals and monasteries. The exceptions were the roughly built houses where uncut stone, or rubble, was used to construct thick walls. The rough version of stone-

This moated medieval house has been added to in the 18th century. A brick mullioned window can be seen on the front, alongside a symmetrical front door and regular windows, which were typically Georgian features. The early use of brick indicates that it was a rich man's house.

A wall of a cottage built of a mixture of flint and chalk. Wherever there is chalk, there is flint, and so the two materials were often combined, making an attractive effect.

An 18th century French farmhouse with farm buildings alongside. Large uncut stones from the locality are used as lintels and surrounds to the doors and windows, while smaller rough stones are used for the rest of the walls. The roof is of stone slates.

This architect-designed cottage, dating from the early 19th century, combines stone with wood for the gable, which has a built-in pigeon loft. The tiles on the roof are of plain clay. Architects rarely designed cottages but, when they did, enjoyed utilizing traditional materials.

built houses has long been used in farmhouses in southern France or Italy.

Whereas stone was used much as it came out of the ground, the most readily available material of all—clay—had to be either dried and packed into brick shapes, or fired to make bricks and tiles. Brick really came into its own around the 18th century. Different minerals in the earth led to an incredible range of tones, from dark plum to nearly white, and varying methods of firing the bricks also ensured that everywhere that brick was used it looked quite

different. It was only in the 19th century that industrially made bricks began to look much the same.

Roofing materials

The roof was even more important to the life of the structure than the walls. Again, whatever was easily available was traditionally the first choice. Wooden shingles, stone or slate tiles, clay tiles in all kinds of shapes, thatch from almost any tough natural material (bracken, heather, reeds, corn straw) and turf were all used.

A simple stable door on a French cottage. The advantage of this type of door is that on a warm day the upper part can be left open to cool the house down. A bead curtain inside keeps out strong light and some insects.

A Tudor window, with timber frame and latticed panes. Although it looks decorative, the brick 'drip mould' across the head of the window was a practical feature, deflecting the rainwater away from the woodwork around the window.

In the Algarve, southern Portugal, chimneys are ornamented by pierced clay hoods which in the strong sunlight throw delightful fancy shadows on to the white walls. This is the only decoration on otherwise very simple cottages.

In these houses the overhanging upper storey or jetty is designed to give more light to the upper windows, a traditional feature of medieval street architecture. Below that is a little slate ledge which gives protection against rain at street level.

ORNAMENTATION

In medieval times people got warm by huddling around a fire in the middle of the room. The smoke eventually found its way through a hole in the roof. But once a solution to that problem was achieved—the chimney—it soon became more than just a functional matter. Builders began to ornament chimneys: in Tudor England, for instance, incredibly intricate twisting brickwork was devised, while in southern Portugal little fretwork ceramic tops were used.

The same process occurred with windows and doors. According to the climate of the area, the openings of the house were made to let in more or less light and air, but once the principle was established then craftsmen began to gild the lily.

Window size

Before the 18th century sheets of glass were very small, and so either the opening had to remain tiny, or the windows had to be divided up—by leading and by wood or stone mullions and transoms. In temperate climates, windows could be quite large and they became an important feature of the way the facade of the house was designed. In the Tudor period glass was still very expensive and so the builders of grand houses ostentatiously used vast windows

An ingenious arrangement in a French village house, where the louvred shutters can remain closed, but a section can open to ventilate the interior without letting in too much light or heat.

This manor house shows a range of Tudor windows: small mullioned lights for the attic, a larger window on the ground floor and an elaborate oriel window projecting from the first floor. A window of this size was a mark of a fairly grand house.

A picturesque detail with a practical function, this thatched porch offers shelter to anyone on the doorstep of the cottage. There was often a seat in a porch, so that the cottager could sit and admire his garden on a summer evening.

A simple cottage door is protected by an ornamental wooden porch, complete with twisted posts, to make it something special.

to emphasize their importance and cost. Before long, others were copying them.

Once it became possible to manufacture much more generous sheets of glass, then the window tended to become simpler, and casement windows and sash windows became prevalent. Later on, when old-fashioned styles of architecture were being revived, the leaded windows were back in fashion once again.

In hotter climates, shutters and screens are essential. The French have made the shutter their trademark, but they *are* practical—cutting back glare and heat in daytime and darkening the room, while it remains airy, at night-time.

Porches and other extras

Although the door is often ornamented, the first and most important influence on the design of a doorway will be the weather. In wet countries a porch, or at least a canopy, is usually provided. Sometimes a little overhang runs all along the house, protecting the lower parts from driving rain. The jettied form of medieval timber-framed houses offered this advantage. Another ornamental touch was the bargeboard, running along the eaves and around the gable end, which was an obvious feature to be decorated. The extras which a hot climate requires, such as balconies and verandas, have tended to be designed very ornamentally.

This late 19th century Rhode Island house is an example of the use of wood not only in construction but also to ornament every aspect. In different areas of the US, certain kinds of traditional ornamentation were developed.

Medieval village houses in Suffolk. Although most of the oak structure is left plain, the corner post (in the foreground) has been decorated with a little carved detail, in the form of a corbel to support the bracket.

Timber framing is confined to the upper storeys of these village houses in Germany. The joinery is different from its equivalent in England and shows how local traditions of craftsmanship influence the end result.

Timber cladding is much more common in the US and Scandinavia than in Britain, but these 18th century cottages in Essex show how attractive simple weatherboarding can be as a surface, as well as providing practical protection for the structure beneath.

In simple stone cottages, colour can make a strong impact. In northwest England and much of Scotland, the stone surrounds of windows and doors are often picked out in bright colours.

DECORATIVE FINISHES

Often the basic materials used for building houses were not high quality and so they were covered, or added to in various ways. Timber-framed houses were generally plastered over, and cheap or irregular brickwork was frequently rendered or clad in another material.

Timber cladding, known as clapboard, is the most widely used material in North America. Often it is painted, usually white but sometimes in the tones used in an immigrant community's country of origin.

Timber framing itself provided an opportunity to make an attractive geometric pattern out of the building materials, and the forms it took varied dramatically.

Plaster lent itself to pargeting, in which the designs were pressed into the wet surface. Plaster could also be covered with a colour wash—originally in soft natural shades. Lime wash coloured russet, gold or dusty pink is characteristic of eastern England, while in Italy rendered walls use a similar warm palette, often ochres and pinks.

Colour is an important part of the outside look of a house, whether applied as paintwork and colour wash, or

Simple oak uprights (or studs) in a Suffolk medieval cottage make their own attractive pattern. The plaster panels between are colour-washed while the timber should be left natural, or limewashed.

Pargeting is the name given to the traditional ornamentation of plasterwork, a speciality of East Anglia. In this elaborate example, flowers and leaves are the theme, but often pargeting consists of a simple repeated pattern.

Faded colours on a shop front and door in southwest France. Modern paints offer a vast spectrum of colours, but traditionally the choices were limited by pigments taken from either vegetable or mineral sources.

A combination of flint and diamond pattern brickwork on an exposed gable wall of cottages illustrates the possibilities of combining two contrasting materials for ornamental effect.

A stone cottage is given a sophisticated touch by this elegant classical porch which has Ionic columns and a jaunty scrolled pediment.

just the tones of the materials as they are. Stone can vary from dark red sandstone to brightest grey, white or gold. Sometimes it is used in bands, to emphasize the effect. Even timber has different tints—for example, the grey of weathered oak. Colour is a bright spot in a dark climate, but equally looks vivid in a strong light—Portugal, for example, is a country in which the architecture is determined by the use of colour. Houses are often painted around the edges, on corners, at ground level or around windows. In the north of England, where the sun is

elusive, the frames around cottage windows are often brightly painted.

Once skilled craftsmen had completed the structural work on a house they might carve a date or the owner's initials above the front door, or make a bit of a flourish of the doorcase itself. Sometimes a main beam would be ornamented with a beautiful band of carving. With cladding the slates or clay tiles might already be shaped, so that the builder would arrange them into a pattern. Even different coloured brick could be set into attractive patterns.

COTTAGE STYLE

Cottages have always reflected the nature of the land—they were constructed by the locals from materials that they had to hand. Simple and unassuming, they reflected the needs of the men who built them—and as their requirements changed, so did their homes. The climate and the local building materials dictated the style: sturdy, functional and down to earth. The joy of these buildings is that they seem to be organic. Rather like a pair of comfortable old shoes that take on the shape of their owner, old cottages seem to reflect the lives of each inhabitant. Cottage interiors have an unaffected style which was originally created out of thrift and economy; today's country folk take the best of the old traditional styles and mix them with modern comforts. A feeling for natural materials and textures and simple furniture predominates. Think small-scale and plan your decorations accordingly.

ACHIEVING THE LOOK

The appeal of the cottage style lies partly in its cheerful mix of the decorative and the functional. Informal and unpretentious, it is characterized by simple, homely furnishings that are as practical as they are charming.

Underfoot

Cottage flooring needs to be sympathetic to the scale and textures of the room, unlike wall-to-wall Wilton which somehow seems too sybaritic. Practical flooring for well-used areas might be quarry tiles, small paviour bricks or slate—all come in small modules which suit tiny spaces.

If your floorboards are decent-looking, you could strip them and then scatter rugs all over them. Wide old boards are often oak or elm, which could be left bare but polished up with beeswax. Deal planking can take a more decorative finish, such as painting or stencilling.

Rush, coir, sisal or seagrass matting is today's equivalent of the strewn rushes of the early cottage floors. Inexpensive and informal, it forms the ideal background for simple rugs—floorcloths, rag rugs and tribal kelims are all types of rug which have suitably homespun qualities.

Walls and ceilings

Whether your style is plain or pretty, make sure that the decorations are in keeping with the architectural spirit of the house. Coloured limewashes produced uneven dappled colour, which is the most flattering for old walls—you can emulate it with a pale and watery emulsion.

In a small cottage, space is at a premium so full use should be made of tiny rooms under the eaves, as in this little bedroom.

Elderly but gracious furniture blends in well with the dark beams, low ceiling and small windows of this home.

Here is cottage style at its most English. The garden theme enjoyed by this room is carried through from the printed cotton curtains to the patchwork and the rose pattern on the carpet.

Cottage dwellers are traditionally hoarders. This collection indicates an interest in textiles and embroidery.

Otherwise, contrast exposed timbers with 'dirty white' walls: buttermilk, parchment and ivory are much more sympathetic in old houses than brilliant white emulsion.

Hand-blocked stencils are the traditional way of adding pattern; or run wallpapers with little all-over designs up wavy walls and across sloping ceilings. Small-scale patterns are useful camouflage for lumpy plaster.

Fabrics and window treatments

Because cottage windows are so small, one of the major considerations is to create treatments that will draw the fabric far enough off the window frame to allow light into the room and yet still close out the weather and darkness. The light butter muslins, sprigged cottons, checked ginghams and lace panels of the summer cottage don't lend themselves to the thick interlinings that will trap the winter chills. Warmer alternatives include creamy calico, woven tickings, heavy tapestry weaves and chunky crewel embroideries. Either way, poles or tracks should be long enough to keep materials well away from the window, and pelmets designed to be neat and simple. Keep frills and flounces in proportion to the size of the window.

Soft furnishings using home-made materials are the most authentic. Patchwork pieces cut from worn-out clothes create charming curtains, covers and cloths for all manner of uses. Knitted throws, cushions and blankets have a home-spun quality, as does the white cotton crochet-work which is most commonly found edging old linens.

This cottage bears the hallmarks of a warm climate: unpolished floors and doors, white-painted walls and a little furniture, all of it free-standing. The lace and crocheted bedcover and tablecover add to the impression of warm wealth.

Perfectly in keeping with the cottage look, this dresser holds a collection of 'cottage' ware: blue and white spongeware with traditional small animal designs and a row of brown and yellow slipware.

Sun streams through a white-painted window to show off a set of commemorative pottery.

In this sunny kitchen, the ceramic sink and hand-crafted solid wood cupboards and furniture go well with the faded blue-and-white platters on the wall.

Furniture

A surprising amount of furniture was built into the structure of the early cottages. You may be lucky enough to inherit some of the original fittings; otherwise, look out for the sort of furniture that was once found in the servants' attics, or below stairs in kitchens and pantries.

Choose small-scale pieces that will earn their keep: fold-away tables such as the gate-leg or the tilt-top designs; low dressers with plate racks and pot stands for storage; and little, rounded, Edwardian-style sofas with drop arms which can double as day beds. Wheel-back Windsor chairs or ladder-backs with rush seats are all in keeping with the style, as is painted furniture of every kind.

Upstairs, buy bedsteads rather than modern divans. If possible, use free-standing wardrobes and linen presses rather than built-in storage.

Warmth of the hearth

Early inglenook fireplaces were very large in relation to the rooms they served. As coal fires became more commonplace, so inglenooks were replaced by small cast-iron hob grates. The small coal basket left room on either side for an oven and a boiler—and this developed into the kitchen range now synonymous with country life.

Whether you're fitting a wood-burning stove or a Victorian dog grate with a tiled surround, make sure that you are keeping to the right proportions. Fire surrounds require a sensitive appreciation of style and period; if in

An entirely suitable collection of artefacts for the cottage: gleaming tin moulds, with, above them, old-fashioned teardrop-shaped oil lamps.

An interesting variety of ceramics with a pastoral theme. Floral and cabbage motifs decorate the jugs and mugs, and a couple of tapestries add to the effect.

Everybody's idea of a cottage must be epitomized in this charming window. Old-fashioned scales and a traditional washstand round off a very satisfactory cottage corner.

doubt, take a look at period examples in similar cottages. The reproduction Adam-style mantelpiece is as out of place in a cottage as is the crazy-paved stone surround. It is equally inappropriate to fit a mantelshelf above a fireplace that was never designed to take one.

Finishing touches

Light for the early cottagers was the flickering fire supplemented by greasy tallow candles—nowadays a combination of table lights, wall lamps and floor-standing reading lights is rather more functional. Wall lights come into their own when ceilings are low, and electrified candle sconces are available in simple monastic shapes, made in wood. Reproduction gas and oil lamps are suitable in style,

as are the converted vases and tin storage canisters which are wired up to make stylish lamp bases.

In a cottage knick-knacks abound. Groups of small pictures and hand-embroidered samplers look perfect on the walls of a small room. Embroidered antimacassars arranged on squashy armchairs add to the homely effect.

Dressers with open racks beg for collections of plates, and deep window reveals seem purpose-built for pots of geraniums. Blue and white crockery looks fresh and un-complicated. Other early pieces of cottage pottery include spongeware and spatterware.

Local superstitions produced household charms such as the corn dolly, and the glass-lustre witch balls which hung at the window to repel evil spirits.

Living and Relaxing

Sitting rooms—even if they do have to double up as dining rooms, work rooms or guest bedrooms—are, above all, places in which to relax. Piles of books, deep armchairs and an open fire add up to an atmosphere that's warm and inviting all the year around.

In the old days, cottages would have had only one downstairs room; life was centred around the fire because it was the source not only of heat and light but also of hot food and water. Later on, the family room continued to be the kitchen, while the front room was reserved for best— furniture was prim and correct, as the room was used for receiving and entertaining 'company'.

Seating is generally arranged around the fireplace in cottages. In early cottages you may find evidence of a wooden screen built at right angles to the chimney to control the direction of the draught, thereby creating a fireside alcove.

These inglenook fireplaces require only a simple stone hearth and fire irons to support the logs and allow the air to circulate. If you do not have fire irons, you can let the wood ash accumulate on the open hearth until the fire is burning well above the hearth.

With the advent of blast furnaces in the 17th century, cast-iron firebacks became the norm. Designed to protect the bricks at the back, they had the added advantage of bouncing the heat back into the room. Most of the modern

LOVING IT FOR WHAT IT IS

It takes courage and a strong sense of history to allow a cottage to remain 'undesigned'. This one is old and now quite unusual with its wattle and daub walls, its wide plank door and floor and its narrow little stairs.

A PLEASANT SUNTRAP

Great thick stone walls, a low ceiling and dependable beams; dark, smooth polished
flagstones; and a bright, asymmetrical window epitomize the older cottage. Here,
where privacy is not essential, curtains have been dispensed with. Autumn leaves in an
earthenware jar blend with the yellows and browns.

firebacks are reproductions of 17th century styles. They marry well with simple, sturdy types of fire basket and dog grate. Look for the plainest—foursquare versions unadorned by brass balls or gilded finials and bandy legs.

In the summer the fireplace presents a rather forbidding black hole. As far back as the 18th century it was the custom to use vases of leaves to fill the empty space—Josiah Wedgwood actually made bough pots for this purpose—and later still, fireboards became all the rage. These were wooden panels tailor-made to fit the fireplace opening exactly and then decorated with wallpaper or a *trompe l'oeil* vase of flowers surrounded by tiles.

These aren't to be confused with firescreens or pole screens, which were smaller panels, often beautifully embroidered, that stood at either side of the fireplace to protect the women from the searing heat of the flames. These old-fashioned firescreens, often separated from their poles, are still to be found inexpensively in junk shops and look wonderful as pieces of needlework hanging on the walls. A firescreen in the right size is also an ideal way of camouflaging an empty fireplace during the summer.

Practical floors

Early cottages had mud floors strewn with rushes. Not surprisingly, earth floors gave way to the more hygienic baked surfaces of tile or brick. Even now these floors make

ROSES, ROSES

A completely different treatment, but equally in keeping, is this small-print-
and-roses theme of a small cottage sitting room. Roses feature in the floor-
length curtains, pink flowers cover the drapes on the plump armchair, roses
stand on the tall chest of drawers and a rose-pink pot sits on the windowsill.

practical sense, especially in areas where the front door opens straight into the main living room. Stone, slate or pebbles are other alternatives, but it's best to be guided by the other building materials in the house. Make sure that the flags or bricks are tightly packed and that the pointing is in a sympathetic colour.

Floorboards in early houses would have been made of oak or elm. The Victorians introduced deal planking, which was inferior in quality and was normally stained and varnished—but older hardwood floors weren't even polished. They were dry-scrubbed with damp sand which helped collect the dust and fluff, and then fragrant herbs were brushed across the surfaces to leave them smelling sweet. Scrubbed boards have a lovely silvery patina which can be simulated by bleaching modern timbers that have been first stripped of varnish. If you are restoring an old floor, it's worth remembering that old floorboards are much wider than today's machine-sawn planks: 30 cm (12 inch) widths were not uncommon then and are practically impossible to find now, so save any sound pieces.

While it would be sacrilege to decorate wide, old oak boards, paint is hard to beat as a finish for the average scarred, pitted and beaten-up softwood planking. It offers all sorts of opportunities for adding both colour and pattern to a room and can be used with stencils to create floors that are either lavish and intricate or geometrically elegant. The most effective stencilled floors seem to be those based on simple motifs.

Painted floor cloths are similar in feel to decoratively painted floors and were the cottager's equivalent of the rich man's carpet. Made from oiled canvas, they were like washable mats and were the forerunner of linoleum. Linoleum is still available in a wide range of muted colours and provides a much warmer and kinder surface to touch than stone or tiles.

Informal mats and rugs

As a covering, matting provides the ultimate country flooring—both practical and informal. The authentic rush matting, with a thick and chunky cabled texture, is still made and can be woven to size, but it will work out as expensive as a hand-loomed carpet. Much cheaper and more easily available are the sisal, coir, seagrass or maize mats, imported from the Far East and made in natural materials which can be stitched together to cover large areas of floor. They do need looking after—the grime seems to sit on the surface while the dust slips through the gaps, so a latex-backed variety is best. Rush and maize will crumble and disintegrate if they get too dry, and the floor should therefore occasionally be dampened using a plant spray.

Rugs—not fitted carpets—complete the look. Exposed

FLORAL PROFUSION
A colourful mix of floral patterns is very well suited to cottage style, and a background of dark wood sets it off perfectly.

EASTER MEMENTOS
Generations of family Easters (and family poultry) have produced these hand-painted eggshells, which will have been carefully 'blown' before painting. Many are portraits of turkeys and other fowl, and there are also one or two members of the family. The case is enlivened with other family heirlooms such as chain-mail purses, an old wishbone, some silver thimbles and other memorabilia.

boards around the edges of the room with a huge Turkey rug in the middle are much more in keeping than a wall-to-wall Axminster, which looks somehow suffocating. An old kelim or tribal rug, worn to a noble thinness, can look immensely distinguished. Otherwise, choose folk rugs, made from scraps of material. Rag rugs were woven from strips of old clothing from the household rag bag, while hooked rugs were made by hooking tufts of fabric through coarse canvas, often to create naive pictorial mats.

Rustic seating

Much of the early vernacular furniture was immovable, either because of its size and weight or because it was part of the architecture. The lateral screen beside the fire often had a bench fixed to it and a long refectory-style table alongside. This was the probable origin of the high-backed settle, often backed by bookshelves and decorated with maps and prints. Some box-seated settles had storage under the seat for keeping sides of bacon.

In these smoke-filled interiors, seating was kept low. Because the floors were so uneven, it was quite customary for stools and tables to have only three legs—'cricket tables' are characteristic in style and often seen for sale in antique markets. In the very poorest homes, there wasn't even a table—merely a thin slab of wood which hung from the wall and was placed on the knee when required.

NAIVE BUT NOT SIMPLE
This cottage dining corner is not so primitive as it may look. The wooden bench is quite carefully designed and put together, the collection of paintings well-chosen and hung with care on the narrowly striped wallpaper. An elaborate silver candelabra adorns the intricately embroidered cloth, and the cushions are silk.

MINIATURE ART GALLERY

Every corner in a cottage must be used to its utmost. This one has been commandeered
as a comfortable resting place and a gallery for a fine collection of predominantly pastoral
watercolours. Every spare bit of wall has been used and underneath sits a much battered
old leather sofa covered in exotic flowered cushions. The paintings have been framed in mainly
plain wood or gilt frames, though some are dark. There's nothing too ornate or modern.

<u>RESPECT FOR AGE</u>

A very old cottage has been treated with the respect it deserves. The beams have been left natural; the rough plasterwork has been painted almost-white. A large terracotta jug stands on a wooden table.

<u>TUDOR COMFORT</u>

This old cottage library with antique furniture has a studious air that spells comfort and warmth. The high-backed settee was originally designed to keep out draughts.

Early chairs were heavy and awkward, but by the 18th century the Windsor chair had become a popular chair for cottages, often painted dark green or blue. Rush-seated ladder-back chairs and, later still, country versions of the elegant cabinet makers' designs began to find their way into humbler homes.

As people today have become used to living in much less spacious accommodation than previous generations, so the demand for small-scale furniture has increased. The bargains in the antique market are to be found in the capacious pieces made for high-ceilinged, well-proportioned rooms—sadly, antique furniture for little cottages is now very expensive.

Multi-purpose furniture

As bedroom furniture is generally designed on a much smaller scale, there are many pieces that are very useful downstairs and do not look at all out-of-place in a cottage-style furnishing scheme. Bedroom chairs, for example, make invaluable occasional seating. Corner furniture such as corner cupboards makes use of space that might otherwise be wasted. Chests of drawers are very under-rated—although chests on chests (tallboys) are collectors' pieces, a low chest with three or four drawers can provide valuable storage in the sitting room. Commode cupboards, sometimes complete with chamber-pot, make useful side

tables. (However, if you're going to use them as lamp tables beside sofas, you should make sure that the heights are compatible, since some modern seating is quite low-slung.) Washstands can double up as pretty writing tables or simply as occasional tables against the wall.

Mixing materials

Even if you're equipping a cottage that is quite old, don't rule out the ultra-modern: a mix of old and new can be most successful but be guided by the materials. Shiny chrome and bright laminates are ungraceful materials unless they are used skilfully.

Invariably, you'll find that some woods clash (although generally, all the native hardwoods—oak, ash, elm and beech—can be happily mixed together). Modern furniture is treated with a protective lacquer varnish, which means it will never really achieve a mellow patina, unlike the old scrubbed and polished pieces which have benefitted from years of beeswax and elbow grease. As a general rule oak antique furniture doesn't sit happily beside rosewood. Arts and Crafts furniture—made at the turn of the century by William Morris and his followers, who idealized the country cottage and designed specifically with it in mind—complements the crude hand-hewn characteristics of country furniture far more successfully than the stained and French-polished Victorian mahogany.

NATURALLY SIMPLE

Natural materials have been used almost exclusively in this cottage to
retain its original character. The warm-toned quarry tiles are all
the friendlier for having seen life, while the furniture is of
solid wood in simple though sturdy shapes. The leather-upholstered
chesterfield has seen many jolly evenings and will see many more.

BLUE AND WHITE

Blue and white forms the basis for a 'garden corner'
where a bold indigo and white floral-printed tablecloth
is a base for three large, bulbous vases, accompanied
by a table lamp in exactly the same tones.

PATTERN UPON PATTERN

A summery decorative scheme based upon a profusion of
patterns works well in this cottage, where a passion for flowers
and bright colours is very apparent. The watercolours over the
mantelpiece echo the summery theme.

Upholstered furniture

It is still possible to buy quite inexpensive little two-seater
scroll-arm sofas, made at the turn of the century, which
were kept for 'best' in the seldom-used front parlour and
are often in remarkably good condition. If you're buying
new upholstered furniture, look out for ranges of small
sofas and armchairs. Scaled-down chesterfields, button-
back library chairs and low nursing chairs all have the
rounded Victorian and Edwardian shapes which have
come to be associated with a cozy cottage style. Modern
seating often has Dacron-wrapped foam seat cushions
which can look artificially plump.

Ultra-modern upholstery tends to come in a larger scale,
more suited to a penthouse than a cottage, but the latest
trend in non-fitting, baggy covers actually belongs very
comfortably with the country scene. There's no reason why
you shouldn't put unconventional covers on a traditional
shape: men's suitings such as tartans, Harris tweeds and
Prince of Wales checks will enhance the most un-
exceptional piece. Leather is the ultimate long-lasting
material—the more scuffed and battered it becomes, the
better it looks. Combined with other suitably masculine
fabrics like Fair Isle knits and herringbone weaves or the
strong patterns of a hand-woven kelim rug, leather has a
very appealing toughness.

Authentic knick-knacks

Although these days we tend to think of cottages as being
bright with all manner of decorative clutter, it is only in the
last century that mass production brought pretty knick-
knacks within the reach of the ordinary person.

Pictures became commonplace as printing techniques

SMALL BUT DIGNIFIED

This is a typical workman's cottage, with small rooms,
a narrow fireplace and bare floorboards.
Without trying to make it what it is not,
it has been given a dignity of its own with
heavy, panelled doors with brass doorknobs, generous
built-in cupboards and drawers, white paint around the fireplace
to give it a simple frame and a hand-painted
wooden chair with a cane seat.

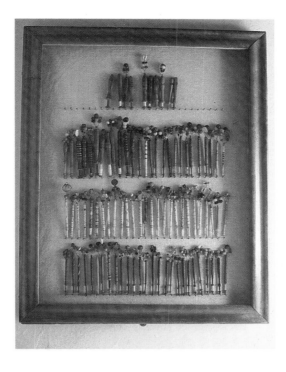

COTTAGE INDUSTRY
Many cottage wives would
have spent time making lace
for the local manor to earn a
little extra money. What more
appropriate collection for the
present cottage dweller than
the infinitely imaginative and
intricate lace bobbins, here
displayed and framed so
prettily?

improved, and 'tuppenny prints'—crude reproductions of popular images—were often hung on the walls. Little pictures like these look more effective when grouped together rather than dotted around the walls of the room.

Books were expensive and therefore very precious, as were mirrors and clocks. Employers in the 'big house', however, often gave very generous presents to cottagers who had been in service.

Sources of inspiration

Every decorative scheme needs a starting point, and one very good one is the building materials of the cottage. It will help you to analyze the idiom in which you are working. A stone-built home that looks as if it has been hewn from the landscape will require a very different internal treatment from a timber clapboard house.

Another good source of inspiration is the changing landscape—in winter and in summer. Country house style is first and foremost a celebration of the countryside.

In winter inspiration might come from the texture of a dry stone wall or the furrows left by the plough, the sight of the fields blanketed in a hoar frost or the silhouette of windswept trees. The typical cottage style corresponds to this in its lean, pared-down-to-basics look which relies on home-spun fabrics, stripped wood and white-washed walls. Cottage-style furniture has an almost classical simplicity;

while it's always comfortable and workaday, it is never excessive or abundant.

Colour in a winter-inspired scheme is limited, for the sun makes only a brief and low arc across the horizon. Contrasting textures are important. Make the most of the wide range of neutrals and emphasize subtle nuances of tone by changing the textures. Think of the varying shades of Berber carpets, the woven ribbing on haircord runners, the wealth of colour in a handmade brick or rush-seated chair—these will guide you towards the perimeter of the winter colour spectrum. This is a look for purists: because it relies so heavily on the basics, they do have to be of the very best quality.

A contrasting but equally authentic alternative scheme is based on summer. Summer in the country is blowsy: the soil is fertile and there's a glut of produce. The sun is high in the sky and the clear light makes a play of shadow. Colours run through the spectrum of pastels and sun-baked tones. Decorating this way involves emulating the quantity rather than the quality of nature. Lay pattern over pattern, use patchwork quilts over chintzy sofas and crowd every surface with pottery, pictures and *objets trouvés*. This is an undemanding style which accepts chips and tears, flaws and stains simply because so much is half-hidden. There is no need for it to be saccharine-sweet because stripes and checks can add a formality and discipline.

Cooking and Eating

The cottagers' world was circumscribed by the struggle to feed and clothe their families, and so their homes sometimes reflected no more than the bare necessities of their lives. At best, the cottagers existed by a simple economy that involved saving, borrowing, bartering and making do: their furniture and furnishings reflected that discipline and had a simple, home-made charm as a result. The cottage kitchen has always been the poor relation of the farmhouse kitchen; built on a smaller scale and humbly furnished, it was often the only downstairs room and therefore the real living room of the family.

The attraction of the cottage kitchen is its down-to-earth simplicity—so think of furnishings rather than fittings. An assortment of old pine tables, cupboards and a few wooden shelves is a much cheaper way of providing storage than any run of kitchen units, and reflects the need for economy and thrift that dominated old cottagers' lives. Cheerful dressers, lath-back chairs, books and pictures, scrubbed pine tables, butcher's block chopping boards, baskets of fruit and eggs, pots of herbs, tin canisters and brass candlesticks are all part of that look.

In a tiny kitchen, every fraction of space has to earn its keep. Some things, like the compost bucket and perhaps the rubbish bin, will need to be kept behind closed doors, but otherwise keep everything to hand and utilize every inch of wall space with open shelves—you can cram far

SIMPLE, WARM SURFACES
Many cottages have low ceilings; this saved on building materials. The far wall is dark green and the ceiling white, to give an impression of height. The red and black floor tiles add warmth to the room, as does the meticulously polished furniture.

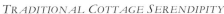

TRADITIONAL COTTAGE SERENDIPITY

This small cottage has remained true to its humble origins, with matchboarded walls and door; an interesting shelf, obviously built specially; a row of wooden pegs, used as cuphooks; and a higgledy-piggledy arrangement of bits and pieces including an old clock, a wire birdcage, some practical pottery and many traditional kitchen artefacts.

A COOK'S KITCHEN

Here is another kitchen which has retained the charm of purpose-built units using white-painted matchboarding. This is obviously a cook's kitchen and every portion of wall and ceiling is crammed with practical, traditional equipment including a butcher's block.

more on a shelf where everything is open to view than when it is tucked away in a cupboard. Wooden draining racks above the sink will mean that crockery can not only drip dry but be permanently stored there. The ceiling can be exploited too: use racks and beams for hanging utensils from S-shaped butcher's hooks.

Simple framed, panelled doors, with wooden or china knobs, are a classic design; matchboarded surfaces, tongue-and-groove or ledged-and-braced doors are also all in keeping. Try to marry up new with old by using ageless materials like salvaged wood, pitch pine, tiles or lino.

From open fire to cast iron stove

Early cottagers cooked food either on a roasting spit which was turned in front of the open fire or in a cauldron which hung on a huge iron arm that swung across the flames. This was a complete cooking and hot-water system combined. Deep earthenware jars were filled with meat and vegetable

mixtures, puddings were wrapped in linen and everything was suspended in the boiling water. An entire meal could be cooked in one iron pot complete with hot water for washing up afterwards.

As coal fires became cheaper and more widely available, hearths and cooking methods changed. Coal had to burn in a basket, and although it could be used for boiling and roasting, it couldn't be used for baking. The kitchen range was the 19th century cooker, filling the open hearths of the old fireplaces—only to be superseded in turn by the cast iron cooking/heating stove, which has now become synonymous with country life.

Many old cottages still have their bread oven intact; built alongside the kitchen range and set into the chimney wall, they were used for much more than plain bread making. The fire was lit inside the oven and allowed to burn for several hours until the floor was thoroughly hot. The ash was then cleared out, the inside mopped and the bread

RUSTIC IDYLL

From the scrubbed kitchen table to the hand-made quarry
tiles and the naive rural scenes painted on the shutters, this
kitchen keeps to its poor but proud origins.

THE COTTAGE DRESSER

Kitchen dressers in a cottage are often designed and built specifically for
the room they are in. Like this one, they may be obviously home-made, but
are invariably of solid wood, are sturdily put together and have their own
quirks of design and proportion, to suit the owner and the space.

NATURAL AFFINITY

Another typical cottage kitchen in which the hand-made units have been designed for the
specific needs of the room. The small wooden knobs are nicely in keeping, and open
shelves divide up the overhead units to show off a collection of china animals. Blue and
white tiles have been fixed as a splashback and are prettily framed by the cupboards.

baked immediately on the hot hearth. As temperatures lowered so were feathers aired, meats preserved, herbs and grains dried, and finally firewood seasoned ready for the following week's baking.

The kitchen sink

Apart from the rain that ran off the cottage roof into a butt below, all the water had to be carried from the well or village pump, normally by two buckets that were suspended across the shoulders by a yoke. Lives were changed by the arrival of piped water—either through a tap in the wall or a pump in the kitchen.

A wide, flat-bottomed stone sink, or slop stone, was built under the tap and against the wall; it doubled as a food preparation area for chopping meat or gutting fish. The sink was set at a slight angle, taking the water down to a drain hole and into a bucket beneath—or better still, to a waste pipe which disgorged the waste through the kitchen wall into the yard.

With the growth of the pottery industry, the old lead-formed sinks and wooden troughs were replaced by white glazed stoneware sinks like the original Butler sink, sadly no longer being manufactured, and the Belfast sink, a very deep rectangular design still in production today. Washing

up was never done in the sink itself but in a smaller wooden bowl standing in the tub. Originally these large sinks were supported on brick piers with shelving underneath to hold buckets and bowls, but nowadays they are successfully integrated into a larger working area by abutting wooden worktops made from a hard wood with a grooved draining section beside the sink.

Food storage and preservation

The great store cupboard of the country kitchen has always been the larder—its function has never been matched by any refrigerator or freezer. Attached to the coolest wall of the house, with a window or a couple of air bricks for ventilation, these old stone larders were designed to remain cool in the hottest weather. Slate and marble slabs, often two or three inches deep, were wedged hard into the thick walls so that fish and vegetables could be laid directly on to the shelves.

Old methods of food storage and preservation were legion, and the larder must have been a rewarding sight with strings of apples dried, cored and strung to the ceiling and with mushrooms similarly threaded like some culinary bunting. Smoked hams, covered in muslin, were sometimes treated to several coats of whitewash, which

PERFECT CHOICE

This French cottage window opens with a characteristically practical but charming metal bolt. It looks out through crisp blue and white gingham frilly curtains on to a leafy garden.

GARDEN PRODUCE IN PROFUSION

In this sunny little window, honesty, everlasting flowers, Chinese lanterns and rosemary are all hanging up to dry; apples, pears, ridge cucumbers and tomatoes are ripening by the windowsill.

DRIED HARVEST SPLENDOUR

A white-painted sash window with largish panes in an old-fashioned shape looks out on to a tall hedge and acts as a backdrop to a veritable celebration of dried autumn flowers, including teazels, helichrysum and asparagus.

A KITCHEN SHRINE TO HORTICULTURE

Another angle on the kitchen with hand-painted shutters. This time you can see a small hand-painted display cabinet, which holds a collection of hand-painted plates with a citrus theme and is hung about with bunches of drying grasses and flowers.

ARTISTIC TOUCH

Obviously arranged by an artist, this hand-made natural-wood dresser, with small and not over-polished brass handles, houses a lovely mixture of pottery and china. A large spongeware jug holds some boughs of hawthorn.

SPORTING PRINTS

Stagecoach and sporting prints as well as a number of hand-decorated plates are often used as wall decorations for a cottage dining room. The picture frames of such prints are traditionally narrow and simple.

formed an effective crust that kept out flies and dust as well as preserving the moisture of the meat. Fruits and berries were also bottled, jellied or jammed.

Between them, the larder and the kitchen housed a great variety of wooden, earthenware, glass and stoneware containers. Herbs were stored in paper bags, while flour and sugar were kept in wooden tubs. Cereals too were stored in wooden bins, raised from the floor on mouse-proof tiles. There would always be some earthenware or glass jars containing some pickled onions or shallots as well as rows of jams and preserves. Salt was often stored in a container known as a wall salt—a wooden lidded box which hung on the kitchen wall.

Bread crocks, salt-glazed storage jars, brick-clay pots, pewter and tin canisters all contained food—hunt them out now and use them to hide less aesthetic packets.

Adaptable furniture

The versatile kitchen dresser only really came into its own in the 18th century with the advent of cheap china, and thereafter it was considered an essential fixture in any cottage kitchen. Before that, a few small shelves or open

racks were used for storage, with saucepans and pots hanging from nails in the walls. Cutlery racks simply sat on the work surfaces. The first dresser consisted of a flat board fixed to the kitchen wall at waist height on which food was prepared or 'dressed'. Soon shelves were fitted above and cupboards below, and gradually regional differences developed. The back of the dresser, which was often as tall as the room, was generally boarded and the shelves of varying depths were set at different heights to accommodate all the different sizes of plate.

Today, a wide variety of old dressers (along with many reproductions) are available, primarily in oak or pine. As well as being one of the most authentic and attractive ways of furnishing a cottage-style kitchen, the dresser is also one of the most efficient. Providing cupboards, drawers, display shelves and work surface, it will be at least as useful as fitted units that take up the same space—and much more in keeping with the overall style.

While a separate dining room is still a luxury in most cottages, there are various small tables that started life as side tables or tea tables in much grander establishments, which would make suitable dining tables in the small

THE EPITOME OF COTTAGE LIFE

An original cream-coloured solid-fuel stove is really the epitome
of cottage life. It dries the clothes which are hung above it; copes
with any amount of cooking, from toast to Christmas dinner;
keeps food warm; heats the room and the water; dries out the
gumboots and seems to have a soul of its own.

SPARSE AND SIMPLE TO COMPLEMENT THE ARCHITECTURE
The big dark beams are allowed to dominate in this
whitewashed cottage. The delightful solid pine cupboards, the stripped
chest and the fine oak table are all left their natural colour,
and the modern ladder-back chairs are in natural wood.

house. The Pembroke table, which has flap-down sides and a central section at one end, is a very useful and adaptable piece of furniture. So is the Sutherland table which has a very narrow central portion, so that the table when folded away is little wider than a shelf.

Oak gate-leg tables with barley-twist legs have been made since the middle of the 17th century, but during the last 80 years they have been commercially produced on a large scale and are therefore readily available and quite inexpensive. When the varnish has been stripped off, they are frequently nice pieces of oak which, with a bit of wax polish, will take on a good colour of their own.

Pine washstands make excellent sideboards; often with marble tops and tiled surrounds, they are really practical in a dining room furnished with other stripped and painted woods.

Sets of dining chairs are among the most expensive items of antique furniture, so buy singly and build up a harlequin set. Choose a country stick-back style or a ladder-back with a rush seat, for these are common styles that will vary only with regional differences. Mismatched chairs have a higgledy-piggledy charm of their own; you could unify them perhaps with tie-on squab seat cushions. Rounded wheel-back Windsor chairs are also prolific, as are the

COZY CORNER
Small solid-fuel ranges something like this are still installed in many modern cottages.
They are used as open fires or closed stoves and are excellent for baking and making pies.
This homely little corner is very cottagey with its wooden chair, commandeered by the cat,
and a wicker basket full of ironing in the background.

robust captain's chairs. You'll be unlikely to find these in sets, as they were commonly made for use in pubs and barber shops. They look good beside the Windsor chair and double up as comfortable and robust armchairs.

Rustic table settings

The earliest plates were bread trenchers made from flat loaves. Wooden platters followed, and later still, polished pewter plates were used exclusively—even in humble households—until cheap china came on to the market. Nowadays, wooden-handled cutlery or bone-handled styles seem most appropriate in the cottage—the former looks its best teamed with chunky pottery plates and bowls, while the latter looks fine with simple earthenware. Many of the early transfer-printed designs are being reproduced on china today—informal patterns of flowers and birds are much more sympathetic to country settings than bone china. A hotch-potch of plates, none matching but unified by style or colour, looks marvellous too.

Drinking vessels would have been goblets or tumblers of handblown glass, horn or pewter. A latterday alternative which looks suitably rustic could be the the reconstituted bottle glass which, with all its lumps and imperfections and greenish hue, does have an authentic hand-made look to it.

Sleeping and Bathing

In the original two-room cottages, the sleeping apartment was no more than a space under the roof rafters often reached not by stairs, but by a ladder. There was no privacy—all the family slept together, with the parents in the middle of the bed and the children ranged either side in order of age. When separate rooms were created, they all led one off another without interconnecting passages. Sometimes bed alcoves were built into the thickness of the walls of the cottage. Otherwise, bed boxes or settle beds were quite common, thus enabling the main living room to double up as a bedroom.

The bed box was either free-standing or fitted into the panelling of the room. It was just like sleeping in a cupboard—ventilation holes in the doors ensured that the sleeper didn't suffocate overnight. Alternatively, it would be curtained off from the main room with a little space beside the bed to afford a bit of privacy for dressing.

Settle beds were a primitive form of sofa bed: high-back settles, used as sideboards by day, had seats that folded forwards to form a sleeping trough. It doesn't take much imagination to see how both these designs could translate into the modern cottage—panelled cots and convertible beds are equally practical today.

The brass bedstead or its cast-iron counterpart was a reaction against the old wooden bedsteads with their heavy stuffed mattresses, which were believed to harbour vermin.

BEDROOM UNDER THE EAVES

There's something secure about a bedroom under the eaves, where birds rustle about pecking at the moss on the slates and the world seems some way away. This room is just large enough for a brass bedstead and a newborn baby's crib.

Brass and iron bedsteads are currently very popular again, and both antique and reproduction versions are available. Painted utility designs, originally produced for institutional use, have an appealing simplicity which looks very appropriate in a cottage bedroom. Simple wooden bedsteads (or even just wooden headboards) are also very much in keeping.

If you're buying an old bedstead, make sure that the side rails are intact: it's all too easy to find pretty head and footboards but they aren't much use unless they can be fitted together. The mattress normally fits on to a lattice frame. It's also safer to stick to conventional modern sizes—otherwise it will prove to be a very expensive business getting a new mattress made to measure.

A LITTLE HAVEN

Cottage bedrooms are a haven from the day's toil. They can be either very simple or a dreamworld of roses and frills, like this one. A narrow brass bedstead commands the rural view through the window. Evidence of nimble fingers lies around in the patchwork, embroidery and lace.

NO NEED FOR FRILLS

There has been no attempt to dress up or disguise this downstairs lavatory, which is small but very functional. The tiled floor is easy to clean, the wooden lavatory seat comfortable, the basin just big enough to wash the hands in and the old photographs amusing and entertaining.

YOUNG GIRL'S HIDEAWAY

This pink and white room is light and feminine for a young girl. The glazed
chintz eiderdown is pretty and warm; the pink and white curtains are perfectly in
keeping. The alcove created by the slope of the roof and the chimneybreast is just
wide enough to hold a pale wood chest of drawers with tiny brass knobs.
A little ladder-back chair has a hand-made cover with stitched-on braid.

A PERFECT SETTING

The double window on the corner of the house creates a wide, wide windowsill which forms a good display cabinet. An old tea-set, a piece of glass, some primitive pigs and a silver dressing set show up well in this setting.

Bedcoverings—a cottage art

Bedcoverings haven't changed that much over the years—long bolsters and feather pillows were listed in the household inventories of Chaucer's day and sheets were commonly made of linen. Many cottagers grew their own flax, and although it was hard work preparing the fibres for spinning, once the yarn was woven it made the strongest, longest-lasting cloth known. The unmarried girls were called spinsters because they had to spin enough yarn to fit out their households with cloth by the time they married. Raw cotton was imported to Europe from America and the East. Not being an indigenous crop, it wasn't used by country folk until the 19th century.

A quilt was, in the old days, a general term for any thick coverlet—at its simplest, two woven blankets with feathers or wool between them. Quilts developed into a cottage art. As women gathered together in quilting circles, they would work communal quilts to present as a wedding gift to a young couple or to commemorate a special occasion.

DARK FURNITURE, DARK BEAMS

The owners of this elderly cottage have chosen traditional furniture, in keeping with the home's age and style. Both mantelpiece and chest of drawers have been used traditionally to display mirror, photographs and a variety of other personal belongings.

BOLD BUT DISCIPLINED

This disciplined arrangement is bold but so very simple that it doesn't
compete with the old and interesting walls. The remains of the red paint
between the oak beams are echoed by the wide red stripes of the
counterpane, and the iron bedstead itself is charming but not fussy.

AN ATTIC BEDROOM

Many cottage bedrooms are tucked in under the roof. Here there is just room for
a small dressing table and a hanging cupboard under the mansard roof. The matchboarding,
walls, shelves and metal fireplace have all been painted white, and the Gothic window is
curtained by seersucker on hinged rods which can be turned into the alcove during the day.

58

Patchwork is also a pauper's fabric—the patches were cut from partially worn-out clothes then stitched together to make counterpanes, chair covers and even curtains. White cotton crocheted bedspreads were another common bed-covering, with feather eiderdowns and knitted blankets providing extra layers of warmth.

Sparse furnishings

Cottage bedrooms were always sparsely furnished. Wardrobes were not a common item until the last century because clothes were kept folded in drawers and chests, rather than being hung up. Although cupboards or 'presses' were often fitted into the alcoves of early houses, it is a shame to spoil the irregular proportions of a cottage room by lining it out with built-in furniture. Instead, use dress racks, rails hidden behind chintzy curtains or free-standing wardrobes; rows of wooden pegs or bentwood hat stands are other ways of hanging clothes.

Other furniture would have included a wash stand, complete with ewer, basin and slop bucket, and the chamber-pot, kept either under the bed or in a cheaply made wooden commode cupboard which stood beside the bed. Pictures on the walls would certainly have included a religious text. Candles would have provided the only form of light.

Today's cottage bedroom demands the same puritan sparsity. Bare floorboards covered in rag rugs or woven dhurries are much more appropriate than fitted carpets. Keep the window treatments simple—use neat roller blinds that sit within the window reveals, or Victorian-style lace panels threaded on to a brass rod which will filter the light and make dappled patterns of their own. Hinged curtain

BRIGHT AS A SUMMER SKY

A generous Adamsez basin is supported here on heated chrome towel
rails. This small corner has the feel of a bright summer's day.
The fresh blue and white scheme is carried through the
pattern on the tiles, the ceramic jars and the towels and linen.

<u>CLEVER USE OF SPACE</u>

When spaces are small, ingenuity can save the day.
Many cottages show clever solutions which are not
too sophisticated. In this tiny bathroom, the basin's
workings are concealed by a gathered skirt.

<u>LIGHT RELIEF</u>

This is another tiny room. It has been painted a darkish blue but the
sun streaming through the window immediately lightens it. Other
relieving factors are the pale colours of the quilt and the patchwork
tablecloth, and the light picture and lampshade.

poles are a useful solution to situations where the walls are
built adjacent to a window, like a dormer; the rod swings
back off the casement so that the fabric can hang against the
abutting wall when not in use.

Small bedrooms often look best when the walls and
ceilings are treated as one, with the wallpaper or paint
running up and over sloping surfaces to blur the divisions.
This is especially important in rooms with lots of irregular
roof angles.

Bathrooms—a modern development

Bathroom design harks back to the mid-19th century, for
by then it was considered a necessity in any gentleman's
home. The deep roll-top baths with claw feet and bulbous
taps, the high-level water cisterns with decoratively
patterned lavatory pans, and the shaving tables with
integral mirrors and basins were all products of the new age
of sanitation.

However, until recently bathrooms were unheard of in
cottages. Baths were taken in front of the kitchen fire,
ablutions were performed at the sink and the lavatory was
simply a privy at the bottom of the garden. Unless they
were built over a natural spring or beside a water course,
these privies were merely earth closets—a wooden seat
over a bucket which was covered with earth or ashes after
each use. While water closets were introduced into polite
society in the 18th century, it was only very much later that
they became part of cottage life, for the high-level water
cisterns which allowed a given amount of water to flush out
the pan had to be connected to a proper plumbing system.

SIMPLICITY IN A WARM CLIMATE

Cottages in sunny climates need very little furniture, as few clothes and belongings are
necessary. There is plenty to startle the eye out of doors so simplicity is welcome inside.
This simple divan bed has a valance and a subtly spotted quilt, the room is painted a
tranquil but not simpering pink and the only decoration is a bowl of flowers.

Baths were portable tubs which were originally made of wood; by the last century, they were of enamelled tin. The hip bath was the most common design; it was shaped rather like an armchair with a rounded base and cut-away sides, so that the bather could sit down deep into the water with legs hanging over the sides. The Sitz bath is a similarly deep, high-sided bath which is still available today.

Comfortably decorated, today's cottage bathroom is something of a hybrid. Often converted from another bedroom, it may well have a little fireplace as well as old built-in cupboards which today could house the hot water tank. The bath and basin might be built into a unit made of old timbers or modern matchboarding—pine was the poor man's timber, while mahogany finishes were for much grander homes. Or, instead of a wooden front, the basin unit could feature a pretty, sprigged cotton skirt—an inexpensive alternative often favoured by cottagers.

Walls of ceramic tiles can often be unsympathetic and clinical, but oil-based eggshell paint or water-based vinyl silk would be a practical finish for walls as well as providing an excellent base for coloured glazes and varnishes. The bathroom floor, like the bedroom, could simply be bare boards, carefully sanded and filled to make sure there aren't any splinters, and then covered with cotton mats; or it could be laid with cork tiles.

Wooden duckboards, a wicker stool, pretty ceramic soap dishes, old-fashioned cork mats and wooden towel horses as well as deep piles of thick towels, huckaback cloths and a bowl of home-made pot-pourri are all finishing touches that complete the picture.

BLUE-AND-WHITE JUGS

Often associated with the country cottage, blue-and-white pottery is more highly sought after than ever. The Chinese were the first to use cobalt blue with painted decoration on porcelain, and as trade with the Dutch East India Company brought Chinese wares to the West, so the traditional blue-and-white along with other pieces of Chinoiserie became increasingly fashionable during the 17th century.

Many European manufacturers tried to emulate the Chinese porcelain—the Dutch produced a tin-glazed earthenware which we know as Delft—but it was in England that the process of transfer-printed designs on porcelain and earthenware was refined and later mass-produced in the Staffordshire potteries. Spode, in particular, started to reproduce the Chinese patterns, but while the designs were oriental in origin they had a naive charm which was definitely European.

The beginning of the 19th century saw a boom in the Staffordshire potteries. Huge volumes of blue printed wares, especially earthenware, were produced. In those days, the copyright laws were very lax and so

Supplied by Sue Norman

craftsmen were able to reproduce the work of various artists—taking topographical scenes from the popular engravings of the day and transferring them on to earthenware shapes. When a Registration of Design Act came into effect in the 1840s, the plagiarism had to cease, and designers turned to romantic pastoral scenes.

Often a popular design of one manufacturer was copied or adapted by another—but some of those designs which originated in the 18th century are still available today. The most famous of all, the

Willow Pattern, was introduced in its earliest form in the 1780s. The Asiatic Pheasant, Spode's Blue Italian and the Wild Rose are all 18th and 19th century designs still being made today.

All the blue-and-white jugs shown here are transfer-printed from hand-engraved copper plates on to white earthenware. The design is printed in a cobalt-blue oxide on to tissue paper, which is then applied in sections on to the ceramic shape. The paper is soaked off, leaving behind the oil-based printed design which is then fired.

FROM LEFT TO RIGHT

Milk jug depicting a tiger hunt c.1870. Helmet-shaped cream jug with faux bamboo handle, acorn pattern design and Greek key border, c.1820. Large jug made by Rogers of Staffordshire, c.1820. 1830s printed jug with 'clobbering'—an overglaze painting in yellows and pinks. Large Dutch jug made in Staffordshire with flowers on a line-engraved background. Small milk jug with Abbey pattern, late 19th century. 19th century water jug by Minton.

Inside meets Outside

The most important outside feature of a house is the front door—in most early cottages it was the only entrance, although subsequent additions have often given rise to a secondary back door. The door would have opened into the main living area of the home. Not only did it serve as a gangway for men—and animals too when they shared accommodation—but it was also often the only source of light. To keep the draught out, an ox hide or coarse fabric was used that could be pulled up like a blind. Heavy door curtains and padded draught stops are still often the only way of keeping wintry flurries at bay.

In its most basic form, the porch was—and is—no more than a hood to keep the rain off the front door step; like a heavy eyebrow above the doorway, it also serves to give emphasis to the frontage. Designs vary—for a rough stone cottage it might consist of a heavy granite slab resting on corbels; for a brick building it might be a piece of slate on wrought-iron brackets projecting from the brick; for an early 19th century plastered cottage it could be a small, shaped lead roof. Pretty trellis-work porches were also quite common during the first half of the last century.

The enclosed porch is more than an additional windbreak. It can double as a hallway, housing all the paraphernalia of outdoor life as well as offering shelter for less hardy plants and a place to kick off gumboots, wipe the dogs and dry firewood. Sturdy little stone porches are

RURAL SCENE
In southern England red brick and leaded panes epitomize rural cottage life. This window opens on to a charming garden and a neighbouring larger house. The window furniture is black iron—brass or chrome would be inappropriate here.

FRAMEWORK FOR A GARDEN VIEW

A dappled decorative wall-finish and
the thick walls of this cottage make an
enchanting framework for a view of
mown lawn leading to open country.
The lead downpipe has been painted a
rural green. The container, painted in
bargeware style, brings the outside in
with a generous supply of pot-pourri.

LETTING IN THE LIGHT

A glass-panelled door and a small window let in
the light to brighten this cottage entrance,
which can be seen from the kitchen.

KEEPING UP OLD TRADITIONS

This cottage has not changed its way of life for
many years. A brick floor leads through a
white-painted door to a brick path outside.

HALLWAY WITH A VIEW

Enter this hallway with its wide but variable wooden boards and you immediately get
a splendid view of well-tended, green and luscious shrubbery. The large window makes
this a very light and seemingly spacious entrance. The wood panelling has
all been painted white, and very fine muslin curtains are simply there for looks;
they will hardly keep the light out, even when drawn closed.

BACK DOOR CHARM

The back door of this brick cottage leads into a white-painted interior where a wide
plank of hooks has been fixed to the wall to store a host of things from family
history, including some headgear from Indian days, and beloved old baskets.

WINDOW DISPLAY

A kitchen or porch window with a less than spectacular
view is a good place to display a collection of bottles or
other glass. The light behind the glass sets it off nicely.
This is also a good place for indoor plants.

A FRIENDLY SPOT

On the terrace, a couple of battered old wicker chairs will
survive the odd rainstorm and make a comfortable stop on
the way indoors with freshly picked herbs. This is also a
good spot for performing tasks like shelling peas.

MELLOW AND RELAXING

A small patio has been built at the back of this cottage using bricks similar in tone to those of the
house. The bamboo folding chair blends into the mellow background, while the white-painted tubs
and Gothic stools create a pleasing contrast. This is an excellent place to relax and enjoy the sun.

frequently found in the more exposed parts of the country—they offer real shelter against the prevailing winds as well as visually engendering a sense of security. Materials would be of the same quality and character as that of the house: faced with a rugged stone or timber lintel, the porch would have a paved floor and perhaps little slit windows in the side walls. The proportions would be quite substantial to prevent it from looking like a little afterthought tacked on to the front of the building. Glass porches date mostly from the latter part of the 19th century.

Extensions to the back of the cottage can vary from a series of passages that link an assortment of outbuildings with the scullery, to a permanent garden room that doubles as an out-of-season store. There's nothing luxurious about this type of room—it serves as the shed and often the coal hole too, where potato baskets and wooden trugs hang alongside generations of work clothes, stiff with baked mud and grime.

The sun room or conservatory is the modern way of creating a transition from the house to the garden. The heat of the house helps to warm the conservatory so minimal energy is needed; while the conservatory in return acts as a buffer between the house and the elements. Even a glass porch without sides will provide enough protection for the tender perennials and shrubs which might not survive the cold months in the open.

While the architectural style of the conservatory should echo the architecture of the cottage, the furniture and fittings could combine the best of both worlds—house *and* garden. The choice of flooring will help determine whether the conservatory predominantly reflects the house in style or belongs more to the garden. For surfaces with an indoor look, but tough enough to withstand frequent wetting and muddy boots, choose quarry tiles or heavy linoleum. Alternatively, bricks and flagstones are more reminiscent of garden paths. Whatever the floors are made of, it is important that provision is made for drainage, since plants in such a warm, sunny environment will require a great deal of watering.

FARMHOUSE STYLE

Farmhouses reveal the personalities of generations of inhabitants. Their interests and tastes, furnishings and possessions create an odd but happy mix—the reason being that every stick of furniture is there for a purpose, to be used, eaten off, sat on. It was never designed like that, it just grew to be that way, and therein lies its greatest attraction. To the city dweller, a farmhouse may mean a dresser full of blue and white china, a cat basking in the warmth of a vast kitchen range, a basket of fresh brown eggs on a scrubbed table, rocking chairs and patchwork quilts. The reality to the farmer and his family may be different. But the farmhouse ideal is close to our hearts because it stands for all that is natural and good. It is the very essence of home.

ACHIEVING THE LOOK

Farmhouses can range from the relatively humble to the fairly grand, but what they all have in common is a practical, down-to-earth quality. Farmhouse style is robust and functional, good-natured and comfortable.

Underfoot

Living on a farm means spending more time outside than indoors, so the first essential with farmhouse floors is that they should be easy to keep clean. Areas under most stress, such as the hall and kitchen floor, are likely to be of local stone, slate or quarry tiles. In a larder or a dairy such a floor serves the additional purpose of keeping the room cool even in the height of summer; inside the house, where a cold, hard floor is less than pleasant if you have to stand around on it all day, vinyl or cork can provide a warmer, more yielding alternative. This is the kind of flooring to aim for when recreating the farmhouse look.

In the living room, the floor can be covered with one or two large square carpets or Oriental rugs; all the kitchen floor needs is a rag rug in front of the range. Coir matting provides a serviceable floor covering in the hall and in children's rooms. For the rest of the house, wide oak floorboards need no embellishment except for the occasional bedside rug.

Walls and ceilings

In a farmhouse, the treatment of walls, ceilings and woodwork is likely to be dictated by the building itself. Unless

A range of useful baskets, a made-to-measure plate rack above the sink unit and a scrubbed deal table all reflect the basic practicality of the farmhouse kitchen. The stencilling on the doors is a lovingly added extra.

Highly polished wooden boards and a mahogany table take pride of place in this room. The starkness is relieved by the wallpaper and framed pictures.

The epitome of farmhouse living: plenty of good-quality, sturdy equipment, carefully stored to be ready for use at a moment's notice. Quarry tiles are easily cleaned, and white makes a good simple background for the inevitable clutter.

you want to plaster over exposed beams, you do not have much choice other than to paint between them, though you should not necessarily limit yourself to chilly white. Warm yellows and deep golds look good against blackened wood, suggesting both firelight and sunshine. To raise a low-beamed ceiling, paint plaster and wood the same light colour. To lower a high ceiling in order to make a room cozier, paint it a darker colour than the walls.

A snug winter room most often used after dark, such as the dining room, can take deep rich colours like wine, rust and purple. Texture will be important here in velvet, tapestry and stained wood, so a darkly patterned paper may be preferable to paint. Use wallpaper, too, in bedrooms, where a fresh, light and delicate flower print will be shown

off to excellent advantage in quirky attics with steeply pitched ceilings and deep window recesses.

An abundance of polished wood is a characteristic feature of farmhouses. Traditionally, the wood is stained dark, but if you like the look of bare wood you could strip the doors and the stairway and treat them with linseed oil to give a deep, natural glow. Alternatively, painted woodwork would look clean and simple.

Fabrics and window treatments

Faded chintz is probably the fabric that springs most readily to mind in association with a farmhouse. Sensible tweed is also a good furniture covering in a house where there are dogs. Flowers will crop up again on the curtains

A purpose-built cupboard, painted green but beginning to fade, holds a formidable array of collected items from past activities on the farm: some carved and painted wooden birds, and a fine collection of stoneware jars.

The ultimate farmhouse still life—but for real! This corner shelf is used for storing earthenware jugs and cooling bread fresh from the oven. On the walls are a charming old family clock, two blue-and-white platters, and a bunch of 'dipped' candles waiting for a power cut.

Stripped pine is not typical of traditional farmhouses, but its unpretentious, mellow look is very much in keeping with the spirit of farmhouse style.

in the living room and bedrooms, but choose each fabric for its individual appeal, and not because it matches another. As long as you like everything for itself, it is bound to make a harmonious, though maybe surprising, whole.

Heavy velvet is essential at ill-fitting doors to keep out the draughts and looks good in the dining room too. Gingham is crisp and fresh in the kitchen. On the whole curtains should be kept simple, avoiding swags, frills and other extravagant effects.

Farmhouses make lavish use of rugs and throws: a quilt on the bed, a shawl or bedspread covering a worn-out chair, a knitted patchwork rug tucked into a small sofa. A lot of the rugs and covers are handmade and many of them are old. Embroidery is much in evidence on the cushion covers, the tablecloths, dressing table mats, pillows and even sheets.

Furniture

Farmhouse furniture is above all practical: the great dresser of oak or pine, the massive kitchen table with its scrubbed top and enough sturdy chairs to accommodate extra workers at harvest time are farmhouse classics. Much of the furniture will have been in the family for generations, which means a good mixture of the simple and the grand. For example, you might find a small elm chair with a painted back and delicately turned legs next to a splendid mahogany bureau.

Seating will be well worn-in and eminently comfortable.

You won't find such creative flair in most farmhouses as in the painted walls and furniture here, but the primitive free-form brush strokes and the bold colours are eminently suitable for a working farmhouse.

This old farmhouse has been treated with suitable dignity and respect. Modern quarry tiles have replaced the original floor, the interior walls are painted white, a solid-fuel stove acts as room heater and the simple wooden furniture is kept to a minimum.

Squashy sofas, sagging chairs and soft pouffes may be covered with faded chintz, and there might be a battered leather chair or two in front of the fire.

Upstairs brass bedsteads, rosewood dressing tables, marble washstands and painted trunks and wardrobes set the tone.

Warmth of the hearth

The kitchen range is probably the most important feature of the farmhouse and is kept alight day and night all the year round to provide both warmth and food. A roaring log fire is traditional in the living room and will be built on fire-dogs in an alcove that is almost big enough to sit in. There might be a padded leather fender seat around the fire,

the ideal position from which to toast muffins or roast chestnuts. The bedroom fireplaces are minute in contrast. In Victorian times it was the custom to fill these tiny grates with hot embers from downstairs upon going to bed.

Finishing touches

Although collections of pottery, paintings and needlework may have grown over the years, embellishments in a farmhouse are not so much objects that have been sought out and bought, as the adjuncts of country life itself. Objects which are practical, such as storm lamps and dairy bowls, and which are inside the house because they are being used for something, take precedence over tables full of fussy knick-knacks and other classic dust collectors.

Living and Relaxing

The room used as the sitting room will have been chosen because it commands the best view in the house—the windows may frame a lush green lawn sloping gently towards a duckpond with an orchard in the distance. Not much used formerly except for entertaining, nowadays a farmhouse sitting room has a thoroughly lived-in, comfortable feel. This is partly because the room has gradually evolved over the years, so that although everything harmonizes, nothing actually matches. It's also partly because it has been turned into a family room, with almost as much time spent here as in the kitchen.

An important aspect of the sitting room is the seating, which should be inviting enough to reassure even the most nervous visitor. The sofas and chairs may have seen better days—a battered brown leather chesterfield could have stuffing oozing from one of its arms, a becushioned wicker chair might be used as a scratching post by the cat, and the armchairs will probably be deeper-seated than their maker intended.

The important thing is to have furniture that you can sink into and put your feet up on after a hard day's work, chairs that will mould themselves obediently to tired bodies and pouffes that will support aching legs. The chintz loose covers may be faded and patched at the arms; the flowered curtains at the window may be differently patterned but chosen to echo the same warm range of, say, pinks and

TIMEWORN ELEGANCE

A very old farmhouse this, whose almost Gothic beams and great slab-stone floors have been complemented with ancient, well-worn oriental carpets and heavy curtains tied back with ropes.

delicate greens, or perhaps rich deep blues and reds and cream. Huge soft cushions can pick out some of the colours in muted velvets; others may be embroidered, beaded, crocheted, or made of patchwork.

A companionable mix

Rather dilapidated seating does not look at all incongruous next to really quite grand pieces of furniture that may have been inherited or perhaps picked up at auction. This is the place to put a solid mahogany sideboard with an imposing mirror set in its majestically carved back. On it could stand a silver teaset on its own tray, or crystal decanters set among recent framed photographs of family and friends. On the wall above such a sideboard is a good place for an array of elegant silver lids from tureens and chafing dishes, a reminder of the days when several courses were consumed at each meal, including breakfast.

You could choose a leather-topped desk of generous proportions to balance the sideboard; its top will undoubtedly get covered in a profusion of papers and objects in daily use, providing another contrast of formal with informal, grand with mundane.

UNPRETENTIOUS AND COMFORTABLE

Comfort without pretensions is the hallmark of the farmhouse. The fabrics and carpet add warmth to the rather stark stone, and the basket chairs are creakily capacious. The fireplace dominates—warm and glowing in winter, the frame for a flower arrangement in summer.

GOTHIC INTERIOR

The Gothic interior of this old house has a sculpted look appreciated by its owners, who have painted the walls a spanking white and kept all woodwork dark in contrast. The furniture is custom-built, purposeful and solid. The pendulum clock also has a Gothic quality.

A pretty, free-standing work basket in wicker or inlaid wood would make a nice addition to a cozy sitting room, as would an old-fashioned radiogram. In a farmhouse parlour a piano and a stack of sheet music would not look self-conscious. A small upright piano in delicate walnut with candle sconces and mother-of-pearl inlay would fit in well. Nowadays pianos can be picked up quite cheaply, and if you have an alcove that would hold one, it can bring liveliness and warmth to a room even if you do not play yourself. If the case is not in good condition, you could paint it in dull greens and reds, picking out the detail with a small geometric border and decorating the panels with delicately worked jugs of flowers.

A roaring fire

Think of a farmhouse and you inevitably think of an inglenook fireplace that shares its enormous chimney with that of the kitchen range and is almost big enough to walk into. A huge log fire, fuelled by timber from all over the farm, burns here and manages to warm the bedrooms above it as well. A large stock of logs saves extra trips to the woodshed. As well as the traditional wicker basket, you

PRACTICAL CONSIDERATIONS

A farmhouse furnished with characteristic practicality.
The economical coir matting on the floor, simple pale
walls and fireplace, and plain country furniture—
including a child's rush-seated chair—are all very
typical of farmhouse style.

DECEPTIVELY SIMPLE
Shelves hung with drying herbs frame a portrait of a prize
bull. The draped fabric is a simple but effective way of visually
linking the painting with the shelves, and the seeming hotch-potch
of items on display have actually been carefully selected
to echo the colours of the painting.

could look out for a more unusual log box: perhaps an old grain bin or a grocer's storage bin.

The warm rosy brick of an old fireplace can be echoed in a well-worn oriental silk rug in front of the hearth. In winter you can draw the sofa up close to the fire. Next to a farmhouse fireplace, set into the wall, there might be a small bread oven behind a painted iron door. This would be the ideal place for drinks and some glasses, or maybe a stack of children's games.

Just as frequently seen in a farmhouse living room as an open fire is a cast-iron log-burning stove. More economical than a fire, its heat output can be regulated, and it can be left in overnight, which means less work. Log-burning stoves give off a powerful heat and are a comforting presence in any room. One special pleasure in a draughty house is that they throw heat downwards as well as in every other direction, which means warm feet and not just a scalding face. Such a stove can also act as a backup to a cooker—the French chimney stoves are equipped with a hotplate and most other types have a suitable surface where

a casserole can be left to cook gently all day out of the way of the kitchen if needs be. Using solid fuel does create a certain amount of dust, but this is a small price to pay for the comfort it generates.

Mellow colours

The sitting room floor in a farmhouse is probably of polished brick (old bricks can be re-laid, sanded and sealed to make them easy to clean), or wide oak boards, or maybe mellow parquet. Extra warmth can be provided by large fringed carpets in addition to the hearth rug, in colours like old rose and much-faded cornflower blue. A beamed living room looks good with the plaster painted white, deep ochre or creamy pink or apricot.

The lighting in the sitting room should be as varied as the furniture—a turned oak standard lamp with a fringed shade, softly glowing wall lights, a practical modern reading lamp, candles and a lantern suspended from the beams ready to take over in a power cut can all find their place in this most harmonious of rooms.

Cooking and Eating

The farmhouse dining room is not used for everyday, and a fire is lit here only when large numbers of family and friends come to eat. One way of making a dining room look more lived-in is to make it a cozy quiet place to read in, somewhere to retire to in peace when life in the sitting room gets too noisy. One wall could be reserved for fitted bookshelves to hold old red and brown leatherbound books mixed up with modern paperbacks. Reading is always more comfortable lying down, and you could have a velvet couch with a rug of multi-coloured knitted squares thrown over it; nearby a little table with a green-shaded reading lamp.

The remaining walls could be papered in a dark colour—crimson or bottle green, perhaps—giving a warmth and snugness that will bring intimacy to candlelit dinners on winter nights, when the velvet curtains are drawn tightly against the elements. On these occasions, a bright fire will cheer the hearts of guests who have perhaps negotiated narrow country lanes and braved ice and snow in order to come and pay a visit.

Soften the formality of an imposing marble fireplace by cluttering the mantelpiece with homely objects such as a pipe rack and tobacco jar alongside a glass-domed clock. Add a lively collection of hand-painted jugs and vases filled with dried flowers and grasses, peacock feathers and coloured spills for lighting the fire.

The Centre of Family Life

A large pine table dominates this kitchen with its dark quarry tiles. Two upholstered and working fireplace chairs sit by the fire, perhaps for pre-dinner drinks. Note that the wooden chairs are related in style but not matching (as, indeed, are the glasses).

CORNER DISPLAY

Corner cabinets make sense when space is at a premium in a busy kitchen. This one with its shaped shelves has been used to display a collection of traditional pottery and porcelain.

FUNCTIONAL BUT GOOD-LOOKING

In this large kitchen, a good deal of space is taken up by the all-important kitchen table, which acts as dining table and worktop. All around are objects collected over the years for their practicality and solid good looks. Though few are matching, they all live comfortably together since they reflect the tastes of their owner and a particular way of life.

The farmhouse dining table is generally large and solid and may have handsomely carved legs. It is usually of dark-stained wood. For a special family dinner it could be covered with a white damask cloth, self-patterned with leaves and flowers, and set with old silver, new glass and perhaps an interesting collection of odd but beautifully decorated plates.

This type of dining room really comes to life at Christmas, when watercolours haphazardly grouped around the walls can be topped with sprigs of holly, a huge bunch of mistletoe hung from the beams and an evergreen garland draped over the mantelpiece. The farmyard goose or turkey might be on the menu, and the family could sip glorious pink sloe gin made with the berries gathered from the autumn hedgerows.

Another possible scheme suitable for a farmhouse dining room is a light, summery feel with blond oak or elm furniture, whitewashed walls and pretty floral curtains. Such a room would suggest high tea with a salad and home-cured ham, the sun glinting on a pewter teapot and lending a bluish tinge to fine bone china. A tea trolly on wheels set with an embroidered tray cloth might stand in the corner laden with egg and cress sandwiches and scones topped with jam and cream.

The heart of the home

But for everyday, the family will gather round the kitchen table. The kitchen is the heart of any farmhouse. It means food, warmth and companionship. This is the engine room of the farm, where the work of running the house and feeding the family is carried out. Farming business is concluded here over a cup of coffee or a glass of beer; good friends drop in by the back door for a chat; children gather after school; and family matters, important and trivial, are discussed over the kitchen table.

Everyone who enters the kitchen will gravitate naturally towards the stove. Though a modern working farmhouse may well have an electric cooker and a microwave oven as well as a kitchen range, it is the range that is traditionally the heart of the kitchen in any self-respecting working farmhouse.

Today's cast-iron ranges are good-looking, clean and efficient—probably the most luxurious practical item that it is possible to possess. The fuel, which can be solid fuel, oil or gas, is enclosed in a cast-iron box, and the stove is so thoroughly insulated that you can comfortably lean against it. It will have either two or four ovens, the coolest ideal for cooking rice pudding or porridge overnight, warming plates or bringing orphaned newborn animals back to life,

DESIGNED FOR ENTERTAINING

Pine gives this kitchen a slightly
more modern look. Instead of a
dresser there are 'library shelves'.
The chairs are sturdy and comfortable
rather than elegant. The enormous
number of glasses and plates
suggests an emphasis on entertaining,
with plenty of good food and drink.

CULINARY ART
This is a dining room geared to eating in comfort.
The walls are a warm butter yellow, the chair and
bench softly cushioned. The table is businesslike and
well scrubbed, with the traditional drawer for cutlery.
On the wall is an enormous painting of food in the
process of being prepared.

MINGLING OF OLD AND NEW
This elderly kitchen has been brought up to date
in a sensitive manner. The small ceramic tiles
and modern set-in hob in no way interfere
with the charming window scene, and they
provide a surface for the many good, natural
ingredients used for cooking.

and the hottest just right for baking bread. The hotplates on top also work at different temperatures. Besides heating the room and cooking, the stove can provide hot water, and the larger ones can run radiators.

The best place for a kitchen range is inside the open hearth, where once food was cooked in a pot over the naked flames, a practice that claimed almost as many women's lives as did childbirth. A clothes horse or airer can be stood over the range to dry the washing on a damp day. Alternatively, an old-fashioned wooden slatted airer could be suspended from the ceiling above the range and raised and lowered by means of a pulley. These are not only useful on washday—you can hang bunches of herbs and flowers from them too.

In front of the range is the place for a traditional rag rug made of colourful strips of blanket or drab bits of men's suiting hooked through a jute backing. The components of these rugs—rags and sacks—being free, they were much in evidence underfoot when carpet was too expensive for most country dwellers. When they became too worn or dirty to be of further service they were thrown on the compost heap and new ones were made.

An efficient workplace

In the centre of the kitchen you will need a great table of well-scrubbed bleached wood, ideally with one or more drawers. Round it could be gathered an assortment of plain wooden chairs, a couple with high backs and arms, perhaps with cushioned pads tied to the backs of the seats with tapes. The tabletop provides a roomy working surface; elsewhere, slabs of slate or marble, perhaps from an old washstand, on top of solid wood cupboards, could be used for chopping vegetables and rolling pastry.

If you are furnishing a kitchen and want to avoid the uniformity of wall-to-wall units but your budget does not run to hand-made wood cupboards, you could create a soft country look quite cheaply by building wooden counters against the walls with shelves below. Tile the work surfaces with unglazed floor tiles, perhaps red quarry tiles or those with a speckled bird's egg pattern, and hang curtains underneath. Look out for secondhand curtains at jumble sales for an old-fashioned feel. This idea is particularly effective in a small kitchen, where a row of doors can make a room feel like a corridor when closed and an obstacle course when open.

Most of the objects in daily use in the kitchen—such as a handsome pair of scales with brass weights; blue-and-white striped china jars for sugar, salt and raisins; heavy, flat-bottomed pots and pans—can be stored on open shelves or hung from the wall. Above the counters you could hang racks of knives and other cooking utensils.

The tableware can be stored similarly on the dresser, that

most evocative and much-copied symbol of the farmhouse style. A farmhouse dresser should be as big as the room will hold, simply fashioned and well worn-in, and then it is the essence of homeliness.

Dressers came about in the 18th century when china started to be so cheaply produced that people could afford to buy it in quantity. Before that, such plates, cups and jugs as they may have owned were kept on a shelf edged with scalloped paper. The dresser grew out of the need for several such shelves, and some large dressers even incorporated a home for the dog—an ingenious use for the central recess between the lower cupboards.

A VIEW TO THE DINING AREA

This enormous room makes the most of old, well-built
equipment, such as the splendid enamelled stove. In the rest of the
room there is an emphasis on natural wood, apparent in the
varnished floorboards, the refectory-style table and set of sturdy
yet elegant chairs, and the pine boarding of the walls.

Massive antique dressers in pine or oak fetch high prices and need plenty of space. Smaller versions in less attractive wood can be stripped and painted in, say, pale green and cream—the main surface, which will get most of the wear, being left bare. Besides holding the crockery in everyday use, a dresser can be used to display eccentric collections of jelly moulds, egg cups or toast racks—the more interesting things you can crowd on to it, the better it looks.

A wall of bare red brick could form a backdrop to a collection of glass and ceramic rolling pins: look out for the delicately hand-painted ones, which were love tokens traditionally given by sailors to their sweethearts. Collections and displays of this sort look charming in the kitchen, but in the farmhouse kitchen they will undoubtedly have a functional bias.

For example, you might find wooden butter pats, heart-shaped cheese moulds, wicker baskets full of eggs and vegetables, stone crocks of wine or cider, wooden and terracotta bowls of fruit, enamelled storage jars and bins and heavy flat-bottomed saucepans of iron and copper. Some new piece of equipment might be a delight to look at, but in the farmhouse kitchen it will certainly get edged out by something more practical unless it is just as much a delight to use.

The kitchen sink

A deep white ceramic kitchen sink supported by brick plinths is preferable to a stainless steel unit. The best place for the sink is under a window, with a sill lined with pots of geraniums that go on flowering all the year round. Choose crisp cotton for the curtains. In summer you could hang a curtain of coloured glass beads in front of the open window to dissuade flies and make it a pleasant place to stand and do the washing up. You may be able to find a scrubbed wooden draining board for the dishes. Above it on the wall you can hang a wooden rack which will serve to store as well as drain crockery.

In the farmhouse scullery just off the kitchen used to be another very large china sink, big enough to soak the sheets in, and a broad shallow one for the vigorous rubbing of dirty clothes. Nowadays the scullery has frequently become a utility room housing the washing machine, tumble drier and freezer, and perhaps a dishwasher too. The scullery floor was traditionally tiled for easy mopping down after washday.

The kitchen floor too may be of tiles, brick or stone. Though easy to keep clean, such floors are cold and hard to stand on for any length of time. A warmer, more yielding surface such as vinyl or cork may be preferred in a modern home and vinyl tiles are available that simulate brick. Nevertheless, if you hanker after a real brick floor, so much the better. Old bricks can be laid in herringbone or block patterns. Odd blue or yellow bricks placed at random in a mainly rosy floor add to its interest. A brick floor can be sanded and sealed to give a regular surface.

The larder, storehouse of plenty

The larder is usually built on the north side of the farmhouse kitchen and separated from it by a thick wall to keep it cool. If you are lucky enough to have a larder, you can make it a pleasure to look into. If not, you can create a similar effect in a kitchen alcove by lining it with shelves from floor to ceiling. Larder shelves used to be covered in printed paper—today you can use washable oilcloth or you could simply paint them. Alternatively, lace or crocheted mats hanging over the edges of the shelves at intervals can look very pretty—and hooks can be added in between them for mugs.

On the shelves, you would expect to find gleaming jars and bottles of homemade jams, jellies and pickles, tinned food, pasta, large enamel storage bins for rice and flour and bread, cake tins and baskets containing eggs and fresh vegetables. The old-fashioned blue-and-white striped china storage jars can sometimes be found in antique shops, and some modern pottery, such as glazed brown earthenware, is equally suitable. Old brand-name tins make an eye-catching display. From the ceiling you can hang bunches of herbs, home-cured hams and some strings of garlic and onions.

People who have the opportunity to produce their own

FITTING OUT THE PANTRY

On this marvellous piece of home-made
furniture stands a collection of
traditional spongeware bowls
and jugs in blue and white.

CUSTOM-BUILT KITCHEN

Why go out and buy faceless units when you
can build your own kitchen exactly as you
want it from wood found in outbuildings?
The worktop here has been hygienically tiled.

A MINIMUM OF CLUTTER

A house whose inhabitants are proud of its
environment and its history has no need of
extra decoration. Here everything is kept to
a polished and cared-for minimum.

CATERING FOR A LARGE HOUSEHOLD

This is one of the working areas in the
kitchen of a large farmhouse, where there
were plenty of people to stoke the range and
keep things running smoothly.

food today are usually as enthusiastic about preserving it as
were previous generations. Vegetables are more often frozen
than packed in salt or pickled in vinegar—in fact, most
modern farmhouses will have an enormous freezer—but
fruit from the orchard and the hedgerows is still boiled up
in a great copper pan to make jam or dipped through a
muslin bag tied to the legs of an upturned kitchen stool to
make jelly.

The harvest over, the farm workers gather around the
kitchen table to mark the end of the farming year before
thoughts turn to sowing the next summer's crop. A harvest
supper is a time to celebrate plenty, and this is what the
farmhouse kitchen is all about. Here you can see, smell and
taste the results of the year's hard work.

The natural materials of the kitchen, the smooth stone
and marble, warm brick and scrubbed wood play their part
in producing an atmosphere that is far removed from the
almost surgical cleanliness of the modern city kitchen. The
farmhouse kitchen has not been planned, but has simply
grown out of long years of working to feed a family,
becoming a homely and comfortable place in which to
cook, eat and relax.

BUTTER AND CHEESE MAKERS

Butter and cheese moulds are very collectable items, and obviously perfectly suited to farmhouse style. The butter and cheese moulds shown here date from the mid to late 19th century—an age when most farms had their own dairy, sited against the north wall of the farmhouse and protected from the sun by a thatched or stone-tiled roof. An elder tree would have been planted close by, as it was believed to ward off the witches' sorcery.

Much activity took place in the 'milk room' or dairy, where big, flat wooden and pottery bowls held the milk. The cream was skimmed off and beaten until it coagulated to form butter. The whey was then drained off and the butter worked with beaters or 'hands' to remove the excess moisture before being worked into shapes—blocks, rounds or rolls which were finished with a decorative pattern.

There are various types of butter prints, from the flat stamps which press a pattern on to the surface, to the little box moulds which punch out a pattern, as well as miniature rolling pins and wheels. Often the prints

indicated what type of farm the butter came from—a swan would denote a river farm, a cow would indicate a dairy farm while others would simply take the English rose or the Scottish thistle.

The dairy equipment was commonly made from sycamore because it was an odourless wood that wouldn't taint the butter; otherwise, local woodmen would carve pieces from available fruitwood—apple and pear trees that had outgrown their usefulness—or boxwood and beech.

Cheese was similarly pressed into shape in a muslin-lined cheese mould or 'chesset'. A heavy board known as the cheese print or 'follower', slightly smaller than the diameter of the mould, was fitted on top of the cheese and weighted down under pressure. As the press tightened, so the superfluous whey was squeezed out through draining channels or weep holes. Although specially carved patterns were sometimes used for cheeses to commemorate special occasions such as a coronation or a royal visit, cheese moulds were generally less ornate than butter makers.

FROM LEFT TO RIGHT

19th century butter scoops in bowl. Butter bat c.1850. Sycamore butter box. On bread board, circular and boat-shaped butter makers; heart-pattern butter maker sits on double cheese print. Small boxwood butter marker with cow print next to small swan print marker. Late 19th century butter scoop and decorated butter scoop with print on handle. 1860s butter hands in bowl. Circular cheese print with quartered patterning and wooden handled butter knife (both mid 19th century).

Sleeping and Bathing

The geography of most farmhouses is mysterious—they seem to change shape depending on where you are standing to observe them. One part of the house mushrooming with attics, the next part long and low—no wonder the upper reaches are a veritable warren of rooms of all shapes and sizes, some colonized as bedrooms, others converted to bathrooms. Still others are left, almost uncharted territory, full of forgotten furniture shrouded in dust sheets and other quaint effects belonging to members of the family long since deceased: junk that will be sorted from time to time to reveal some covetable object or other, a real piece of treasure that will once again find a home among the living.

In general, the larger rooms for the working members of the family are to be found on the first floor, the smaller rooms under the eaves being the domain of children and visitors. The first-floor rooms may lead off a corridor with many surprising twists and turns—such a passage is difficult to negotiate safely in the dark, for the floorboards probably slope alarmingly, and have been thoroughly polished by generations of stockinged feet. Unless it is a grand house, the upper hall will probably be whitewashed or painted in a light colour to contrast with the exposed beams.

A charming aspect of many a landing in a rambling old house is an unexpected corner where, weary of housework

CHARACTERISTIC PRACTICALITY

The farmhouse bathroom is often a late conversion of an upstairs bedroom. As with all farmhouse decor, materials and equipment will be practical and of good quality and there will be no truck with unnecessary 'design'.

CREATURE COMFORTS

After a hard-working day on the farm, nightly comfort is very welcome. The farmhouse bed is soft and spacious and the bedroom in general lovingly furnished, though not overly fussy. This bedroom is fresh and bright, with space for make-up and hairdressing, but nothing built-in.

SUBTLE SIMPLICITY
In this bedroom the muted colour scheme, delicate
stencilling on the walls and intricate quilting of the
bedspread create a subtle effect that complements
the decorative panelling.

or bedmaking, you can rest for a while. An old wicker chair draped with shawls might offer a downy cushion, or there could be a padded window seat. On a little table nearby you could keep a collection of oddments to muse over—shells, faded photographs, old postcards, glass beads—while a pot of hyacinths would scent the air under a softly shaded lamp. This could be the place to write a diary—or to read someone else's. A rich velours cloth hung on the banister would give a pleasant feeling of taking sanctuary in a private nest.

The rest of the upstairs hall can be lit with candle wall lights or electric lanterns hung from the ceiling, as long as they are high enough to clear the heads of tall people.

The larger bedrooms

Bedrooms in farmhouses used to be rooms in which you spent most of the time with your eyes shut and entered and left in a hurry—it's hard to drag yourself away from the glowing embers of a cozy parlour to a room that might have ice on the inside of the window, and harder still to leave a warm bed at cockcrow, unless you move swiftly. They were thus furnished in a functional style, not meant for much gazing at.

The bed would be of painted iron or brass, polished until its knobs gleamed in the light of the candle before it was snuffed out. A high bed which had to be climbed into gives a sense of security; under it would be a chamber-pot, or

there might be a mahogany commode in the corner with a tapestry lid. A simple washstand with a jug of cold water on which you had to break the ice in the depths of winter, should you be reckless enough to want to wash in it; a basin and matching soap dish, a rough cotton towel on a rail and a pail for the slops would complete the picture. On a night table by the bed stood the candle, matches, a prayer book and a glass of stale water.

Over the generations the furniture in a typical farmhouse bedroom has been added to, though the family's rooms are generally still fresh and simple. The old feather or horsehair bed has given way to an orthopaedically recommended interior-sprung mattress, but the eiderdown may still be filled with the feathers of the farmyard geese. Under it is a traditional patchwork quilt, which would have been made during the long winter evenings by the local women, sewing together colourful scraps of material, each one rich with memories, as a present for the friend who was getting married. Feather pillows may be covered in fine lawn embroidered with the couple's initials, and with sheets to match, still going strong, though now 'turned' to bring the worn sides to the middle.

Simple decoration

A simple sprigged wallpaper and flower-print curtains, not necessarily to match, would contrast well with the bare or painted floorboards and their woollen bedside rugs. These rugs, speckled with many colours or with bold geometric or naive flower patterns, were hand-made by men and children as much as by the women. Two people could work at a hearthrug, one at each end, with sometimes surprising results. Rugs like this are real treasures and can often be picked up quite cheaply.

Bedroom furniture, generally plainer than that used in the best rooms downstairs, was ripe for decoration. Today painted chests, mirrors, washstands and wardrobes are much sought-after and command high prices. Anyone with the confidence and skill to paint their own will have something unique at a fraction of the sum. Artists' acrylic paints are easy to apply and can be washed off if you are not satisfied with the results. Marbling, ragging, stencilling,

sponging—all the techniques that are being used today with such enthusiasm were used in the past to great effect; indeed, itinerant decorators travelled from one neighbourhood to another taking their stencils and colour pigments with them and hawking their skills.

Another decorative touch is to be found in the tiles at the back of a marble-topped washstand and in the fireplace, though in Victorian times bedrooms tended to be equipped with only the smallest of grates under a plain wooden mantel. These were not designed to have fires built in them and were in any case far too small to heat a whole room— the idea was to bring up the embers from downstairs as you went to bed and tip them into the fire basket. This saved 'wasting' them, though it is doubtful whether it made

SIMPLE ATTIC BEDROOM

Here an attic bedroom has a large
traditional stove for heating.
Its matchboarded walls are painted grey,
blue and white. The simple furniture has
deliberately been kept simple, and
plain rag rugs keep the feet warm.

BRIGHT AND FEMININE

A young woman's room, bubbling over with signs of life and
vitality. The cheerful bedlinen and cushions pick up the colours of
the patchwork bedspread, which are echoed in the rug, hand-
painted chest-of-drawers, and ewer-and-basin set. The many
different floral patterns manage to produce a harmonious whole.

much difference to the temperature of a freezing bedroom. The temperature of the bed could be improved with a warming pan full of hot coals or several stone hot-water bottles, called 'pigs'.

The delicate touch

With the introduction of more soft furnishings into the bedroom you might find a covered ottoman at the end of the bed in place of a painted trunk—this holds extra blankets and eiderdowns, as well as providing a useful surface to take breakfast trays, newspapers and general clutter. Alternatively, a small two-seat sofa could be placed in this position; piled with cushions, it makes an inviting place to sit if the household cats don't get there first.

The dressing table, in any case a more frivolous piece of furniture than a solid chest of drawers topped by a free-standing mirror, might be trimmed with a full skirt of crisp cotton. On it you could put a set of brushes and a hand mirror backed in tortoiseshell, ivory, beaten silver or painted wood, together with a melee of scent bottles, family photographs and a preserved bouquet alongside day-to-day jewellery, lotions and creams.

Look out too for lace mats and runners and hand-stitched samplers to frame for the walls. Something else to hang on the wall would be a small oval mirror garlanded in painted plaster flowers. A wicker laundry basket, a wooden towel rail and a screen (perhaps covered in tapestry or découpage) on which to throw discarded clothes completes

CAREFUL PLANNING

Though again majoring on the floral, this room is much more disciplined with its white fitted carpet and its basic rose-pink colour base. Bedspread, curtains, dressing table skirt and backing have all been made to measure specially for this room.

TOP PRIORITY

The hand-embroidered Jacobean design of this
bedspread goes well with the slightly Gothic
arch of the window. As always, the emphasis is
on physical comfort after a day's work, so the
bed and the dressing table are the two most
important items.

FITTING IN A BATHROOM

Another instance of the way old farmhouses
have adapted to modern plumbing. This
bathroom is under the sloping roof. It has
comfort and style, but no nonsense about built-
in bath panels, though the space under the eaves
has been panelled-in for storage.

the furnishing, though you might add a deep old armchair
in a faded chintz loose cover.

Bedrooms in farmhouses often smell faintly of lavender—
there might be lavender bags hanging in the wardrobe or
slipped under the pillows or between the linen in the chest.
A guest will be welcomed by a delicate potpourri or the
heady perfume of a bowl of full-blown roses. The guest
bedroom might well be grander than that slept in by the
farmer and his wife, especially in a house that has been
added to at different periods.

The children's rooms

Often situated under the eaves, with steeply pitched walls
and deep window seats, the children's rooms can be very
different in atmosphere. A suitable floor covering is hard-
wearing coir matting, fitted wall to wall to avoid slipping
and tripping. The walls and paintwork look best in white,
cream or pastel colours and you can buy cheap secondhand
furniture in undistinguished wood and paint it in a bright
cheerful colour or to match the woodwork. A large nursery
table where children can sit to do their drawing, a chest of
drawers for their clothes and a toy cupboard or chest are
the basic requirements. The chairs can be low and squashy

and covered in chintz or blue-and-white striped ticking.
For safety a brass-railed fire guard should enclose fire irons
and coal hod as well as the fire. No nursery is complete
without a much-ridden rocking horse, a collection of rag
dolls in a wooden buggy and a doll's house. If these
belonged to, or were made by, the children's parents, so
much the better.

Often children's bedrooms are only big enough to hold a
bed, a night table and a chair full of stuffed animals, with
perhaps a bookcase under the window. There might be an
iron crib for the baby that can be rocked gently from side to
side in its ribbon-trimmed frame, or a wooden crib on
rockers, or a hooded wicker crib. The smaller children can
sleep in wooden truckle beds, the larger ones in beds with
painted wooden headboards or, where space is short, in
modern bunks.

Farmhouse bathrooms

The farmhouse bathroom is usually a converted bedroom,
though there might be a purpose-built bathroom in an
extension on the ground floor. This will be compact and
modern and fitted with a shower. It is the bathroom used
by the farmer when he comes in from work and is essentially

functional—a cork-tiled floor, short print curtains, a good light to shave in by a mirror over the hand basin and a transistor radio for listening to the weather forecast will fit the bill.

By contrast, the upstairs bathroom may be a room of character that invites you to linger over your ablutions. If the bathroom was once a bedroom, the chances are that it will have a fireplace, next to which you could put a wing chair in faded velvet with a crocheted cushion and a footstool. A fireplace recalls the days when a tin bath would be placed in front of the bedroom fire (the ancestor of the 'en suite') and filled with pitchers of water lugged upstairs from the kitchen by the maid. Above it an elaborate overmantel with a large mirror and a lot of tiny shelves crowded with coloured bottles and jars of bath oil and body lotions would look good.

Decorative additions

Choose restful colours for the bathroom, such as muted greens and sea blues. Keep the lighting subdued, perhaps with wall lights behind pink opaque glass shades in the shape of shells; sometimes you could have candles flickering. Hot-house plants enjoy a steamy bathroom and a wrought-iron garden table or bench by the window could hold an exotic collection of ferns, flowers and shells. Prints featuring watery subjects may adorn the walls. The walls themselves could be covered with a vinyl wallcovering, or, if a non-vinyl paper is used, it could be varnished as protection against the moisture. But even polyurethane will not guarantee to keep wallpaper permanently flat and unstained; and, though it looks colder, it can be more practical to tile up to the dado and paint beyond it. Plain tiles with a starkly geometric border look effective against fitted rush matting and the intricacies of ancient plumbing. If you are keeping the room plain, choose venetian or roller blinds in white, parchment or dark green rather than the heavy drapes that belong in a more romantic bathroom.

Victorian tiles, old Dutch tiles or modern Italian ones, matching or a happy mix of colours and designs, can be collected for the splashback behind a washbasin or to cover the panel of a fitted bath. In fact the bathroom is a good place to house any interesting collection of objects that don't find a natural home in the other parts of the house. Pebbles, glass marbles, preserved fish in glass cases (even live ones in an aquarium), rows of jugs on a high shelf under the cornice—there should certainly be plenty for the eye of the bather to rove over while relaxing.

The centre of attention, and often situated in the centre of the room, is the bath itself. Deep-sided and generous enough to hold two people or several children, the bath stands on its own clawed feet. Gleaming white enamel inside, the outside could be painted and stencilled—the bathroom is as good a place as any to let your imagination run riot. The bath may have brass fittings and at the side of it you could put a woven cotton rag bathmat.

A toilet with a high cistern and a chain may stand regally on a platform at one end of the room. Perhaps it will have a blue-and-white patterned toilet bowl; certainly there should be a mahogany seat. Some people are still nostalgic about commodes and have them built over flush toilet bowls, though others do not want to be constantly reminded of the days of such primitive sanitation.

The washbasin can be decorated ceramic, but more likely it will be plain white and very large. Old-fashioned concertina-type radiators would look in character here and keep the room warm, as the fire will be lit only on special occasions. It is possible to buy these radiators secondhand, and reproduction models are now being manufactured also. A heated towel rail will provide the bather with hot towels; fresh ones can be stacked in a built-in airing cupboard. Some bathrooms are large enough to accommodate a dressing table and a padded stool for a lengthy toilette; others can be equipped with a glass-fronted corner cabinet and a mirror in a good light.

Keep the window treatment simple, with fresh print curtains or a roller blind, and avoid fussy frilled tablecloths and other draperies elsewhere in the room, which may in any case get tangled up with discarded clothing. Let a small wicker chair or a folding screen act as a clothes-horse, and hang the dressing gowns on hooks behind the door.

Inside meets Outside

Farmhouses are likely to have several outside doors, all of them in constant use, but the stranger will be welcomed through the front door—perhaps of ancient oak, studded, latched and bolted with iron—into the hall. Boots are left behind in the porch, coats and hats are sent to roost on pegs on the wall and the visitor is free to take in his surroundings. The first thing that strikes the eye will be the transitory nature of the hall's contents: most of them are waiting to be taken outside, like dog leads, guns, garden twine, walking sticks, riding tackle and golf clubs.

The furniture in the hall is kept simple: perhaps a polished table, a bare wooden chair, a grandfather clock ticking sternly, a glass-fronted bookcase full of dusty Victorian novels. There might even be a fireplace with a dog basket in front of it—a fire would blaze a welcome here at Christmas, but for the rest of the year the grate would hold flowers and green branches. Above the mantelpiece there might be framed school photographs and sepia likenesses of members of the family no longer remembered well enough to put on the sideboard in the dining room. The walls in this part of the house could be papered and dadoed. Coir matting is a serviceable covering on the hall floor, which may be of brick, stone or tiles. There may be shutters at the window; and velvet curtains, perhaps in faded maroon and brown, some of them richly patterned, may be hanging snugly over the doors from brass poles.

THE ROUGH AND THE SMOOTH

Many farmhouses have a simple working back door but a spacious, even grand front entrance. This rough door with its businesslike latch opens surprisingly on to a polished and cared-for interior with a marble-topped table, oriental rug, and paintings.

<u>UNEXPECTED MIX</u>
This is a good example of the juxtaposition of practical with imposing
often found in farmhouses. Colourful all-weather clothes are hung up in
a small vestibule, but through the door can be seen a spacious room
with a generous arch, a grandfather clock and some fine furniture.

Sturdy and functional porches

The romantic notion of rustic life stops short at the back door of the farmhouse. Beyond it is the swampy reality of the farmyard. To protect the house from the muck of the yard as much as to keep the wind and the rain out of the living quarters, farmhouse doors—back, front and side— are usually equipped with sturdily built porches. There may be a hose on the wall outside the back door to wash the worst off the wellingtons, and outside the front an iron foot scraper embedded into the ground. These scrapers can often be quite decorative, and the free-standing ones make attractive doorstops inside the house.

Under the doormats the porch floor may be of stone or concrete covered in linoleum—it must be easy to wash and preferably quick to dry. A bench running the length of the porch would provide somewhere to sit down and take off muddy boots. No matter how tiny the porch, it will inevitably get filled with a variety of outdoor clothing to fit all members of the family and to share among visitors who find themselves ill-prepared for the weather.

In a larger porch you might find buckets of feed that have been mixed in the kitchen and are on their way out to the animals, together with goats' cheeses, buckets of milk and trays of eggs waiting to be brought inside or to be sold at the door. There will probably be Tilley lamps hanging on the wall. Farm dogs and cats can be fed in the porch outside the back door and if there is a sunny window it may have a shelf for a few pots of herbs or a couple of tomato plants. There is seldom time to look after a greenhouse.

Outbuildings

Farmhouses are often blessed with a number of rooms neighbouring the kitchen, perhaps an old dairy or scullery or grain store for the hens. Such rooms can still be

WARM AND FRIENDLY

The front entrance to the farmhouse is warm and welcoming.
The cat has chosen to lie on the upholstered armchair by the fire.
A straight staircase with a natural wood banister leads upstairs
and a full basket of logs is waiting to replenish the dying flames.

A CENTURIES-OLD VISTA

This lobby with its ancient, cracked floor and diamond
window panes leads through a charming arch into
the world outside. The doors are heavy and studded.

PRACTICAL STOREROOM
From the kitchen, an outhouse leads into the farmyard.
Farm implements are carefully stored here,
each with its own hook.
The floor has been concreted and the walls
left in their natural state.

invaluable for old-fashioned or modern activities. In good farmhouse tradition a room like this could retain its dairy identity and be used for making cream cheese and yogurt—and even bottles of ginger beer using a live culture. It can serve a double purpose and be used for hanging and plucking game. Shelves can be given the old-fashioned alternative to cupboard doors by having clean white muslin hung in front of them.

The easily washed floors, usually of stone slabs or perhaps chequerboard quarry tiles, are perfect for a modern laundry room with washing machine and tumble dryer, airing line on a pulley, a sink for handwashing and plenty of space to store detergents, starches, iron and ironing board.

A smaller room would be ideal as the traditional 'flower room'—a real luxury in modern times, with a shallow sink and draining board, shelves for various vases, scissors and secateurs, trugs and ornamental baskets.

Such a room is also a godsend as a bootroom with boot and shoe trees; shelves for trainers; polishes, brushes and cloths and perhaps even fishing rods, and various other pieces of leisure equipment.

Backyards and courtyards

If the farmer has not got round to building a porch at the back, the kitchen will probably have a stable door to the yard. The top half can be thrown open in summer while the bottom stays shut to keep the animals from wandering into the house. Because of the mess made by the cows and the chickens, the backyard is not the place to take a deck chair. Besides, it may have all manner of things stacked in it awaiting eventual relocation to a more suitable permanent

TRADITIONAL COBBLES

This charming cobbled area delineates the end of
the house and the beginning of the garden.
This is a sheltered spot for summer drinks or for podding peas and
topping-and-tailing gooseberries. Various hoes and
bunches of onions are neatly stored here.

site, such as building materials, old doors, piles of slates, wood to be sawn into logs, and furniture and machinery that need repairing.

But if the farmhouse has outbuildings ranged at either side of the back door, the space they enclose could form a courtyard to be separated from the animal yard by a gate. Once the area is chicken-proofed (and this is not as simple as it sounds), it can be set with tubs of flowers and perhaps a trellis for a grapevine. The farmyard can offer all kinds of containers for planting, the more miscellaneous the selection, the better. An old wheelbarrow, a painted oil drum, ceramic sinks of all sizes, a water butt sawn in half, disused animal feeders, hip baths, a water trough—even a dough trough—can make a charming and eccentric display filled with tumbling nasturtiums. Runner beans can be grown up strings against the wall outside the back door—the brilliant red flowers will provide a feast for the eye before the beans are ready to eat.

Terraces and verandas

Outside the living room, beyond the French doors, there may be scope for a more civilized terrace. In summer when the grate is empty and the chairs are pulled up to the windows to catch the sun, the garden doors can be thrown open to the mossy flagstones. Here battered cane chairs could be set around an old elm kitchen table ready for lunch. Or there may be a handsome wooden veranda finished with Victorian bargeboards and fitted with rocking chairs, loungers and a day bed. This is the place to sip drinks as the sun goes down or breathe in the perfume of night-scented stock. In winter the veranda can be enclosed by shutters and act as a storage room.

MANOR HOUSE STYLE

The fascination of the manor house style lies in its unique blend of grandeur and informality. A manor house suggests a building that is important and sometimes even grand, but first and foremost a solid family home passed through generations of people born into wealth and privilege. Beautiful furnishings of widely varying styles and periods have been lovingly collected over the years, and constant use has given them an air of faded glory. Few manor houses these days are owned by their original families; but the influence of the manor house style continues as a basis for the kind of comfort and security many of us wish to have, whether we live in the town or the country. It is a style based on very high values, skilled craftsmanship, a dislike of pretence or pretension combined with a down-to-earth realism and a warm-hearted sense of family life.

ACHIEVING THE LOOK

In the manor house style, rich, mellow colours, sophisticated designs and polished antique furniture are part of day-to-day life. Evident everywhere is the love of the countryside and traditional country pursuits.

Underfoot

Floors are vitally important to the manor house look. They should be made from high-quality, long-lasting materials which age gracefully and improve with loving care and attention. This used to mean plenty of polish and hard work but these days it needn't if you make the right choices. The often cluttered and busy rooms of the manor house style give no great scope to large, plain areas of flooring, except perhaps in an entrance hall or corridors.

Halls and downstairs passages might once have been made from marble, large-scale tiles, stone or slate flags. Nowadays some of the superb look-alike vinyl flooring could recreate the effect more practically. Fine polished wood in reception rooms and bedrooms looks warm and welcoming; layers of rugs and carpets should be added at random or in strategic places such as in front of a fire or beneath a favourite sofa. A soft, washed Indian carpet would make a good basis with smaller patterned rugs added at will.

Kitchens, pantries and work rooms would have had tough sensible floors such as stone, terracotta tiles, slate or brick. Most kitchens now, however, are multi-purpose and more than just places to cook in, so floors should be adjusted to suit your needs.

An entirely practical room: the game larder, one of the hallmarks of the country manor house.

Eating is a major aspect of manor house living so at least one purpose-made dining room is a sine qua non. This room is obviously a 'second' dining room for small parties. It is quite informally arranged with a stack of logs in the immense fireplace.

Manor house style is epitomized in this hall, with its mellow tones, timeless furnishings, well-proportioned design and pervading sense of comfortable elegance. As always, the countryside is much in evidence.

Upstairs the needs change again and comfort takes over. Floors would mostly have been made from polished wood, usually covered or scattered with warm and luxurious rugs. The nursery and servants' quarters would stay bare and the only concession to comfort here might be a plaited rag rug beside a bed or a square of carpet in front of the fire.

Walls and ceilings

The decoration of walls, ceilings and woodwork in a manor house would have taken its inspiration from far and wide. A house from the Tudor or Elizabethan period might have had simple wood-panelled rooms made by a local carpenter, or plain stone walls covered by rich tapestries and hangings. In later centuries, some of these houses would have been given regular redecoration in the latest styles. Classical plasterwork, complicated mouldings and delicate carvings appeared. The very size and height of most manor house rooms demands a grandeur of surface treatment in scale with the house. Rich and sometimes strong paint or wallpaper colours are needed to show off fine paintings and portraits, or dark stained wood with elaborate detailing for a more Gothic style.

Fabrics and window treatments

Rooms are generally large and well-proportioned in the manor house and windows follow this pattern. The manor house had elegant expansive windows positioned to enjoy glorious gardens and sweeping landscapes. Curtain

Another informal corner, this time more enclosed and cozy for evening entertainment. The chairs are old, comfortable and shabby; the piano, the pictures and the large overmantel mirror have been in the family for years. The marble fireplace has been filled with dried flowers grown in the walled garden and herbaceous beds. A primitive metal chandelier gives adequate but not glaring light.

The manor house kitchen was usually built in the bowels of the house. It was large enough for the cook and several kitchenmaids to cook for parties of 30 or more and to manhandle enormous pieces of equipment and pans.

In this manor house bedroom, every detail contributes to the overall effect of opulence, from the richly coloured floral motifs to the backdrop created by the splendid tapestry.

treatments should be bold, dramatic and luxurious, and it is important always to be generous with fabric, even if you use the cheapest. If windows are large-scale then they can happily take large-scale fabric designs plus plenty of detailing such as pelmets (either severe or draped), tie backs, tassels, braids or even frills.

Furniture

Furniture for most manor houses would have been an eclectic mix according to the history and fortunes of the family. Always of the finest quality it would have ranged from small, everyday locally made pieces to elaborate items ordered from the best cabinetmakers of the day. Chinoiserie and other foreign pieces were often brought back from travels abroad. To recreate the feel, antique furniture is important. Good solid English oak always looks right, as do the fine and rare hardwoods imported from abroad. Never buy post-Edwardian furniture except for odd items which hardly change in style, such as wicker. The emphasis should be on comfort and generous proportions.

The dining room, having such an important part to play in family life, should be furnished with a table large enough for the biggest party of people you are likely to entertain, complete with sturdy dining chairs. They don't have to be a matching set but they should match the wood. Flimsy bedroom chairs look quite wrong and should be avoided. Bedroom furniture continues the theme of comfort and

The lady of the manor house became adept at making large rooms comfortable and friendly and at creating small areas to relax in within larger rooms. Heavy patterned curtains may be slightly faded, and paintwork pale to reflect light.

Manor house walls invite large tables or sideboards to stand up against them and serve as display cases for collected pieces.

elegance with the four poster bed summing up for many people the manor house look, whether it is draped in folds of fabric or solidly made from plain, simple wood.

Warmth of the hearth

A fire burning in every room evokes the manor house style, so retain or make fireplaces with either simple oak lintels of giant proportions, classic carved wood surrounds or something grander in stone or marble. The space inside must be large enough to take wood if possible, burned on a bed of ash with a fire back and fire dogs rather than a grate or basket. Other fireside effects include a fender with seats to perch on and perhaps a tapestry fire screen to cover the fireplace in the summer months.

Finishing touches

Over the years a typical manor house would have acquired collections of paintings or special ornaments, stemming maybe from one person's fascination with a subject such as horse breeding or a passion for beautiful porcelain. Paintings of ancestors, animals, pastel drawings of children hanging beside landscapes and romantic views are all in the classic manor house style. Glass and china might be kept in special display cabinets but a few beautiful pieces should be left out to be used as containers for pot pourri and flower arrangements. Halls and studies and little tucked away rooms could display collections of objects like walking sticks, hats, silver trophies, mackintoshes—any piece of paraphernalia for living in and enjoying the countryside.

Living and Relaxing

The inhabitants of a manor house would inevitably have been involved with the running of the estate, even if it was in a very minor way, but their rank and social status in the neighbourhood would have demanded that they had a full social life. Houses were therefore built on a scale which easily absorbed extra people at any time and the numbers of servants kept were capable of looking after house guests for an afternoon or a fortnight. In the days before transport was easy and reliable, parties of guests might have stayed in the house for several days at a time so space for their entertainment and relaxation was important. Even without guests, families were usually large and were naturally expected to provide their own amusement—everything from music to billiards.

We tend to think of an Edwardian or Victorian house party as epitomizing the manor house style of relaxation, with guests coming and going, using the house almost like an hotel, amusing themselves throughout the day and meeting for meals, particularly in the evening. This went on in earlier centuries, too, though people may have dined at four rather than eight and hunted all day rather than play genteel games such as tennis or croquet. Early evening, however, was always the focal point of the day when everyone, freshly bathed and dressed for dinner, would meet in the most important room in the house which was usually the drawing room (in earlier days this might have

TASTEFUL BUT CONSPICUOUS CONSUMPTION

Large though the manor house is, it is nevertheless liable to be over- rather than under-furnished, as generations of owners collect furniture and works of art from travels throughout the world.

A DELICATE TOUCH

No continental manor would be without its tiled room heater or *kacheloven*. This one is tall to make good use of the high ceiling. The view through the wide doorway into the light and airy rooms adjoining, together with the delicate colours and furnishings gives a sense of spaciousness.

SIMPLICITY AND HARMONY

This room with its large windows has been given a modern treatment, both simple and luxurious. Brown and white ceramic tiles complement the lavishly draped curtains in an Italianate manner.

been the library). From the drawing room, people moved off in couples to the dining room to eat. After dinner and the rituals of port and smoking and the ladies leaving the men, everyone would reassemble in the drawing room (which was originally known as the withdrawing room because of this practice) to spend the rest of the evening singing, playing music, dancing or playing communal games or cards.

The drawing room

For the modern equivalent of this relaxed and gracious way of life there are several essentials. The rooms you relax in must be warm, but not necessarily enormous, comfortable without being messy, smart but definitely not forbidding. An open fire is a must to create atmosphere and act as a gathering point, whether it is to stand and warm your back with a pre-dinner drink or to sit and toast bread for tea.

A PEACEFUL READING ROOM

The blue paint on the panelled woodwork, combined with the painted panels,
lessens the masculinity of this traditional library and so do the
glass chandelier and the silvery-grey sofa. Valuable books are kept
in this peaceful room opening on to the garden.

COMFORT WITH TRADITIONAL ELEGANCE

Here is an English manor house given traditional furnishings which are both comfortable
and gracious. A pretty floral chintz covers the little sofa, curtains are pelmeted
and heavily lined to hang well. An ornate table covered in objects is
reflected in the large gilt-framed mirror. Small antique tables are dotted about
the room and there are bowls and vases of roses and herbaceous flowers.
Note the panelled shutters at each window and the delicately decorated oval ceiling.

Informal Coziness
A good example of a 'small' room used
as a morning room or study. Here
comfort and coziness are paramount.
The chair seat is comfortably, but not
recently, upholstered, and an unkempt
plant presides over all.

Objets d'Art
Small displays in the manor house tend to
be of rather beautiful objects rather than
jolly junk. On this highly polished table the
hand-painted porcelain is arranged with a
bowl of lilies. On the wall are works of
art collected from abroad.

Seating of several different kinds is needed—from a hard upright chair for playing chess and card games to soft squashy armchairs for losing oneself in a book. Sofas and chairs should be large and roomy, remembering that a two seat sofa never comfortably seats two nor a three seater three people. The shapes of sofas and armchairs are best when simple and classic. Choose a timeless design built with a sturdy hardwood frame and feather cushions for the proper depth of comfort.

Chairs should never look over-stuffed or hard and awkward but accommodating, a little worn out, even saggy. This look is always best achieved with loose covers rather than close upholstery. Evocative flowery prints of blowsy roses and summer flowers make beautiful covers, as do crisp ticking stripes. Strong plain colours work well, too, but show creases and dirt more than a patterned fabric. Pure natural fibres such as linen, cotton or mixtures of both are practical and look right. Keep brocades, tapestries, dupions and richer fabrics for dining chairs and pieces which are used less often. Loose covers make sense in a house where children, dogs and cats are much in evidence.

Sofas arranged in pairs either side of a fireplace look good in well proportioned rooms but the overall aim for the manor style is to achieve a slightly haphazard look—as if furniture could always be moved to wherever someone wanted it. Cushions are vital to this look so there should be plenty of them and they definitely shouldn't match. Cover feather pads with handstitched petit point or tapestry, silk brocades or scraps of old, rich-coloured fabrics. Small-scale geometric prints or stripes work well as a counterpoint to larger floral chintzes. They should all make a glorious jumble of colour and texture and through their various styles link times past with the present.

There should be plenty of tables in the drawing room— tables for books and magazines, for jigsaws and games of chess, for lamps and collections of photographs, for the piece of tapestry or sewing currently being worked on— with space on them too for bowls of flowers and room to put down a drink or cup of tea. Waist-height tables look best, especially alongside or behind a sofa. A low modern coffee table, very much a 20th century invention, invariably looks quite wrong.

Drawing room lighting should be warm and general with pools of specific light near seating, probably provided by table lamps as opposed to standard lamps. A large room can have several different areas lit at different levels for the many types of activity.

Window treatments

The fabrics used at windows in the living rooms of a manor house may be quite subtle if they are to decorate rather than dominate the windows or they can be the flamboyant

FOREIGN PLUNDER

Another display this time demonstrates
unashamedly the booty of visits abroad, as well
as collections of birds' eggs from a previous
generation—not even the lord of the manor
may collect eggs like this today.

118

A CRAFTSMAN'S ART

Hand-painted panels like these would have been executed by
a local craftsman or someone brought in from abroad.
No other decoration is really desirable or necessary,
although the wall-hung wooden clock with its
charming face fits in quite nicely. On the low,
polished sideboard sits a porcelain urn.

DARK MEETS LIGHT

Sunlight streaming through the window
catches the golden wood of this antique
desk with its little collection of inlaid
wooden boxes and porcelain. Behind it,
heavy dark panelling makes a backcloth
for a rural tapestry.

element in a room lacking in strong points. In either case, they are unlikely to truly take over in rooms which are invariably full of furniture and cluttered details unlike in a cool, empty, modern space where fabric can be used to set the whole theme of a room. Manor houses generally have well proportioned, even beautiful, windows which need little embellishment and often no fussy dressing at all. A sense of scale is vitally important for window treatments, and generosity is often the key word. Plenty of width and folds in the fabric, deep hems, generous turnings and large-scale poles, swags and pelmets are essential. Trimmings, braids and borders along vertical and horizontal edges give an extra richness, and cord and fabric tie-backs provide opportunities for different curtain shapes and effects.

For today's version of all this luxury you can copy the ideas to suggest a more splendid window than you have. Setting curtains well above and beyond the frames can create the feeling of large windows. Be sure to make hems drop to the floor even if the windows do not, as nothing looks meaner than short, fussy sill-length curtains. Many manor houses would have had wooden shutters which were used at night and these are well worth restoring if you have any hint that your house once possessed them. They look smart and are useful for both security and insulation.

Years ago curtains would have been changed from season to season but few of us do that now so choose a fabric suitable for warm summer evenings and firelit winter nights. Always line, and preferably inter-line, curtains, partly for insulation but mainly for the body and shape this gives to the humblest fabric. A cheap fabric used generously and then lined well can look as if it cost the earth, and with some careful and individual trimming can look sensational. Pictures and references from the past of curtains and window treatments in large country houses have inspired another generation to see the window and the way it was decorated as a crucial part of an overall scheme.

Upholstery fabrics for chairs, sofas and stools can be chosen to blend with or even match curtain fabrics, or they can be in complete contrast, depending on the size of your room. A large room can happily take several designs and colour themes but a small room is likely to look best if the scheme is more controlled and built around a single idea.

The library

Up until the early 19th century the library was often the room most commonly used for living in throughout the day, containing enough books on every subject to

UNCLUTTERED ELEGANCE

This very ancient house makes the most of its dark oak
beams by contrasting them with white walls. A long
Persian runner is placed in front of the very stately
fireplace and on a highly polished quarry-tiled floor.
The furniture is elegant and there is not too much of it.

INFORMAL MORNING ROOM

Here is another example of an informal morning
room, its floral chaircover counteracting the
dark panelling which might otherwise be rather
overbearing. The vase of flowers also helps
to make this a comfortable corner for relaxing.

TRADITIONAL HARMONY

Another very traditional treatment of a manor house drawing room.
The large painting in three panels at the back covers a complete wall.
Comfortable sofas and chairs, in harmony with each other but not all
matching, are well-supplied with stools and tables for newspapers and
books. An elegant table lamp gives a soft light.

FAMILY COLLECTIONS
This is an elegant room almost full of several generations'
worth of collected furniture and objects. Heavy floor-
length curtains, portraits, a large mirror with a curly gilt
frame, an exquisite chess table, and views to the garden
are all very much in character.

entertain, divert and inform any guest for days on end.
Later, when the drawing room took over as the main living
area, libraries changed their emphasis and became more
personal rooms with a masculine emphasis, perhaps
doubling as a study for business, as a room in which to
pursue hobbies, or as a smoking room exclusively for men.

A small library room could become a warm, pleasing
sitting room and a perfect place to escape to from the large
spaces and noisy chatter of the drawing room. A room
lined with books certainly has charm and though few of us
these days would cover every bit of wall space with shelves,
a book-lined area in any room adds a mellow, lived-in look
of safety and security and other-worldliness which is very
pleasant to be in. Shelves do not need to be elaborate. If
they are fitted into alcoves then they should be simply
constructed from timber of generous proportions which is
best painted unless the wood is a fine-looking timber such
as oak. Free-standing bookshelves should also be plain,
using generous shelf thicknesses and end boards. It is
almost certainly worth getting bookshelves made to
measure for your particular room, rather than buying
anything which is ready-made.

The morning room

Many manor houses through the centuries had smaller, less
formal, rooms than drawing rooms for living in during the
early part of the day. Often known as morning rooms, they
would be built in a part of the house which caught all the
morning sun and they were a practical and pretty place in
which to spend the hours after breakfast. Used by the
women of the household rather than the men, this was the
room in which the lady of the manor might sit and organize
her day and menus, plan a social event or talk with her
dressmaker. The children, too, might be allowed a free rein
in such a room whereas their presence in the drawing room
would have been frowned on except during prescribed
hours.

A morning or breakfast room should be fresh, light and
cheerful. One or two comfortable armchairs are essential,
plus a good-sized table on which to spread out garden
catalogues and suchlike. A desk or piece of furniture for
writing letters and dealing with household affairs is essential
to the look. The colour scheme could be summery and
bright with sky blues, yellows and white or corals, peaches
and pale greens. Fabrics should be fresh and simple—candy

SIMPLICITY AND FRESHNESS

This small sunny room, a good example of the
manor house morning room, has been decorated
in a simple Scandinavian style with sheer
curtains, softly striped wallpaper, elegant chairs
and a polished wooden table.

A QUIET SPACE

A built-in glass-fronted cupboard, a small desk
and a quarry-tiled floor in various shades of
terracotta combine to make a pleasant
housekeeping space in what could once have
been the butler's pantry.

stripes, checks or small geometrics mixed with neat, all-
over florals. Wicker and basketware have just the right feel,
and can be incorporated perhaps as a cushion-filled armchair, a little two seat sofa, or some roomy baskets.

The games room

Games rooms designed for special pursuits such as billiards
were quite commonly built in, or added to, large country
manor houses. Usually meant for the male members of the
family, though many wives played billiards too, they were
often richly and sombrely furnished in what has come to be
thought of as a masculine style. As these rooms were
mostly used at night, in artificial light, the colours and
textures of walls and fabrics were chosen to enhance the
warm, intimate atmosphere with a lavish use of plush,
velvet, leather and brass. Colours were rich and tended
towards deep green, plum and tobacco brown, with no
florals, chintzes or fussily designed fabrics. Nowadays,
rooms specifically designed for billiards are rare indeed,
though the ambience of dark polished wood, darkly shaded
lamps and strong velvety colours still appeals and can look
good in certain rooms.

THE ART OF ARRANGEMENT

Horses and manor houses go together.
This elegant sculpture is grouped with
great artistry with two blue and white
china plates, an arrangement of
flowers, and two portraits.

TAPESTRIES AND EMBROIDERIES

Today, a collection of 19th century tapestries and embroideries—still within reach of the ordinary collector—is a splendid evocation of manor house style.

Antique textiles and fabrics are often so damaged and worn that they are beyond repair and cannot be put to their original use. However, small pieces of tapestries and amateur embroideries which may have started life as firescreens, tea cozies or pot stands make superb cushions, complemented with old braids and tassels, or appliquéd on to worn velvets.

Up until the beginning of the 19th century, embroideresses often drew their own patterns or traced them from the sketchbooks of friends. But by the 1830s a wide range of little books containing instructions for the working of pictures, clothes and miscellaneous fancy items were generally available. Embroidered pictures, bell pulls, mantel borders, pelmets, even tablecloths were all embellished by hand.

A printer in Berlin conceived the idea of printing embroidery patterns on to squared paper, from which they could be copied

Aubusson and crewelwork supplied by Danielle Hartwright; other cushions from Patricia Harvey

stitch by stitch on to a mesh canvas. Berlinwork, as it was known, had become such a craze by the middle of the 19th century that it virtually superseded all other forms of embroidery (including crewelwork, traditionally worked in wool on linen).

In Berlinwork, counted-stitch designs were worked in tapestry wools on the canvas; individual squares were joined to make larger pieces. Silk was sometimes used to highlight parts of the design, and this combined with chenille threads and beadwork to produce exotic effects.

Early Berlinwork consisted of elaborate copies of popular paintings of the time, or lavish designs of roses, paeonies and lilies together with parrots, peacocks and other exotic birds. By the end of the century, geometric patterns based on 16th and 17th century designs became fashionable.

Beadwork too was exceptionally popular in the 19th century. While it was most often used on clothes, by the 1850s entire objects such as table tops, firescreens and cushions were embroidered with tiny glass beads on canvas grounds.

FROM LEFT TO RIGHT

Mid 19th century beadwork tea cozy opened out to make a cushion, with artificial jet, gold and bronze beads on a silk ground. Fragment of a border of mid 18th century French needlework tapestry finished with old trimmings and made into a cushion. Berlin woolwork tapestry probably made as a tea cozy, mid 19th century. English 19th century crewelwork cushion. Fragment of 20th century Aubusson tapestry made into a cushion. Early 19th century Aubusson table carpet used as a background.

Cooking and Eating

The dining room in any large country manor house has traditionally been spacious, comfortable and masculine in style. This has developed through the years with the idea that the drawing room is essentially feminine—a place for chatter and tea drinking—while the dining room is a place for serious eating and drinking, conversation, and cigar smoking. The women would leave the men alone at the end of the meal, to be joined later in the drawing room (formerly called the withdrawing room) for the rest of the evening.

If a room is used only as a place to eat in, it can be simply arranged and lavishly furnished. The decorations can be bolder and more elaborate, and the colour scheme stronger and more dramatic, than in a room used for relaxing or working in. Traditionally, warm reds, pinks, plums and golds were used, as they were seen as more conducive to good digestion and appetite than the cool greens and blues. The choice of colour these days may rest more with the need to tie in with rooms leading off the dining room, or to counteract a chilly atmosphere in a north-facing room, for example. If the proportions of the room allow, it is a perfect place to use a dado rail with pattern above and plain below. Also called a chair rail, this rail originally had the practical purpose of protecting the wall when chairs not in use were kept against it.

Window treatments can be lavish. The fabric will be

IN THE GRAND MANNER
This formal dining room with its mahogany table and Georgian chairs leads through a series of panelled doors into the drawing room. The lack of a sideboard indicates that meals would be served by kitchen staff.

A TOUCH OF CLASS

A small manor house can look very much like a prosperous farmhouse: this one, with its great stone flags on the floor, its Windsor armchair and its spinning wheel might equally well be found in a rural farm. The difference is perhaps in the very large collection of pewter and other fine objects.

important in this room as it will probably be the greatest area of fabric on show. The view from the windows is not very important when people are arranged facing in towards each other at a table, but a green and flowery garden can be delightful glimpsed through open windows or French doors on a warm summer evening.

A sense of occasion

Ceremony has always played a great part in the manor house meal, particularly at the most important meal of the day which was usually held in the evening. Lunch parties tended to be informal, with guests often helping themselves to food from a buffet. For important meals there would be plenty of servants to attend to guests, at times one for each diner. Meals containing course after course were served on exquisite china accompanied by wine in

sparkling glasses and eaten with shining cutlery. On the table there would be polished silver, fresh scented flowers and maybe fruit from the hot-houses, all set off by perfect linen. Candles, though superseded by oil, gas and then electricity, remain today one of the best ways of introducing atmosphere to the simplest meal.

An oval or round dining table seats more people comfortably than an oblong one of the same area. A very long table breaks up general conversation into small groups or even restricts it to a diner's immediate neighbours, as at a formal dinner. This happens less on a round table but can still do so with a very large one. The size of table you choose will eventually be decided by the space you have and the maximum number of people you are likely to want to seat for a meal.

A well-polished mahogany, rosewood or oak table is

chairs. Many households feel that a dining room is wasted space if it is only used occasionally—but even if it is just for week-end lunches, family celebrations and seasonal feasts, it lends a sense of occasion and tradition to everyday life.

The groaning sideboard

One very important piece of furniture in the manor house dining room was the sideboard. All the food from the kitchen would be put there as it came in and then served to guests by the servants. Later, in Edwardian days, elaborate heated buffets were positioned just outside the dining room for serving and keeping food warm, but the sideboard was still used. The main dish if it needed carving would usually be placed in front of the host to deal with. Empty glasses were removed from guests and filled at the sideboard.

As the numbers of servants declined in households, methods of serving food changed. Nowadays we are likely to help ourselves from dishes on the table or serve straight on to plates in the kitchen. But a sideboard is still a useful piece of furniture, especially if it has drawers to store napkins, serving spoons, table mats and other odd bits of equipment. It can also be an important decorative feature in the room, with perhaps a large mirror or painting behind it and space for flowers, a table lamp or candlesticks and a beautiful bowl of fruit arranged for dessert at the end of the meal. Plates and puddings, cheeses and extras for each course can wait happily on the sideboard. Many restaurants provide this kind of display for the sense of theatre it adds to a meal.

The Edwardian manor house breakfast sideboard groaning with silver-covered chafing dishes has passed into legend. It was provided as a kind of running buffet to suit the variable hours of rising and different tastes of a house filled with guests.

The preparation of all this food was done in a spacious kitchen and little satellite rooms such as a scullery. This area was usually well away from the dining room to keep cooking smells at bay. From the kitchen food was transported by servants down winding corridors and was then warmed up in a serving room adjacent to the dining room.

very typical of the manor house style and is a perfect foil for flowers, food and china. But a less than perfect surface can be covered with a floor-length cloth and still look sumptuous, so a beautiful antique piece isn't imperative. Early dining tables commonly had gate legs to support the solid timbers and large sizes but pedestal legs were used later when table tops became lighter through the use of veneer finishes and a general daintiness appeared in furniture. The legs of the table may influence the size and type of chair you use.

Choosing the right type of chair is very important. If you cannot find a suitable set which match or are the right period for your style of room, then choose the simplest shapes possible. A mix of periods is fine if the woods are similar in colour. If the seats are upholstered, then cover all the chairs in the same fabric; this can be a less practical fabric—such as brocade or damask—than for living room

REFLECTION OF BYGONE DAYS

The manor house is always spoiled for space. This room is used as a laundry room and also a small
museum of manor house life as it was lived. The huge great press sits beneath an old-fashioned clothes
airer on a pulley. Old implements for goffering (ironing frills into a garment), ironing and pleating are
displayed along with other laundry tools and bottles. All it needs is the laundry maid.

A PERSONALIZED DINING ROOM

Here is another example of a small manor house dining room. This is a highly
personal room in which much of the decoration has been hand-painted, perhaps by a
local artist, or one whose work has been seen and admired elsewhere. Green predominates.
The large, purpose-built dresser has a trellis pattern echoed in the table. A very
fine porcelain dinner and tea service and set of glasses complete the 'manor' look.

The kitchen—a hive of activity

The manor house kitchen from the very earliest times has
been highly functional, benefitting from the latest tech-
nology of the day. Feeding a household and frequent guests
all the year round meant that the kitchen and all the services
connected with it had to run like clockwork. There was
always plenty of servant power for every meal, but apart
from regular meals there were all the other things to be
done before the age of electricity and refrigeration. Dairy
work, brining and preserving meat for the winter, pickling,
smoking and drying foods, baking all the bread and usually
brewing ale as well—all had to be done in the kitchen.
There would have been still rooms, lamp rooms, pantries,
storerooms, meat safes, sometimes ice-houses, cellars and
game larders, all clustered near the main kitchen.

This was a separate world from the rest of the house and
the family might never venture into the kitchen. Soundly

built with the best money could buy, it nevertheless lacked
comfort and was not designed for living in but simply for
work. The elements of this style of kitchen which have
remained today and which are still relevant are in some
cases truly fashionable again: the use of honest materials—
china, wood, brass and marble—and no unnecessary colour
except that which is inherent in warm wood, polished
copper or bricks.

One large free-standing table—used these days for eating,
working at and every kind of activity—would once have
been the basic work space for the cook. Plain scrubbable
wood was the best surface, with boards and cool slabs for
special cutting or rolling jobs. Fire-glazed sinks are enjoying a return to popularity and they look good let into a
solid wood surface or cool black slate. They of course
demand traditional pillar taps in brass or dull chrome. Plate
racks appeal nowadays for their decorative quality but in

A GOTHIC GARDEN ROOM

Here is eating in a grander, rather more Gothic manor house fashion, using the shelter
and light from a conservatory-like extension to give a garden-room feeling. 'Skeleton leaf'
wire chairs are arranged around a marble table. A clematis clambers up the trelliswork, and
elegant stemmed glasses and polished silver create an atmosphere of leisure and graciousness.

RESTRAINED ELEGANCE

This Scandinavian manor house is kept warm by a traditional ceiling-high tiled stove with
hand-decorated tiles. The room's simple lines, white-painted woodwork and plain blue and white
floral wallpaper add up to an interesting yet unconfused feeling, both elegant and restrained.
The white-painted table has a blue and white woven runner and a bowl of garden
flowers. Brass candlesticks and candelabra add a touch of extra luxury.

SUNLIT INTIMACY

Manor house eating can be a moveable feast. An intimate meal for four has
been laid here on a small oval table in front of the classical fireplace. Sunshine
falls on the plain coir matting over polished, dark-stained wooden boards.

the manor house kitchen were used as a sensible means of draining and storing plates.

Other furniture designed for storage was usually built as an integral part of the kitchen, so large built-in dressers with cupboards below and open shelves above were more common then single free-standing dressers. The manor house version was often painted white or cream and made a splendid backdrop for rows of burnished copper saucepans and jelly moulds or collections of giant-sized meat plates and serving dishes. By Victorian times the manor house kitchen had almost become the model for a fitted kitchen, with everything in its place and the latest gadgetry in use. The enormous open fires with roasting spits and great black ranges and ovens of earlier days do not fit happily into our modern way of life, but few country manor houses

today would do without a large range of some kind for cooking and heating.

Much of the messier preparation work such as washing vegetables went on in the scullery, and the fine china and glass was washed elsewhere and stored in safe china storerooms. Each day baskets of fresh fruit and vegetables, eggs and game would arrive from the garden and fields to be used by the cook. These fresh foods still make the finest decoration, albeit fleeting, for a country kitchen.

A cool separate larder for other foods, leftovers and the day-to-day storage of cheese and groceries is a luxury in many houses these days but wonderfully practical if you can arrange it. It is one of the soundest ideas passed down through the years, leaving space in the kitchen itself for the multitude of activities that take place here.

Sleeping and Bathing

Country air has always been conducive to sound sleep and the manor house bedroom has first and foremost provided a large, comfortable bed, warmth from an open fire in winter, and an idyllic view to wake up to each morning. Spacious and restful, it is a room which is welcoming enough to linger in but usually vacated early for a long day of outdoor pursuits and the sociable life downstairs.

Through the centuries the arrangement and position of bedrooms in the house altered according to fashion and social codes, and the importance of anterooms and dressing rooms beside bedrooms waxed and waned. Bedrooms changed from being places to entertain and talk with others to more private and personal chambers, which were often a haven to escape to for peace and quiet. At one time guests in grander houses might be provided with a suite of rooms.

It used to be common for bedrooms in a manor house to be decorated in very individual ways, often based on a colour or a theme such as Chinoiserie. Guest rooms were known as, say, the blue room or the Chinese room. The main bedrooms were more likely to be decorated in a personal way, reflecting the lady of the manor's love of, say, Indian fabrics or perhaps birds as a decorative motif.

Whatever your starting point, you can afford to indulge in a little decorative fantasy in a bedroom. For example, you could base your scheme around a favourite *toile de Jouy*

A WEALTH OF FINE OBJECTS

This bedroom is an excellent example of manor house style with its wealth of collected objects, all now valuable antiques. The heavy four-poster is sumptuously 'dressed' in printed cottons, scalloped edges, and a dark velvet bedcover.

fabric. (This is a French chintz which is usually printed in a single colour like violet, blue, red or sepia on a white background. It originally became popular in the English manor house in the late 18th century.) Or you could create a soft, romantic, all-white room with draped voile or spotted muslin. A glorious fabric used for curtains could be the beginning of your theme; ideally, choose a design with the feel of country gardens. Be generous with fabric, and aim for an impression of opulence and indulgence.

Suitable furniture

The manor house bedroom should be furnished with just the right amount of useful furniture—including some beautiful pieces—without being cluttered. The most suitable woods are oak, mahogany, walnut or similar fine hardwoods. Pine is not grand enough for this look.

If there is a separate dressing room, then wardrobes and cupboards for hanging clothes can be kept out of the bedroom itself. Otherwise, attractive free-standing wardrobes will be more in keeping than the built-in type.

In addition to the usual bed, dressing table, bedside cabinets, chest of drawers, one or two small bedroom chairs and perhaps a stool, a comfortable armchair or two would be welcome. If there is room, a washstand and a full-length, free-standing cheval mirror are very traditional.

In Edwardian times it was very common to provide guests with a writing desk in their bedrooms, as people staying in the house were expected to fill the mornings with letter writing. Paper, ink and everything that was needed were replenished each day. If there is space in a bedroom these days, it is a perfect place to continue this tradition. Positioned with an inspiring view over the garden, it could become a favourite sanctuary in the house.

The bedroom floor should be soft and warm underfoot but not necessarily luxurious. If you are blessed with beautiful mellow polished floorboards, then don't cover them entirely with fitted carpet; just have a few rugs or a small carpet square as an oasis for bare feet. If the floor is not worth exposing, then carpet entirely with a plain velvet or smooth pile carpet and add rugs if you wish.

The important four-poster

In many people's minds a bed in a country manor house must be a four-poster. The four-poster bed was originally designed for practical reasons in the days before satisfactory windows were built or curtains were generally hung, and certainly before bedroom heating was introduced. The thick folds of fabric surrounding the bed were a very effective way of protecting the sleeper against draughts. However, this type of bed continued to be made long after the need for drapes diminished. By then they were seen as a decorative device, and the curtains could be used to show off fine needle skills on rich fabrics similar to the exquisite dresses of the time.

It is possible to buy reproduction four-posters now and also modern versions that simply echo the idea. You can have a plain, severe, wooden structure left unadorned by fabric to make a bold statement, or you can indulge in flights of fancy with complicated fabric confections featuring frills, canopies, tassels and swags or any amount of decoration. Soft folds of gauzy muslin contrast beautifully with a solid, plain wood frame.

It's possible to use fabric to create a four-poster effect on a modern bed. Stand the bed facing into the room with the head against the wall then use fabric above the pillows. This can either be in a canopy fixed on to a frame cantilevered from the wall, or simply attached to the wall centrally above the headboard and draped softly down to the edges of the bed. The folds of fabric can be caught back against the wall with a tie or bows.

An existing bed could turn into a four-poster by adding four posts and possibly a canopy, but be sure that the proportions of your room can take the imposing dimensions without looking out of scale and awkward. Single beds often look too tall and top-heavy with the four-poster treatment.

A relatively easy way to create the opulent manor house effect is with cushions piled casually on a bed. Hand-embroidered silk and lovingly stitched petit point can mingle with antique fabrics and heirloom lace. Scented sleep pillows and sachets of lavender and heady pot-pourri

AN HEROIC BATHROOM

Only a manor house is likely to have a room tall enough to house this fascinating bath with its heroic shower cubicle. This room was probably once a bedroom and the plumbing and 'furniture' are free-standing and sculptural. The brass taps turn on the water for both bath and shower. Everything here is very basic and yet 'of the best'.

PLUMBING AS FURNISHING

The manor house does not attempt to hide the plumbing away. Instead its basics are chosen with care and incorporated as part of the furniture. In this large bedroom the marble basin is quite at home in the midst of elegant mahogany furniture. One concession to 'the toilette' is the white-painted wooden floor.

slipped into tiny pockets on the cushions will scent the room with a fragrance reminiscent of summer days.

For an authentic look, bed linen is best in white and can be delicately edged or embroidered, initialled or frilled. Ideally made from the finest pure linen or, alternatively, hard-wearing cotton, it should look crisp and inviting. Blankets can be chosen according to personal taste but a bedcover of some kind is important for the manor house look. This might be a downy comforter in bleached and faded colours or a thick, textured, woven-cotton throw in the palest pastel. It could be a strictly tailored cover made from the same fabric as the curtains to bring cohesion to the whole bedroom scheme. Patchwork quilts generally suggest a humbler home than the manor, but an intricately quilted cover in a single fabric or plainest white can look totally luxurious.

Pretty details

Details in the manor house bedroom are likely to be personal and intimate—a delicate pastel drawing of a child

asleep rather than large, dark ancestral portraits; a touching memento or treasured photograph rather than fine porcelain figures. Pictures should be fairly lightweight in style and content; flowers and romantic landscapes have long been great favourites and botanical prints and soft watercolours preferred to serious oils.

While plates might not be an obvious choice for a bedroom, they can look very pretty grouped above a piece of furniture or dotted amongst a patchwork of pictures. A collection of several prints in matching frames can be made into a stunning display hung vertically from wide ribbon or fabric strips down a wall.

A popular way of decorating the walls of manor house bedrooms and small sitting rooms two centuries ago was to glue engravings to plain-papered walls, then decorate the engravings with paper borders and bows printed in black, white and grey. Paper swags and other classical motifs were added to the walls as well. Rooms decorated in this way were known as print rooms, and the idea is easy to copy today for an authentic look. For a similar effect you could

FLOWERS AND LIGHT IN THE BATHROOM

Manor houses can choose rooms which get lots of sunshine to turn into bathrooms. This one, with its white marble bath surround and panelled sides, brings sunshine and the garden right inside. The curtains are springlike and floral, and the rose pattern appliqué quilt accentuates the garden theme.

visually link a group of pictures by means of a fabric bow atop each frame.

Lighting in any bedroom should be totally flattering to the furnishings and people alike, so table lamps are to be preferred to overhead lights. Bedside lamps are best with simple shades in cream or parchment but lamps for general lighting can be elaborate and less functional.

One of the nicest finishing touches in a bedroom is an open fire, and fireplaces were an essential element of older manor house bedrooms. If you are lucky enough to have one (or more), it would be a pity not to make the most of it. Sometimes an original fireplace has been removed and the opening sealed up, but it is not too difficult to install a replacement. Ideally, it should be the right period for the house; bear in mind also that bedroom fireplaces tended to be simpler than those downstairs. In fact, it was in front of the bedroom fire that many people took their baths until the bathroom was introduced to the grander houses in the early 19th century and gradually incorporated in humbler homes over the next century.

The bathroom—seclusion and splendour

The manor house bathroom is large and luxurious, splendid and elegant, yet often with a hint of the spartan, as if to remind the user that the important thing is to concentrate on getting clean, not simply to enjoy oneself.

This is softened, however, by the special details which are always carefully chosen for total comfort to the body and a joy to the senses. An endless supply of the softest, whitest towels, bath oils and delicious soaps and colognes is always to hand, along with natural sponges, proper scratchy loofahs, bristle brushes and shaving soap in a bowl.

Well-lit and carefully positioned mirrors should be provided, and there should be some space near the bath, whether on a table, shelf or bath rack, to park the bathtime reading and reviving drink. After a long, muddy day in the country a bath is a welcome ritual.

The room itself should feel safely private, even cut off from the rest of the house. A view of the garden, though not essential, can improve the whole bathing experience,

BATHING IN LUXURY

A copper bathtub must be the most luxurious of bedroom conveniences. Here it
has been given pride of place with a fine window view over garden
and grounds. It is complemented, as it deserves, by the great swathes of
dark-red brocade curtains belonging to the four-poster bed and an elegantly
patterned carpet. Past generations look enviously down on such modern luxury.

COZY WINTER NIGHTS
Comforting on cold winter nights, this old-
fashioned stove charmingly fills the old fireplace
niche and should keep alight all night.

but there should always be totally efficient curtains, blinds or shutters.

Because manor house bathrooms are generally spacious, there has always been room for those extras that make it resemble a private sitting room—an armchair for relaxing in after a bath, a rug and, originally, an open fire (opposite which the bath was traditionally positioned).

The materials used in the manor house bathroom, as elsewhere in the house, should be of a high quality and made to last. Tiles are chilly and perhaps best suited to small bathrooms, while plain, painted, wood-panelled walls or surfaces painted in vinyl silk look fine. Marble has the right touch of grandness for floors or surrounds, but where it is used good heating is crucial.

Good-quality imitations are also a possibility for materials. For example, a hard-wearing, modern, man-made material called Corian, which resembles marble but resists staining and can be cut and moulded to any shape, could be used instead of marble for panelling, for the basin surround or even for the basin itself. For floors, a less authentic but very practical alternative is vinyl. Available in imitation marble, tile, stone or wood, it feels softer and warmer to bare feet and is much easier to lay.

Traditional bathroom fittings

The claw-foot cast-iron bath standing in splendour in the middle of the room has enjoyed a recent revival, and reproductions are widely available. For the manor house look, a white roll-top bath is ideal. It can be built into a panelled surround of dark wood or even marble, or the outside can be painted so the bath can stand gloriously alone. Taps and fittings should be in keeping with the style of bath and there are plenty of reproductions on offer now; brass, china, chrome or nickel would all be suitable.

Showers were popular as far back as Victorian times; but, unlike baths, very old-fashioned showers are rather ungainly and not widely available now. It is nevertheless possible to install a shower that would fit into the manor house style of bathroom. One solution would be a shower installed in an alcove or built-in cupboard, with a door in plain or etched glass. Another possibility would be a period-style shower-mixer to use in the roll-top tub, with a shower curtain hanging from a curved, ceiling-mounted pole. Rather than a modern plastic shower curtain, you could use fabric backed with a clear plastic one.

The basin, which ought to be white, should be generously proportioned. It can stand on an imposing pedestal, be built into a suitable surround of wood, tiles or marble, or be set into a piece of period furniture such as a washstand with a marble top.

An old-fashioned toilet with a mahogany seat and high-level cistern looks very authentic, but a plain white low-level toilet is also perfectly suitable.

The giant chrome or brass heated towel rail is a traditional fitting in the manor house bathroom. A relic from the early days of country house plumbing, it nevertheless is an important detail and usefully provides all those warm towels.

Inside meets Outside

How a house makes the visual change from interior to exterior is vitally important in a country setting.

Though a hall is invariably the room, or part of a house, you first come into from a main entrance, it has been used for many different purposes—including as a general living room during the day, which explains the huge size of many halls found in country houses. In medieval times, when the house was really just one large room or hall, most activities had to take place in it but eventually by the late 19th century whole strings of ground floor reception and living rooms were built for people to use throughout the day. The hall then became a rather busy and uncomfortable place to be, with servants and guests coming and going. Many Victorian and Edwardian manor houses, particularly those built or refurbished in the Gothic style, re-introduced the idea of the hall as a large space for gatherings and a place to play games and have entertainments.

How closely you can conform to the original manor-style hall, will depend on the size of your present hall. A country manor house hall might contain all the paraphernalia needed for walking, even riding, if other rooms at the back of the house were not provided for this storage. One or two chairs are also needed.

A side table, for flowers and odds and ends, is important in a hall and if you have space perhaps a round polished wood table too. These are probably the only pieces of

An Intriguing Mix

Inside this manor lies the expensive and desirable clutter of centuries of acquisitiveness. Outside, there is evidence of wealth of another kind—a carefully landscaped environment, which requires a team of full-time gardeners to keep it all in order.

PALE COLOURS FOIL WELL-POLISHED WOOD
Beautiful flagstones, pale colours and polished
wood greet the visitor to this spacious hallway.

COLLECTION OF ODDITIES FOR ALCOVES
When architecture offers you an alcove like this, you can but put
something marbled inside and decorate with the trappings of
leisured life. The ornamental ceiling light is quite in keeping.

A WARM WELCOME
Here, a white ceiling and sunny yellow walls
give a warm welcome, while easily cleaned stone flags
acknowledge the possibility of muddy feet.

furniture needed because, although a hall should look furnished and welcoming, it shouldn't be cluttered.

Mirrors should be strategically placed. Decorations here tend to be less exotic or valuable and more mundane than in other parts of the house. Shooting trophies, stuffed birds or fish in cases and general landscape paintings or maps seem most suitable for the surroundings. A longcase clock and barometer might also be put in the hall.

The main staircase would generally have led off from the front hall and, depending on the age and status of the house, might be made from stone, marble or wood. Once the practice of having state rooms on the first floor died out after the 17th century, there wasn't the need for really magnificent and eye-catching staircases. Even so, the stairs would have been as wide and generous as it was possible to make them, with perhaps a sweep or curve to add elegance and often a half landing with a window for light.

The outdoors comes in

The fashion of having doors opening at ground level on to the garden from a living or drawing room became popular in the late 18th and early 19th centuries, once the important

EXOTIC SHRUBS AND TREES
A conservatory for a manor house should be tall and generously proportioned.
Supporting pieces should be made of wood and should be many and slender so they
don't dominate the glass. This conservatory is used to grow exotica as well as small trees.

reception rooms were built on the ground floor and not at first floor level as was once the case. These doors, which often looked more like windows, gave unhindered views across magnificent gardens and elegant parkland. The French window also gave access in and out of the garden and on to a terrace without the need to call servants and use the formal front entrance.

Today, of course, French windows are still widely in use, whether in the original Georgian manor houses or in their 20th-century counterparts. The impression they create remains the same—the feeling of being in touch with nature, separated only by doors that can be thrown open spontaneously on a lovely day.

In the 19th century, large and often exotic conservatories leading from a drawing room or dining room became popular in many country manor houses. Some were designed to be used as extra rooms, particularly for parties, soirees and entertainments. Others housed collections of tender plants or caged birds and were added as just another curiosity in the garden, along with ferneries, grottos or statue lawns. These days, a conservatory can stretch the space in your house and provide an extra room.

GOTHIC VIEWS

This little side entrance is a Gothic porch cum garden room from which
to view the garden. The brick area between room and lawn provides a place to sit when
the sun comes out, while the glass-paned door offers a view of the garden even on dull days.
The curtains have been cunningly held back at the top to accentuate the Gothic quality of the room;
they allow the door to open yet they drop down warmly in the evening.

<u>LIGHTENING A SOMBRE ROOM</u>
Another Gothic eye on to the garden, but the white
paint and exquisite view prevent the Gothic
imagery from being overbearing.

<u>CATCHING THE LIGHT</u>
This upstairs landing, with its white-painted surfaces,
catches so much sunlight and is so airy and bright
that it has been used as a picture gallery.

The design and period detail of a conservatory must suit the house to which it will be attached. While it makes sense to paint the structure white from the point of view of light reflection, there is no reason why a conservatory shouldn't be a less obvious colour, such as a very dark holly green, or stained natural wood, which ages to a silver grey.

Try to decide very early on in the whole process how you intend to use the extra space, since the choice between, say, an extra living room or a place to grow a palm collection will have a definite effect on the basic details such as ventilation, flooring or shading.

Furnishing the conservatory

Flooring must be practical if the conservatory houses plants which need watering or even damping down overhead on hot days. Even if you plan to live in the extra space, floors must still be easy to clean, as they are the first to receive outdoor footwear on its way indoors. Tiles make an obvious and beautiful choice—Victorian conservatories often had wonderfully elaborate and colourful floor designs, but you could choose simple, pale, glazed or unglazed terracotta tiles, or classic black and white tiles laid chequerboard-fashion. A suspended wooden floor is another possibility but only practical if there isn't going to be much water sloshing around.

Furniture in the conservatory will obviously have a distinct outdoor feel to it. Wicker or rattan furniture always

looks good; and soft, squashy cushions will add the comfort cane can lack, protecting skin from the rough or sharp edges which often protrude. Basketware chairs and tables seem to relish the steamy atmosphere. Real wooden deck chairs, still available from the original Edwardian cruise ships, also look very natural in the manor house style of conservatory.

Metal filigree—real or reproduction—looks right in a conservatory too. Original cast iron is extremely heavy, expensive and prone to rusting but there are plenty of copies in cast aluminium which don't have this problem. Think about painting metal furniture, or better still have it sprayed or stove-enamelled, in something other than the ubiquitous over-bright white which often jars in a northern climate. A few dainty white pieces can look charming in a lushly green conservatory, but often a pale green, a soft greyish greeny-blue, or a dark inky green looks best of all.

If you want to include a table for meals, it can simply be a wooden top fixed to trestle legs or to a cast-iron base, or it could be an all-metal version. Lacy cloths for summer teatimes or a practical sturdy cotton fabric thrown over for everyday will hide a less than perfect table top.

Lighting is important too and looks particularly good if it is a little fanciful, such as an ancient chandelier or wooden candelabra. Candles always create atmosphere. Lighting concealed among plants can be cunningly used for special effects, but try to avoid glare from the glass.

Perfect planting

If a conservatory is to be used mainly for growing plants, then either spaces must be left for planting things directly into the ground, with paving round the spaces; or the whole floor area must be covered with a hard surface, with staging and stands used for the plants. Large, heavy pots will need sturdy wooden or metal slatted shelving or staging, built in as the conservatory is put up.

In the 19th century, elaborate metal wirework stands and cache-pots were made, very often in several tiers, in which to stand collections of plants in small pots. Painted white or green, these stands were usually very decorative, with fancy twists and curls and frilly edges. Nowadays they are very highly priced, but plainer, sturdier versions are available, usually made from flat strips of metal which are practical if not quite as decorative as the antiques.

ANCIENT BEAMS AND FLAGSTONES
An old manor house may have a room which was once the 'grand hall' featuring ancient wooden beams—the beams shown here have simple carving at the ends, and there is also a tiny minstrel's gallery. The flagstones on the floor are no less attractive for being very cracked with age. The furniture and furnishings have been kept sparse and plain, in keeping with the architecture and the age of the house. The metal plates of the wall lights reflect and so double the light therefrom.

TUDOR TREATMENT

In this Tudor home, the length and height of this space allows some monumental
furniture to be ranged side-by-side along the wall. The paintings have been carefully
chosen to complement the heavy, dark, Tudor feeling of the interior.

For a sense of scale in the conservatory you will need some permanent larger plants to stand on the floor, and these should be planted into simple wooden tubs, either round or square, or plain terracotta pots standing in saucers.

Wherever possible banish plastic from the conservatory or garden room—this more than anything will help achieve the manor house look. Avoid plastic flower pots and containers, any plastic furniture, watering cans, even plant labels. Instead look for old battered wooden trugs, ancient flower baskets and wooden-handled garden tools. A crumpled linen gardening apron and an old straw sun hat are the details which set the mood, while a galvanized metal watering-can rather than a gaudy orange or green plastic one evokes the manor house style straightaway.

A conservatory with no living green plants looks sad and sorry for itself. Even if you concentrate on one type of plant to grow—such as ivy, simple geraniums (pelargoniums) or one or two standard trees in pots—your conservatory will look furnished. Trying to grow too many different varieties of plants can be tricky when they all demand different temperatures, light levels and humidity.

The garden room

Another room which spans the break between indoors and outdoors is the garden room. It is the kind of room which simply develops over the years. Perhaps starting out as a corner between two outside walls, it becomes filled in with glass to make a lovely, sheltered sun-trap halfway between the house and garden. Usually attached to the house, it is entirely covered in, with doors to inside and out.

The garden room is the place where all the paraphernalia needed for outdoor enjoyment has a habit of collecting. Furniture simply arrives there when it has seen better days elsewhere, and strange bits and pieces occasionally appear and then are never removed. It is likely to be the place that the family dogs slink off to for peace and a snooze in the sun.

Definitely not a smart room, it is meant for the family and very close friends to use for relaxation and be themselves when they have no guests. Without as much glass as a conservatory, it might not produce perfect plants but would make a good home for resting indoors plants or overwintering geraniums.

COLONIAL STYLE

Born out of a spirit of improvisation and adaptation, colonial style reflects the settlers' need to create a home from home in the 'new world'. The style represents so many different looks that it is simplest to follow furniture guidelines. Generally speaking, there's an ornamental look which embraces the heavily carved furniture of the 17th century and the early settlers. Another, more functional look takes in the undecorated simplicity of Shaker furniture along with rough-hewn country pieces. There is also a decorative style which uses paint and stencils to create pattern and emulate grander finishes as well as borrowing from folk art traditions of other cultures. Colonial Georgian is based on the pattern books of the English cabinet makers and includes the well-to-do classical interior which was fashionable across the world from Philadelphia to New South Wales—in America this developed into Federal style.

ACHIEVING THE LOOK

The early settlers, arriving in the 'new world' with little more than they could carry with them, used whatever materials they found to hand to recreate the familiar furnishing styles of their motherland.

Underfoot

While the earliest floors were simply packed earth, these were succeeded by stone and finally by wide boards of oak, pine or chestnut which were either dry-scrubbed with sand and herbs or grained to emulate other rare timbers. Since floorcoverings were minimal, wooden boards were painted to represent woven carpets, tiled pavements or parquet floors. This is a look that is easily copied today. Hardwood strip flooring also looks very appropriate.

Rag rugs, woven out of worn-out clothes, became a new art form still very popular today. Rugs made from fabric remnants used elsewhere in the home will help to pull together colour schemes. You can use either tufts of fabric hooked through large-mesh canvas, or long strips of fabric plaited into a rope, coiled and then laced together.

Walls and ceilings

Matchboarded walls and beamed ceilings are intrinsic to this style, as are high rafters. American colonials used paint and stencils to decorate their homes. Travelling artists would transform timbered walls by emulating the patterns and wallpapers of wealthier houses. Nowadays advice on these decorative paint techniques is freely available; stencil

A typical New England bedroom with a matchboarded interior and plain varnished floorboards, a hand-woven rug and traditional quilted patchwork bedcover. The slatted blinds let in (or keep out) the sun. A narrow, panelled door leads on to a little veranda.

Painted woodwork and white walls are characteristic of colonial style. Here they provide an ideal background for displays of glassware and other prized possessions.

A very simple, beautifully proportioned Shaker interior. Most items such as chairs were designed to hang on wooden pegs fixed to a wooden rail on the walls.

kits abound and shortcuts have been devised to make it easy for the least artistic. Choose the simple folk art motifs used by the early settlers, based on fruit, flowers or animals—some symbolic, like the tulip, the pineapple and the heart, others purely decorative such as borders of foliage swags or ribbons.

Seldom was wood left bare. Sometimes it was grained, marbled or stained to give it the look of costlier timbers; otherwise, it was painted in strong flat colours to offset plain walls. If you want to emulate the spare style of the religious communities, keep colours muted. A deep blue-green combined with burnt sienna and yellow ochre was a traditional and popular scheme, but nowadays shades of indigo, ox-blood red and all the dirty greys look marvellous.

Fabrics and window treatments

For the early settlers, patterned fabrics were limited to a few imported silks; otherwise, hand-embroidered patterns were worked on to basic homespun cloths. Wool and flax were combined to make linsey-wolsey, while cotton mixed with linen became fustian—both hard-wearing cloths used for bed and window curtains. Cotton was used extensively in the home. Plain calicoes, denims, self-striped dimities, muslins, ginghams and fine wool veilings are appropriate today—and so are rough cotton duck, woven hessians and sacking.

Window treatments should take their style from the type of fabric used. Basic cloths demand no more than a couple of lengths of hemmed material threaded over a metal rod,

Simplicity and comfort: a white painted wicker rocking chair set out on the porch so that the evening sun may be enjoyed after work. The hand-knitted shawl thrown casually over it is a reminder that the evenings can become chilly.

Colonials soon learned how to achieve comfort and security in what often started out as harsh conditions. Here, a comfortable armchair placed next to the fireplace, with a view through the low window, make this bedroom a cozy place in which to sit and read.

The prettily rayed slats of wood which form the arch to this little window alcove are typical of colonial imagination and craftsmanship. From the comfortable upholstered window seat, through the art nouveau stained glass, one can watch the world go by. The sheer fabric curtain is held back just by a ribbon.

or tied with fabric or leather thongs. Chintzes and calico prints might lend themselves to tiers of frilled café curtains or flounced swags bedecked with bows.

Window treatments in early colonial houses varied from straight curtains with fabric loops hung on slender wooden poles to elegant swags and slatted blinds topped by wooden cornices which concealed the blinds when they were raised. By the mid 19th century these cornices were decorated with landscape scenes, often stencilled in bronze powders against a dark green background.

Furniture

Although most of the early colonial furniture was based on the Jacobean styles, expelled religious communities formed settlements which had distinctive styles of their own based on puritanical simplicity and practicality. American Shaker furniture is much admired for its lean, spare lines. Imported styles such as Chippendale, Sheraton, Hepplewhite and Empire lines also found their way into rural communities, the designs coarsened by the village carpenters.

Warmth of the hearth

Early designs of fireplace are based on the inglenook— simple, large-scale recesses in the wall which combined an open fire with all the cooking apparatus. The proportions are always generous, with high mantelshelves standing at shoulder level. Brick hearths are authentic, as are cast-iron firebacks and delft tile surrounds; but coloured pigments

In this haven from the sun, the sturdy wooden columns are quite ornate with fretwork brackets. The slatted rocking chairs are reminiscent of old cruise ship deck chairs.

Typical of colonial practicality: a built-in wooden dumb-waiter, pulled up by a rope. The cupboard doors are made with care, as are the panelled kitchen door and the small solid wood table next to it.

Here is another pretty little room with all the signs of colonial taste. White is much in evidence, with fresh white paint over walls and ceiling, white woodwork, a white cane chair, white muslin curtains and a white radiator. Home handicrafts feature in the framed embroideries on the wall and the hand-woven rug.

An amusing conceit: a group of miniature colonial-style houses on stakes 'planted' in the garden. Authentic details like gabled roofs, shuttered windows, weatherboarding, and windows with contrasting paint finishes add a certain fascination. Their setting is a delightful informal garden with wild roses and a feathery herbaceous border.

added to modern cement mixes can make an effective alternative, and patterned tiles will make a decorative focus. Modern fireplaces could have simple plastered surrounds with chunky mantelshelves of salvaged timbers.

Settlers from mid-Europe brought cast-iron, pot-bellied stoves with them. A low squat stove with a long black flue rising to the upstairs rooms is a style detail associated with the Shaker homes—these proportions make for a strong design which is equally appropriate today.

Finishing touches

Simple wrought iron chandeliers, with curving metal branches to hold candle lights, or wooden cartwheels drilled to take bulb holders, are appropriate modern

alternatives to rushlights and the simple oil lamps known as betty lamps. Wall sconces, either mirrored or made from tin cut in animal shapes, are also available today. Improvised lamp bases always look good in the country—outsize wine casks, salt-glaze storage jars and stencilled biscuit canisters can all be wired to take light holders.

Patchwork quilts and woven throws—whether hung on the wall or used as tablecloths or casual coverings for sofas, chairs and cushions—are essential accessories. So too are samplers; you could embroider your own using patterns based on antique samplers now found in museums. There is a wealth of early folk art: look for any simple, naive patterns, paintings with irregular perspectives and un-tutored pots that have a chunky crudeness.

Living and Relaxing

The earliest colonial houses were built with one main hall downstairs which was used for cooking, dining, living and sleeping. Gradually, as the living quarters developed into separate rooms, so the living room became a more formal parlour, furnished with the best pieces that the family owned, and used for receiving the clergy and other important guests. Since the old parlour furniture was never designed to be comfortable, 20th century colonial-style rooms tend to combine well-upholstered modern pieces with antiques, folk art and country accessories.

The earliest country furniture dates from the mid-17th century—provincial versions of English and Dutch styles of that era. Every home would have had a heavy chest or court cupboard, made of native oak or maple, and a high-backed settle, often made in white pine, maple or oak, that had a swing-over hinged back which came to rest on the arms, thus converting it into a table. There would have been an assortment of wooden chairs made of a mixture of hickory, ash, maple and elm; and candlestands, little circular-topped pedestal tables supported on tripod legs.

Subsequent furniture styles also emanated from England, based upon William and Mary, Queen Anne, Chippendale, Hepplewhite and Sheraton styles. French Directoire and Empire furniture was popular in the early 19th century, with Duncan Phyfe emerging as America's leading cabinet maker of the Federal period.

THE WARMTH OF WOOD

Spots are not particularly colonial but the contrast of pale walls and dark wood is. Each piece of furniture has a personality of its own yet is in happy harmony with its neighbours. The solid, confident dresser complements the two chairs well.

Rather than slavishly following any one period or style, however, concentrate on collecting an irregular assortment of chairs and sofas, covering them with throws, blankets and quilts to create layers of pattern.

Upholstered comforts

While Windsor benches, high-back settles and lath-back chairs are all authentic, they are hardly relaxing, even with the addition of squab cushions, so mix old seats with modern upholstery in traditional shapes. Limit pattern choices to stylized floral designs and simple geometrics. Woven stripes and checks will add a crisp definition to any form. There are some marvellous facsimiles of ancient hand-blocked linen prints, where the colours are deliberately faded on backgrounds that are built up of blotchy tones.

TRADITION ADAPTED

This room is typical of many of today's colonial-style homes. Traditional colour schemes and furnishings have been combined with both modern upholstered furniture and antiques to create a comfortable and very distinctive ambience.

LEGACY OF THE PAST

Here a large but elegant wardrobe in a typical brick colour perfectly complements a fine patchwork quilt, a little painted table and chair, and a stack of traditional wood boxes.

THE COLONIAL LOOK IN A CORNER

One little corner of this room epitomizes the colonial look, with matchboarding a quarter of the way up the wall, painted white; a hand-made cupboard/sideboard; an oil lamp, a wicker basket and a couple of ancient wooden-handled paintbrushes; a hand-made wooden box and a delightful painting of pansies.

A SMALL COLONIAL DESK

This window is very colonial, up in the eaves of the roof. So are the little hand-made desk and the oval Shaker boxes with their characteristic swallowtail joints.

Use generous-scale chesterfields for conversational seating. More formal styles include pert little high-back sofas with wing sides and cabriole legs; covered in a linen plaid or a stencilled print, they make an upholstered alternative to the fireside settle. Chippendale-style wing chairs and sofas, covered in pin-dot twills or herringbone weaves are other possibilities.

A more modern interpretation of colonial seating could include wooden day beds, platform seating and built-in seats fitted into deep window reveals—minimal-style seating to fit around the perimeter of the room, leaving the fireside free for the occasional antique chair.

Occasional chairs

Upright chairs, country carvers and bentwood rockers as well as bent twig and wickerwork basket furniture will give a strong colonial identity to any room. The Windsor chair, which was very popular in colonial homes, has become a country classic. Carver and Brewster armchairs were earlier designs named after two of the Pilgrim Fathers and based

COLOURFUL STORAGE
Lightweight wooden boxes were widely used in
colonial times to store everything from buttons to
nails; the different colours often identified the
contents. The boxes were originally made of
steam-bent wood, but balsa-wood versions are
available today. They make effective and colourful
containers and are very much in keeping with
colonial style.

on English Jacobean styles. Later on, spool-turned furniture was another popular style, based on the English
bobbin furniture—legs, spindles and stretchers were decorated with a succession of machine-lathed shapes resembling
spools.

No colonial home is complete without a rocking chair—
an American invention which became something of a
national institution as people had local carpenters cut down
the legs of their old chairs and fit them with wooden
rockers. The Boston rocker, made in the early 19th century,
resembled a high-back Windsor chair with gently curved
bends. The flat comb piece and front edge were often
decorated.

As fashions moved away from darkened timbers towards
painted finishes, so furniture was manufactured for decorating. 'Fancy chairs' became popular, such as the Hitch-
cock chair, which came ready-stencilled from the factory.
While it would be sacrilege to paint a fine period chair,
many an undistinguished piece of Victorian pine has been
prettified by a coat of colour.

Cooking and Eating

As with the rest of the house, the colonial-style kitchen could be decorated in various styles, each inspired by different colonial looks. These range from a very basic, primitive kitchen using natural materials and roughened textures, worktops supported on brick piers along with open shelving, to a fully fitted kitchen with dark hardwood units disguising modern conveniences. Some of the most interesting schemes are based around regional styles or relatively simple period details. But whatever look you choose, make sure you are setting a style that you can sustain elsewhere in your home.

If you hanker for fretwork carving and fancy wrought iron hinges and handles, you could base your kitchen on the homes of the German settlers in Pennsylvania, whose well-developed folk art traditions were one of the main sources of American folk decoration. Known as Pennsylvania Dutch (a corruption of Pennsylvania *Deutsch*), the style featured highly patterned surfaces and motifs like little hearts, weeping willow trees and doves, often set out in a paired symmetry.

Shelving units based on this look might have scalloped sides or chipwork decoration with little V-shaped nicks taken out of the wood. Barley-sugar twists on timber supports and arched panelling might combine with shuttered windows featuring heart-shaped ventilation holes. Cooking is done on decorative cast-iron stoves made bright

A ROOM FOR FAMILY AND FRIENDS

Preparing food and sharing it with neighbours
was an important part of colonial life.
This warm, friendly room is absolutely right for
entertaining, with its inviting open fire, its sturdy
and well-polished table, its comfortable rocking chair.

SPACE AND NOSTALGIA
Wooden columns and fretwork instead of a wall give a pleasant open
feeling to this spacious Australian dining room. The matchboarding is painted
white as is all the rest of the woodwork. The dark marble fireplace with
its ceramic tiles is surely a nostalgia taken from the Old Country.

with enamelling and curlicue patterns and fitted with brass rails, pot hooks and trivets.

Surprisingly, much Victorian kitchen pine shares these decorative details, and modern reproductions would look good painted with some of these stencilled motifs. Designs could also be stencilled or hand-painted on to salt boxes, spice racks or even picture frames; tulips, grapes and other flower and fruit motifs are the most traditional.

Shaker style

A much more disciplined, classical look might owe its inspiration to the Shaker homesteads, where everything was designed to fit into prescribed spaces, decoration was considered superficial and floor areas were kept free and tidy. Outward appearances, they believed, conveyed every-thing about the inner spirit.

Seek out simple, strong and perfectly plain jointed furniture. Organization is the key factor here: be over-generous with cupboard space and storage areas to ensure as much as possible is out of sight. Set a continuous wooden hanging rail around the perimeter of the room with dowelled rods forming chunky hooks. Shakers hung everything on peg rails like these—from wooden lath-back chairs to clocks, mirrors, brooms and baskets. Deep batten-ing, set at head height around the walls, will not only make a strong visual statement but will also help align units and equipment of differing sizes. Paint it in a contrasting colour so that it stands out from the walls; drill holes through wooden implements and stitch loops on to cloths in order to hang up attractive items.

Oval boxes in gradations of size, made of finely shaved ash, are another Shaker style detail. These boxes, of distinctive design with extravagantly forked swallowtail joints, were often given a coloured stain to make the

A GARDEN VIEW

A small corner of a colonial kitchen showing the generous window with a view of the garden, the small, much-used wooden table in front of it, the positive dark green paint of the built-in cupboards and the collection of early 20th century enamelware.

SOLID SHELVES FOR STORAGE

These made-to-measure solid-wood open shelves are used to store a collection of baking tins and old-fashioned rolling pins and other baking equipment.

contents identifiable. Balsa-wood copies of these boxes are available and make unconventional containers for storing packets and pulses or herbs and spices.

Period detailing

Colonial food cupboards and larders also have an interesting pedigree and are often particularly decorative because of the ventilation holes rendered necessary by their contents. Some have pierced tin doors, punched with circular and geometric patterns. Others feature open panelled doors which might contain rows of small turned wooden spindles, or wooden latticework set at the diagonal, or fine chickenwire or metal gauze which could be painted or gilded in the period manner. Take inspiration from these old styles to create alternatives to standard door fronts.

Flat colour, stencilled pattern, or ragged, dragged and stippled surfaces are all ways of adding interest to kitchen furniture, while crazed and crackled finishes will add a look of age. Don't stop short of painting factory-made units. While lacquered finishes can be broken down and distressed by rubbing with wire wool and white spirit, sometimes it is possible when purchasing new units to buy them unvarnished. Even laminate-faced doors can be painted once the surface has been sanded. In all cases, a heavy-duty type of oil paint is recommended, ideally containing a polyurethane hardener.

Early colonial dressers consisted of sideboards with plate racks—sometimes called delft racks—on the wall above. Shelves that were to take china were often covered with a strip of linen which had a decorative edge that hung over the side: patterns for crocheted shelf trims in the old style are still available. To make a new dresser fit into an old setting, chunky architrave and moulding could be added to the front edges of the shelving; modern pine could be painted in deep brick red or teal blue—or charcoal grey simply rubbed into the grain.

Kitchen basics

Whatever style of storage you choose, the basics should follow the theme. Worktops of heavy maple blocks can be made to measure and could incorporate a grooved section by the sink for a draining surface, as well as a marble-topped pastry board. Marble, slate and tiled surfaces are all equally practical natural surfaces, while look-alike laminates and simulated marbles are for those who want easycare tops. Deep fireclay sinks are normally set into purpose-built units or sit astride brick supports; stainless steel sinks will look less modern set into old pieces of furniture.

For flooring, stripped wooden boards strewn with rag

rugs would be traditional, as would a stencilled border or even a stencilled 'carpet'. Plywood and chipboard sheets, or tongue-and-groove panels, set chequerboard-fashion, would also look good. Terracotta tiles, brick paviours and flagstones are part of a more ethnic version—a large rush mat or a runner of coir matting alongside the working areas will make it less tiring on the feet.

Painted matchboarding, the classic wall finish in the colonial home, is very practical in the kitchen. It can be fixed vertically, horizontally or even diagonally. Ceramic tiles are another traditional finish for working walls. Copies abound of the old Dutch picture tiles, either in the traditional blue and white or in the less well-known magenta glaze. Of the modern designs, look for patterns that are reminiscent of the country house larders and dairies. Modern washable wallpapers are another option for the kitchen; American stencil motifs and Scandinavian checks and stripes will echo the various colonial looks.

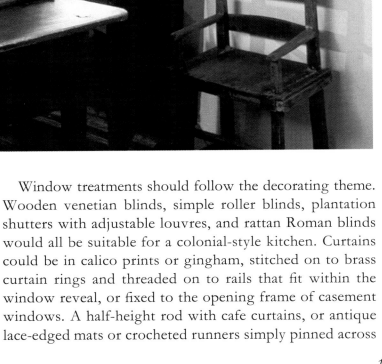

FLOWERS AND WOOD

This 'flower room' part of the kitchen epitomizes the colonials' appreciation of wood. The wooden worktop runs from the window and is expressly designed for drying or arranging flowers and for drying and storing herbs. There are trugs and jugs, clippers and shovels and even a tray saying 'herb rooms'.

LIVED-IN COMFORT

Here's a kitchen surprisingly 'busy' for a colonial one, but it has all the right ingredients: a collection of obviously much-loved baskets; a little Shaker chair hung up on wooden pegs; an open fire; a comfortable wingback chair; white walls with contrasting green woodwork and polished wooden floorboards.

Window treatments should follow the decorating theme. Wooden venetian blinds, simple roller blinds, plantation shutters with adjustable louvres, and rattan Roman blinds would all be suitable for a colonial-style kitchen. Curtains could be in calico prints or gingham, stitched on to brass curtain rings and threaded on to rails that fit within the window reveal, or fixed to the opening frame of casement windows. A half-height rod with cafe curtains, or antique lace-edged mats or crocheted runners simply pinned across the frame are seemly ways of blocking an unattractive view, especially on smaller windows.

Dining styles

A separate dining room did not become a feature of colonial homes until the emergence of Georgian architecture in the 18th century. Until then—and even after that time in most rural areas—eating took place in the all-purpose hall, around tables that could be taken apart,

VARIATIONS ON A THEME

This charming room looks as though it has remained unchanged for
generations. The colour scheme is predominantly blue and white,
but with variations in the blue, so it is by no means sterile.
The spongeware pottery fits in perfectly.

CONVENIENCE AND TRADITION

Another specialist corner showing an
appreciation of different woods and all
things made with it. The bucket hangs on
a peg rail, in true Shaker tradition.

turned into seats or made smaller by dropping the leaves at
the end of the meal. The family assembled around the table
on simple stools and benches, with a chair reserved for the
head of the household.

Space-saving, multi-purpose tables, both antique and
modern, are still popular today, particularly because dining
has once again merged with the living, cooking and
'family' spaces. Old board tables made from long planks of
oak set on thick bulbous legs are the earliest style; these
would have been partnered by three-legged stools or
tavern-style benches.

If space is tight, long narrow refectory tables with
benches either side are a surprisingly economical way of
seating a great number of people: check that the construction of the table will allow the benches to be pushed
well underneath. Otherwise, look out for low-backed
dining chairs, like the Shaker-designed rush- or rope-seated
lath-back chairs that would actually push right under the
tabletop.

Other colonial seating includes the wagon bench—
designed to be used in both the wagon and the home—and
the Windsor settle, a two- or three-seater version of the
familiar Windsor chair. Single, late-Victorian kitchen

chairs, either painted in authentic green, yellow, brown or
'heavenly blue', or grained, then stencilled and given a tie-
on squab cushion, make excellent informal dining chairs.

Gate-leg and drop-leaf tables are so adaptable in design
that they have been in constant production since the 17th
century. While they look good with all the rough country
versions of the Georgian chairs, they could also be teamed
with the earlier high-back Queen Anne style chairs with
flowing lines, and cabriole legs ending in ball-and-claw
feet: a more formal style which is nonetheless in keeping.

Dressing the dining room

Old country equipment can often be adapted to modern
needs yet still retain an authentic period flavour. For
example, a bread trough, or dough bin—a type of deep-
bellied chest which stands on four splayed legs, with
internal compartments to house the flour and the dough—
makes an excellent rustic sideboard or hinged-top drinks
cupboard.

Accessories can go a long way towards creating the right
effect. Take old household equipment with strong graphic
shapes like wooden sieves, bent twigware and split-cane
carpet beaters and hang them on the wall. Start collecting

A WARM AND SUNNY ROOM

The visitor enters through the front door straight into this sunny dining room, where an antique gateleg table has pride of place on the bare floorboards. The warm tones of the wood and the blend of different periods and styles of furniture create a cheerful, homely atmosphere that is very welcoming.

A SOMBRE LOOK

This tall room has quite a Victorian air about it with its dark doors and furniture and lace tablecloths. The matchboarding, the woodwork above the door, and the rocking chair remind us that this is colonial. The wooden board dividing the wall horizontally on the left looks as though it might once have held pegs for storing furniture.

WHERE HOUSE AND GARDEN MEET

This charming room makes best use of a good climate, with wide glass doors opening on to
a patio where one can sit and have a cool drink on sunny afternoons and evenings. Indoors,
some talented member of the family has painted the dresser (just visible), table, chairs, cupboard, and
the little basket on the table in that particular almost-blue green which is so popular. Garden
and house really meet in this room where the tree is indoors and the chairs outside.

ASSORTMENT OF WOODS

Very narrow matchboarding in this kitchen cleverly conceals a
door, only given away by its neat little hinges. On the pale
wooden floor stand a rocking chair with an assortment of
cushions; a small stool with a blue budgie in a dark-green
birdcage; and an old barrow used for storing a selection of bread
boards, chopping boards, cheese boards and pig-shaped platters.

baskets of all shapes and sizes—there's a great legacy of
country baskets woven to individual designs according to
their uses.

Antique folk-art is now very expensive, but a lot of
ethnic figures, boxes and baskets from the Far East as well
as wooden implements and platters from India have a
similar crude and native charm which comes a lot more
cheaply. For example, cheerful copies of Pennsylvania
Dutch enamelled tinware, robustly painted and bright with
fruit and flowers, could be made using modern enamelled
tea and coffee pots, and inexpensive ready-stencilled tin
plates and bowls are also available.

Colonial table settings

Eating utensils followed a European tradition—wooden
and pewter platters for humble homes, followed by blue
and white exportware in the traders' homes. Spatterware
and spongeware are particular types of pottery which are
currently enjoying a revival of interest—they are distinguished by the fact that the pottery looks as if it has been
flicked or dabbed with colour.

Of the everyday pottery, two types are especially
associated with colonial style: the blue-grey or tan stoneware, which is often given a salt glaze to make it watertight
and is still being worked by craftsmen potters today; and
redware, which is often used in conjunction with sgraffito
decoration (where a design is drawn into a contrasting
cream-coloured clay 'slip' to expose the red clay body
underneath) or with slip decoration (where the redware is
decorated with slip after shaping, using a tube or quill—
this is known as slipware).

Wooden-handled cutlery marries well with this pottery,
as do simple turned wooden candlesticks and salt and
pepper mills: experiment with unconventional settings and
use a variety of tablecloths to ring the changes. Paisley
bedspreads or striped and chequered sheeting make outsize
cloths to cover large tables. Or simply add pattern by using
a runner of plaid linen down the middle of the table.

Sleeping and Bathing

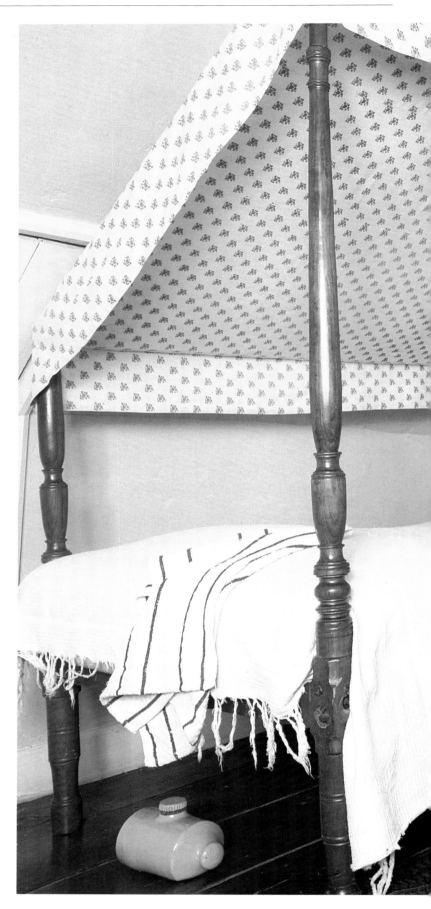

Today's colonial bedrooms combine the spirit of the old styles with modern comforts. Many antique bedsteads are too short and narrow by today's standards, and modern reproduction bedsteads offer greater flexibility. Even an interior-sprung divan set can be adapted to give it the spirit of the age. Because modern beds tend to be too low for period rooms, the legs can be raised; high-level headboards, wall-mounted panelling or even the serpentine back of a Victorian chiffonier will give them dignity.

Open-posters and half-testers were developed from four-poster beds. While some colonial beds continue the four-poster tradition of swathing the bed structure in fabric, others rely on a frame of sculptural simplicity. Particularly common are the open-post beds where the leg columns of the wooden bedstead rise to become four slender turned posts finished with a decorative finial; the height of these bed posts would depend on the proportions of the room. Half-testers are less invasive: they have a canopied roof which extends only a third of the way down the length of the bed, supported from two head posts.

Classically inspired Empire-style beds with curving head and foot boards in cherry or mahogany were popular at the beginning of the 19th century; these also make elegant daybeds. Spool-turned beds, known as Jenny Lind beds, were fashionable in Victorian times. Wrought iron cots, wooden cradles and low-level truckle beds are old-

A TESTER BED UNDER THE ROOF

Colonial homes were more generous in height than the cottages they often emulated. This one has room for a four-poster bed with a simple calico tester, or canopy, neatly fitting under the steeply pitched roof.

fashioned styles for children which make highly decorative accessories today.

Authentic chests and wardrobes

In the main, clothes were kept folded rather than hung up. Free-standing storage pieces of every nationality found their way into colonial homes, from the elaborate French *armoire* to the simple linen presses and chests-on-chests from England. These mahogany or fruitwood 'tall boys' were often partnered by 'low boys', which make graceful dressing tables and desks in Federal-style bedrooms.

The Pennsylvania Dutch rooms housed enormous wardrobes, distinguished by heavy mouldings and ornate with boldly carved or painted fruit and flowers. The painting was always very exuberant, uninhibited and two-tone— often a deep yellow ground applied with crumpled cloth or newspaper with a contrasting topcoat of terracotta or conifer green, which was worked into patterns with the finger while the paint was still wet.

Another classic piece of furniture associated with Pennsylvania Dutch is the dower chest. Decorated with symbolic stencilled motifs such as hearts and flowers, the tree of life and the unicorn (the traditional guardian of maidenhood), dower chests were presented to girls when they reached marriageable age, and the girl's name was part of the decoration. Dower chests—or tin trunks or blanket chests—are ideal to stand at the foot of the bed. Modern whitewood chests make perfect apprentice pieces for freehand paint and stencil techniques.

Candlestands and commode cupboards can double up as

PRETTY DETAILS

The colonials certainly knew how to make a bedroom pretty and inviting. In this room very narrow cream and red striped wallpaper is the background for a white-painted curvy metal bedhead whose curves are echoed in the frills of its very large, fat pillows. A small hand-painted chest of drawers with ceramic knobs holds an old-fashioned washbowl and jug.

THE MASCULINE LOOK

A more masculine room this, with the colonial matchboarded walls and
lots of wood. The wooden bedsteads feature turned posts and grey check
woollen bedcovers with star and zigzag patterned patchwork quilts.

bedside tables, but as they don't provide very large surfaces, circular chipboard tables covered with full, sweeping cloths or old quilts are more practical.

Simple rugs

Keep bedroom floors as simple as possible. Traditionally, the rag rugs and straw matting were confined to the best rooms downstairs—upstairs, bare boards were the norm. While wall-to-wall carpets are not really suitable for modern colonial-style bedrooms, there are various patterned carpets which could be used as a large rug in the middle of the room, offset by an edging of floorboards. Small geometric designs, such as crisp checks, stripes and pin dots, look much more in keeping than a plain wilton weave.

The choice of rug is legion—braided, hooked, crocheted and knitted designs were made out of the rags of old household fabrics. These days, striped cotton rag rugs made from random, dip-dyed and twisted fibres are easily found. Embroidered needlepoint rugs—Berlinwork—were popular in the more affluent colonial homes and, while the old pieces are collectors' items, modern copies are available. Traditional designs include exotic birds and animals, full-blown roses and peonies.

Typical colours and patterns

One of the most typical colonial colour schemes is based on a particular shade of blue-grey, offset by accents of vivid colours or held in suspension by other colours of similar weight. If you're using a variety of patterns, link them with matching background colours: patterns reversed out on darker grounds have a more colonial feel about them than the more conventional white backgrounds. Authentic reproductions of old colonial wallpapers and fabrics are available; otherwise, look for patterns that have a childlike simplicity and directness about them.

Because wood was so readily available, panelled walls were a common feature. While these provide opportunities for lots of different paint finishes, one of the most effective is the classical three-tone use of flat colour, with framework, panelling and architrave all finished in different densities of colour. Flush walls and doors could be enlivened with mouldings—cut and mitred into false panels which might form frames for stencil borders. Treat vertical tongue-and-groove walls to alternate stripes of colour or pick out the beams, architrave and skirtings in strong glowing colours to provide a contrast to light walls.

Stencilled patterns work well on any surface—plaster, paint or wood—but they seem particularly appropriate in

SERENE SIMPLICITY
A very traditional, very elegant
tester bed in a serenely
simple room with dark floorboards,
dark beams and white paintwork.

PEACEFUL IMPERFECTION
This little room is peaceful in white and
not too perfectly decorated to be
intimidating. The only furniture is a bed,
bedside table and rocking chair.

LIGHT, FRUIT AND FLOWERS
Two rattan lounging chairs complete with crisply starched red
gingham covers and quilts are well-supplied with reading matter,
light and fruit from the octagonal wooden table between them. The
bottom half of each window is screened by a muslin curtain.

the bedroom where cupboards and chests as well as the walls provide flat, unbroken surfaces. Use a small, free-flowing border to delineate the junction of wall and ceiling and to frame individual motifs. Choose motifs that echo the stylized images that frequently occur in the folk patterns used in colonial homes. They were all symbolic—the willow was thought to bring immortality; the oak leaf represented long life; and the three-petalled tulip, the Holy Trinity. The pineapple, a novelty fruit in the 17th century, symbolized hospitality; there was the pomegranate of fruitfulness, and clematis and grapes of prosperity and plenty. Other images were abstractions of local observations: the popular Log Cabin design, for instance, was derived from the view of the roof of a log cabin.

Traditional quilts and bedcoverings

Because quilts are such an intrinsic part of a colonial bedroom, they make a good starting point for a colour

AQUATIC ATMOSPHERE

A soft blue-green colour scheme creates a suitably aquatic atmosphere for this
bathroom. The old-fashioned bath with its pair of brass pillar taps is positioned in the
traditional way, at right angles to the wall. The hand stencilling on the door and bath
panels and the wall complements the bare floorboards and simple furnishings.

scheme. As well as patchwork quilts, there are also appliqué
quilts (in which the material of the motif is sewn on to the
background fabric) and plain quilts. The latter are patterned by the tiny hand stitches of the quilting.

Young girls used to start making bedcoverings from a
very early age so that they would have at least twelve quilts
in their 'hope chest' by the time they became engaged.
Quilting bees were a welcome distraction, especially in far-
flung rural communities, where women would gather around

the quilting frame to sew together. Album quilts were co-
operative efforts, often made as commemorative gifts, each
square designed and stitched by a different person.

Every community had its own distinctive style of quilt.
The most individual quilts of all were those of the Amish
people, a radical religious sect who settled in the Midwest.
Since their religion prohibited all forms of decoration, their
patchworks were made as simply as possible from geometric blocks of plain dyed colours. As they were limited to

PICTURESQUE EFFECT
A bent-twig bed has its own tiny bent-twig bedside table on one side and a more
conventional table on the other. Otherwise, all there is room for is a narrow bench and a
tiny stool. The bed is clothed in layers of fresh-looking cotton and a traditional very finely
quilted patchwork cover, whose red and white match the stripes of the hand-woven rugs.

three or four colours in any design (a particular favourite
being a deep lavender blue), the overall effect was so strong
and uncompromising that they look surprisingly modern.

At the turn of the century patchwork took a freer turn,
and 'crazy' patchwork made of silks, satins and brocades
turned up, not just as bedcoverings but also as throws on
the arms of sofas or covering the piano.

Another traditional colonial bedcovering was the all-
white candlewick bedspread, originally made from an inexpensive type of white cotton similar to that used for the
wicks of candles. Today they are still being made to
resemble some of the old quilting designs. Woven coverlets are also very traditional, often featuring an eagle motif,
the symbol of American independence.

Old linens, lace and nettings are all suitable for colonial
bedrooms. Search antique stalls for outsize cotton tablecloths with cutwork borders and scalloped hems, for they
can be made into bedhangings and coverlets. Add edges of
cotton crochetwork and tatting to percale sheets. Use old
lace place mats and table runners as cushion covers.

Start collecting amateur works of art. Needlework
samplers and pictures cut out from black or white paper
were just two of the stylized arts taught in the girls'
seminaries during the 19th century. Baskets overflowing
with fruit, or vases of flowers, were painted in watercolour
or oil on velvet, silk or satin as well as on paper. Instead of
being drawn spontaneously from nature, these 'theorem
paintings' were built up using stencils to create arrangements of painted fruits in painted bowls. The boys worked
at penmanship, developing writing styles using fine steel-

A QUALITY OF RICHNESS
Another example of polished dark wood
predominating. The narrow four-poster bed,
the little cupboard and the polished floor are
accentuated by the rag rug and the patchwork.

tipped pens. This was particularly so among the Pennsylvania Dutch communities, who developed the art of calligraphy to its highest form, working 'fractur pieces'— illuminated manuscripts, certificates and bible texts set out in the manner of the old medieval documents—which hung on their walls.

Country colonial bathrooms

When it comes to fitting out the bathroom, take your guide from the furnishing style of the rest of the house. There aren't any strict historical precedents—a tin bath in front of the kitchen fire together with a privy at the bottom of the garden sufficed for the original colonial homes.

Victorian-style fittings constitute a traditional style bathroom, so use high-sided cast iron baths with claw feet and bulbous brass taps; generous-scale basins set on chunky pedestals or wall-hung from decorative wrought iron brackets; lavatories with old-fashioned, high-level cisterns. Open shelving units might be set with apothecary jars and ewers filled with dried flowers. Modern sanitaryware can be given turn-of-the-century style with traditional surrounds— baths can be panelled with old salvaged timbers or tongue-and-groove boarding, for example, while basins might be set into old cupboards or washstands. Elm, maple and pine are more appropriate than mahogany for country colonial.

Wall finishes for wet areas like the shower might include slate tiles or even wooden shingles sealed with a polyurethane varnish. In the same way that ceramic tiles with a matt glaze are more sympathetic than high gloss finishes, vinyl silk paint is more suitable than gloss.

Inside meets Outside

The earliest colonial homes consisted of only one downstairs room, which opened straight on to some sort of veranda, or sun-porch. Later, with the development of more specialized rooms, a hall would often separate the main room from the veranda.

Provided it is in keeping with the style of the rest of the house, the hall more than any other room can benefit from the early colonial ascetic look. In the hall, practicality is more important than comfort. Simple furnishings and natural materials, especially wood, are the keynotes, with perhaps a single antique chest or console table. Hard-seated chairs with decorative backs, often shield-shaped, and also long settles were commonly made for colonial hallways, where visitors would wait to be received in the main reception rooms, and these still look good in today's less formal halls.

The wall space in the hall, especially at the top of the stairwell, makes an ideal place for a picture gallery. Primitive paintings, stencilled theorem pictures, reverse paintings on glass, 'fractur pieces' and silhouettes were all popular forms of wall decoration in 19th century colonial homes. Displays of china look good in the hallway too, either hanging directly on the walls or arranged on a pretty wooden plate rack; collections of colonial spatterware, spongeware, majolica, sgraffito or slipware would all be very much in keeping.

CAST IRON GRANDEUR
Australian colonial style is often on a scale appropriate to the size of the country, and its balconies may run right along the length of the house, sometimes with little jutting out 'viewpoints' from which to gaze over wide open spaces.

HOUSE GUARDS
The edge of this balcony is fenced in by
a motley collection of cocks, horses, bulls and squirrels
collected from far and wide. They sit on the stout
wooden fenceposts and keep the countryside at bay.

A PLACE IN THE SUN
A 'rising sun' patio chair sits snugly on the
gravel, a cushion of blowsy cabbage-rose design
covering its slatted seat. The sea-green colour
of its paint is a popular one in colonial style.

The veranda—an outdoor sitting room

Whether the colonial house contained a hall or not, it was likely to include a veranda, or sun-porch. In early colonial homes, verandas provided a meeting place for community life—for example, the men might congregate on the veranda for a drink after a day's harvesting; the women might hold quilting bees there. Verandas helped to create an informal lifestyle. In some parts of the world, they were (and still are) used not only as outdoor sitting rooms but as sleeping-out quarters and cooking areas too. The layout of the colonial veranda around the world varied as much as the uses to which it was put, ranging from nothing more than a deep porch for a front door, to a wide structure completely encircling a house. But whatever the style, the veranda was an integral part of the design of the building.

The hotter the climate or the rougher the life, the more the veranda was used. In the tropical north-westerly parts of Australia, for example, early houses were based on a square bungalow plan which was surrounded by a balcony. Gradually this became more than just a shelter for the rooms and grew in width until it became a three to four metre (10 to 15 foot) encircling space which could be used for dining, sitting and sleeping. In the driest seasons, verandas were elaborately furnished; dining tables and chairs, bedsteads and mosquito nets, even pictures and flower vases were moved outside into the heavily shaded open air, leaving the little knot of enclosed rooms in the centre of the bungalow for washing and dressing. Beyond the balustrade grew frangipani, bougainvillea and palms; while on the veranda, tropical pot plants flourished in huge planters. Ceiling fans pushed the sultry air around. Oiled and polished hardwood floors were scattered with rugs.

Various techniques were adopted to screen the sun but not the breeze and at the same time keep the insects at bay. The lower part of the veranda was composed of balustrade, with open timber slats, trellis work or even an expanded metal grill. Above this there was a gap to the low eaves of the roof. Sometimes this gap was left open, while at other times it was filled with latticework or wooden louvres or was inset with screens of fine wire mesh to keep the insects out. In the very hottest countries, solid metal or wooden shutters were used, hinged along the top edge of the window opening so that they folded out like wings to form their own canopies. During the rainy seasons the shutters

PERFECT VANTAGE POINT

Colonial verandas have always been important architectural
features. Often spacious and extensively furnished, they provided
useful additional living space—as well as excellent vantage
points for viewing the surrounding countryside.

COOL ELEGANCE

Wall-to-wall windows, a door opening on to
the garden, a pale tiled floor, and white
walls create a light and airy atmosphere
in this elegant room. With windows as splendid
as these, curtains or blinds would be sacrilege.

SUN AND SHADOW

A long, winding veranda catches the sun in narrow stripes through the wooden bars. The design has been carefully worked out to give a feeling of elegance and dappled shade. All the woodwork is painted white to reflect the heat.

POTS OF PLANTS

A little wooden summer house forms a bower where pots of young plants can revel in the shade, vines can clamber over the white-painted wooden bench and a *trompe-l'oeil* tree reaches for the sky.

GLASS ROSES

A local glass-artist has devised and made this art nouveau rose to enhance the window in a colonial conservatory.

A PLACE FOR EVERYTHING

This little porch-cum-conservatory has tall windows bringing in lots of warm light and makes the perfect place for drying herbs. Through the door is a tempting view of the deep blue of the swimming-pool with its brick surround. A home-made bench holds leisure paraphernalia and hides the shoes and boots.

on the weather side could be dropped and latched, and the perishable furniture moved inside. The owners didn't choose to follow suit—they sat outside in cane armchairs, sipping rum and combating the mosquitoes.

Buildings like these were often raised up on stilts, sometimes because of steeply sloping sites or because of possible flooding, their elevated positions offering spectacular views over the rolling countryside.

Classical and Gothic revivals

Verandas of Australia and the southern states of America share a particularly wide range of designs and decorative form. As the colonials became wealthier, so the façades of their homes became more ornate.

The formal Georgian-style homes built by the old families and the new merchant classes had classical façades modelled on the old Palladian plans. Symmetrically placed windows balanced a central front door which was in turn sheltered by a long portico—a type of veranda built in the style of the Greek Revival, with stately columns, stone balustrading

and a shallow flight of steps. The colonial versions were much simpler than the grand stately homes of England on which they were modelled. Sometimes the stone detailing was replaced by carved timbers—reeded columns and simple wooden railings and chunky banisters might front an 18th century clapboard house with twelve-paned Georgian sash windows set with slatted shutters on each side. Occasionally, to add weight and greater impact to the design, the porticoes ran up two storeys of the building so that the main bedrooms as well as the rooms downstairs enjoyed the benefits of a shaded balcony.

The Gothic revival of the 1840s led to a break with these classical traditions. A variety of scrollwork patterns began to be commercially produced, and exterior detailing such as wooden railings and trelliswork became fancier, while window frames and veranda friezes were shaped into pointed Gothic arches.

By the end of the 19th century, cast iron was readily available and was used for everything from umbrella stands to balconies. Sturdy columns were replaced by slender iron

WOODEN GEESE AND FRESH APPLES

A beautifully shaped hall table stands under a tapestry portrait of
the house. Two wooden geese with metal legs welcome all visitors.
They are faithfully painted and remarkably elegant. A metal dish of
apples picked from the apple tree is the only other decoration.

pillars. The lacy balustrading, frilly friezework, ornamental
trellis and iron railings were of such delicacy that the style
has often been likened to the icing on a wedding cake. The
early designs were geometrical, but patterns of flora and
fauna and even patriotic themes and colonial coats of arms
soon became popular.

At the turn of the century, there was an Australian vogue
for the English picturesque style. Terracotta roof ornaments were popular on buildings that had clay-tiled roofs,
and often a decorative porch would be finished with scalloped tiles and finials in animal shapes. The wooden wind
whirligigs and the original tin cut-out weathervanes of the
early settlers' homes are now collectors' pieces, but reproductions are being made today.

BOLD COLOURING

A stroke of genius has emboldened the owner of this house to choose a
darker version of the ever-popular green to paint the woodwork of the
staircase as well as the built-in dresser and wall panelling. The set of
hand-decorated plates and cups shows up wonderfully well against it.

Creating the effect today

It is very important that the architectural detailing of the veranda is in keeping with the rest of the house. Classical columns and balustrading are now available in reconstituted stone—its soft porous composition encourages lichen and mosses to establish themselves, giving it a nicely aged look, but a coating of liquid manure on the new stone should help to speed the plant growth. Ornamental bargeboards and decorative porches with turned supports and balusters do sometimes turn up in breakers' yards, but there are enough surviving originals to be able to take a copy and get them made. Victorian cast-iron work is still being reproduced to the old pattern book styles, and nowadays epoxy-coated aluminium offers a solution to the problem of rust.

A HAVEN FROM THE SUN

Jigsaw patterns on this wooden balcony with cast-iron railing give a peaceful
haven from the weather and a glimpse through columns and leafy trees of cool water
and sunsoaked garden. Battered old wicker chairs are waiting to be sunk into.

THE HEIGHT OF RELAXATION

This stately balcony is almost as
big as a house. Its height and depth
give a feeling of relaxation and a sense
of grandeur. Odd bits of furniture
invite rest and comfort.

SHADE AND LEISURE

Grecian columns survey the countryside from a height,
and a cast-iron balustrade is reminiscent of the
grandeur of large, old railway stations. Under this
imposing structure can be found cool shade and
the promise of leisure in the hottest part of the day.

DRAMATIC CONTRASTS

Through this sombre wooden doorway with its stained glass, there is
just a glimpse of the hot garden beyond. The heaviness of the interior is
deliberate, to separate the house from the glare of the hot sun.

Patterned tiles and bricks set in geometric patterns were popular for porch floors in the second half of the 19th century, but replacements for these are hard to come by. Reproduction tiles are available; though expensive, this may be the only solution for patching up a damaged floor.

Furniture for the colonial-style veranda

In the same way that architectural detailing of the veranda must take its cue from the style of the rest of the house, so the furniture should ideally follow suit. Windsor chairs and benches as well as rocking chairs of every type are the archetypal early colonial styles. In those days, indoor furniture was simply taken outside, so ladder-back chairs and refectory tables are authentic even for quite classical colonial buildings.

Wickerwork was popular throughout the Victorian period and was used inside and out. Neat basket chairs with an openwork base rather like a shuttlecock were the earliest designs, but cane loungers—long easy chairs which incorporated a footrest and a semi-circular back that curved around into the arms—became very popular for afternoon siestas.

Much of the furniture that would now be described as period-style garden furniture was originally designed to be used on board the old cruise boats. For example, the steamer chair, which is still being reproduced today, is an elegant folding armchair with a curving back either of slatted wood or woven cane and a seat to match, supported by six arched legs. Canvas or netting hammocks slung between the veranda posts make traditional and relaxed couches—they were used as far back as the early 18th century as hanging beds for sailors on board ship.

Elaborate cast-iron Victoriana, overflowing with bunches of grapes, interlocking leaves, ferny fronds or intricate Gothic tracery, is too heavy to be easily transported, so make this seating permanent. You'll need to add thick cushions to make it comfortable. Lighter-weight wrought-iron work drawn into finely spiralling designs, rustic bent twigwork pieces and Lloyd Loom or wicker chairs are other decorative styles to use outside as well as indoors.

DECOY BIRDS

Decoys are a significant form of colonial folk art: they were carved and painted by untutored hands to lure the wildfowl within range of a gun. The huntsmen who made these birds were attempting to reproduce an impression of a particular bird rather than creating an exact replica; and the decoy had to be practical and appropriate for the hunting techniques and conditions in which they were to be used.

American Indians were the first to devise decoys, using mud, rushes and vegetable paints to entice the birds within the range of

the bow and arrow. Until 1918, when the indiscriminant shooting of the birds on their migratory flight was prohibited, there had been a huge market for the commercially slaughtered game.

The decoy carvers experimented endlessly with types of wood and methods of carving, with relationships of contour and volume, and with colour tones and patterns. They were trying to create not a replica, but an illusion, of the living bird. Realistically carved details were not needed to catch the eye of the flying bird; at any rate, they were

liable to break—simple smooth lines were much more durable. Complex plumage patterns were also unnecessary and were tricky to repaint season after season—a few key strokes of the right colours in the right places sufficed. Details that did count were the set of the head on the body, the shape of the bill, the angle of the neck and the way the bird rode the choppy seawater and nestled in the island bays.

Variety comes from regional differences as well as from variations in wildfowl species. From the big, bold eider ducks to the small graceful teal, decoys can be found in an almost infinite variety of style, sculptural form and colour—stately swans, belligerent geese, gaudy mallards, intricately painted waders and herons poised to snatch unwary fish are just a few of the varieties to be found.

Decoys are not only American. Wader decoys from the Camargue, a large marsh area in the south of France, are very collectable, as are the British wood pigeons which were made from the mid 19th to the mid 20th century.

FROM LEFT TO RIGHT

Tiny French shore bird c.1930. Large Canada goose made in 1890 by Henry Grant from New Jersey. American merganser hen c.1870 from Massachusetts. French curlew stick bird c.1910. Old squaw drake made in Connecticut at the turn of the century. In the foreground, a widgeon drake from Chesapeake Bay, Maryland, made in 1915 by Noah Sterling.

FRENCH PROVINCIAL STYLE

All over France the quality most observed and enjoyed is the proportions of the architecture. Buildings are large and generous. The entrances may be wide arches, originally designed to be wide enough for a pair of oxen. Doorways are tall, walls are thick and windows reach down to the ground. In northern France, the climate may be cool, so the thick walls keep out the cold. Southern French country houses are blessed by the sun. Their colour-washed walls are a vibrant echo of the russet and ochre earth; neatly pruned vines provide dappled shade in the shimmering noonday heat. The sensuality of the landscape invades the cool interior through elegant windows and is apparent in the natural materials which make up the French home. The clarity of light inspires interiors with a sense of spaciousness. Walls and floors are allowed to remain bare; no clutter distracts the eye from the graceful proportions.

ACHIEVING THE LOOK

Created mainly by prosperous farmers, French provincial style is practical but with a sense of graciousness. Ceilings are high, materials solid and furniture well-built, often with a strong individuality.

Underfoot

In northern France, floors are generally either stone or boards. But in the south, terracotta tiles are the characteristic flooring throughout the home—not only in the kitchen and bathroom, but in living rooms and bedrooms too. Stones and floor tiles are usually large and slightly uneven. Tiles come in many shapes and sizes but the classic is the plain faded-red square. Glazed tiles can be used to spectacular effect and are often seen escaping from the floor and running up the walls and along table tops and work surfaces. 18th and 19th century glazed tiles, even when cracked or chipped, are particularly sought-after for renovations and can also add grace and character to new rooms.

Whatever type of flooring you choose, make sure it is a natural material and leave it bare for preference. Rugs are kept to a minimum as they break up the floor space and impede progress across it. Where a carpet is needed for softness, pick something that will not interfere with the proportions of the room, perhaps a large Persian or Turkish rug in faded pink and gold that will almost merge into the tiles, or an Indian dhurrie in textured neutrals to tone with the walls.

One of the charms of French provincial style is the personal element—the individual style imposed on large buildings by their owners. This small corner is a delightful example.

French provincial houses are often large, with outbuildings which form a sheltered area for outdoor leisure activities: anything from playing boule to serving a slap-up meal.

This is a room where meals are taken seriously. The table takes pride of place on the diamond-shaped ceramic tiles, and up to 14 people may sit around it.

Walls and ceilings

Walls should be as plain as possible. Old stone or brick can be left uncovered. Plaster can be washed in white, cream or pale ochre. Avoid strong colours. Avoid wallpaper too (except perhaps in the living rooms, where pale papers could be used)—if the surface is irregular so much the better: it adds character.

A French provincial farmhouse may well have a ceiling punctuated with hefty beams. In former times these were covered in plaster to serve as a protection against fire, especially in the kitchen, where a fire burned in the hearth all year round for cooking by. Nowadays beams are being exposed to reveal the beauty of the old wood and more of the structure of the house.

Woodwork and panelling can be stripped or painted white or cream. But throughout France the trend is to use a smoky sea-blue, or sometimes a bluish-grey. This may start out as a startlingly bright colour but it soon fades to a comfortable dull tone.

Fabrics and window treatments

You can give any room a feeling of the south of France by the liberal use of vividly coloured Provençal fabrics for curtains, cushion covers, upholstery, tablecloths and throws.

Keep window treatments simple so as not to obscure the shape of the window. Avoid ruffles, frills, swags and heavy voluminous drapes. If using a print, hang the curtains from

This very typical French provincial room has elegant proportions, a high ceiling and tall doorways. Plenty of light comes in through generous windows and this is maximized by painting the walls white. The door height is emphasized by giving the opening a wide frame. The furniture is free-standing and fairly primitive but with some decoration. The blue of the door beyond is common in French provincial houses and fades to a wonderful pale colour in the sun.

poles and keep them unlined. Draw them against a flood of sunlight for a delicate gauzy effect. Lace is also a popular curtaining. Hunt around for lace tablecloths, runners and bedspreads. Traycloths or large dressing table mats can make exquisite curtains for tiny windows. Remember that the window treatment should always be subservient to the window and not vice-versa.

Furniture

French provincial furniture is unmistakable. At once solid and graceful, it celebrates the French enjoyment of the grand but practical. Utilizing local skills, it suits the confident spaciousness of French homes. Many classic pieces produced in the 18th and 19th centuries are growing

increasingly difficult to come by. If the originals are out of reach, aim for furniture that shares the same exuberant spirit. Avoid anything cumbersome, impractical or over-wrought. Choose old pieces that were made to last in wood with a deep patina and some simple decorative carving.

The large upright cupboard or *armoire* is the most important piece of furniture in a French country home, and this can be used in the kitchen or living room to store food, linen or china. Tall cupboards with glass-panelled doors, possibly former shop fittings, can be painted in a pale matt colour and used to hold anything from books to bath towels and toiletries.

Rush-seated benches and chairs are the traditional seating for reception rooms, but the French country spirit

This is not quite a sink, but it acts as a good place for vegetable and fruit preparation because of the 'drain' in the wall.

This wall of small tiles has been carefully arranged with a central focal point. The tiles are old and cracked but that is part of their charm. The small flower motif is traditional in flavour.

The rather fine stonework on wall and fireplace has been kept in its raw state in this fine room. Simple floor-length curtains suit the room's dignity. The white quilt is beautifully laundered but obviously an old friend.

can be recreated in cane or bentwood with comfortable cushioned seats.

Warmth of the hearth

Monumental stone or marble fireplaces are a characteristic feature of French provincial rooms, bedrooms included. Enormous and often quite ornate, they are inevitably the main focal point of the room. The mantelpiece can hold an eye-catching collection of pots.

For rooms without such fireplaces but with a chimney, a free-standing cast-iron stove would be perfectly in keeping with French provincial style. Much more efficient for heating than an open fire, they are available as antiques or reproductions in a variety of traditional styles.

Finishing touches

In northern France, ornaments tend to be large, individual pieces which are elegant rather than jolly. In the south, chunky glazed earthenware—hand-painted or finished in iridescent enamel—is more typical. This should be stored where you can see it on open shelves and not hidden away in a cupboard.

Large pottery bowls of fruit and colourful jugs of garden flowers are the simplest and best decoration any room could have. Aim to avoid suffocating under clutter. A flourishing lemon tree in a tub looks handsome standing on a tiled floor. A gigantic terracotta urn on a small table is a dramatic visual surprise and more pleasant to look upon than a slithering heap of magazines.

Living and Relaxing

French provincial homes—whether in the north, where they are set rather uncompromisingly in the middle of a field or a hill, without much of a planned garden around them, or in the south, surrounded by lush growth and a vista of disciplined vineyards—all turn their living room faces outside. Large French windows may open on to a stream, a courtyard or an escarpment.

Windows are always generous except in the far south, when they may be very small to keep the heat out. From these large windows you get a good view of the countryside or more immediate garden, and the furniture is often faced towards them to make the most of this view. Very often a desk may be placed by such a window.

The living room is for visitors and for weekends. (In France even the mayor is inclined to put his feet up and relax in the kitchen rather than anywhere else in the house.) It can be quite austere in its elegant simplicity, but it is never cold. When life is conducted outside in summer, the living room becomes a garden room, somewhere to retreat away from the glare and to watch the goings-on outside. On winter evenings the room will be lit by lamps and the glow of the fire in a huge fireplace made of marble or stone. In fact, in all of France except the south, it is cool in the evenings until Easter, so the great fireplace is in use for several months.

The pleasing proportions of the windows in a French

SIMPLE AUSTERITY

This entrance lobby with the living space beyond is a good example of French simplicity coupled with an elegance which is very typical of provincial homes. The slightly rough walls are painted an uncompromising white but are softened by the warm hexagonal tiles.

SIMPLE ELEGANCE
This interior is not as basic as it seems. The furniture,
though simple, is of excellent quality, and the tapestry
rugs almost certainly hand-worked.

provincial living room will not be obscured by heavy
swags of fabric. It could be that only shutters are necessary,
either stripped or painted in cream or white. Venetian
blinds are spare and elegant, with dramatic possibilities for
adjusting the natural light, which is something that appeals
very much to the French character. Where there are curtains
they will be unlined so the sunlight can filter through and
so they can be pulled back without bulking. They will be
made of lace (in white or cream), muslin or perhaps a
cotton print. The effect is gauzy and delicate. Poles are
slender and, like the curtain rings, of wood or dull brass.

The walls of a French provincial farmhouse are very
thick. They are painted either white or pale shades of
yellow or apricot, with a faded look. Woodwork, in contrast, may be painted a characteristic bluey-green, which
again looks its best when allowed to fade slightly, or it
could even be painted brown. All paintwork is matt; gloss
is never used. Wallpaper may be used in living rooms—if
so, it will be a pale, neutral colour, with possibly a smoky-
blue naive floral motif or pale stripes.

A dynamic space

The floors will most likely be of fine wood, perhaps
parquet, if they are not stone slabs or terracotta tiles. The
tiles are usually hand-made, very thick and large, and
reddish but not absolutely uniform in colour. The space
and the plain surfaces encourage movement. There is no
reason why you should not pull a chair across the floor to
sit where you want, because there is no rug to impede your
progress, no formal arrangement of furniture to break.

The ceilings are typically supported by a criss-cross of
massive beams, sturdy timbers that give a cottage-like
charm even to large rooms. Traditionally the ceilings, like
the walls, were plastered over, but now in France, as
elsewhere, beams are being exposed to make a valued
decorative feature.

The proportions of the room matter above all else. The
natural materials and lack of clutter serve to emphasize the
generous lines on which the room was built. The use of
natural light from sun and fire is supplemented by
judiciously placed lamps, possibly ultra-modern ones.

REFLECTED LIGHT
Warm sunlight filtered through long lace curtains lights up a collection of blue and white French earthenware.

MELLOW TONES
Light falls through the windows to reveal spacious rooms and very tall doors, painted a blue shade which is already bleached to a paler hue.

The way the furniture is arranged in the French provincial living room is important. Instead of a tight circle of chairs around the fireplace or a formal grouping in front of the window, which would force people to sit in pre-ordained relationships to one another, the furniture should feel as if it can be moved. Sofas or *banquettes* on two adjoining walls, a chair in the corner between them and a further chair in the middle of the room that can be turned to face in any direction is a configuration of seating that looks informal and fluid. It opens out the space in the room and gives a feeling of mobility. It's hospitable, because it invites you to come in and sit where you want.

Chairs of character

Typical French provincial chairs are of willow with slatted backs, wooden arms, spindle legs and rush seats. Their light construction makes them easy to move around. They can be painted or left plain and the seats can be of natural or coloured straw or both, combined in a simple pattern. The more commodious examples of this style are called *fauteuils*

à la bonne femme. On the whole, French provincial chairs are quite basic compared to the *armoires*, *buffets* and other more solid pieces of local furniture.

The *banquette*, which seats three or four people, looks like several chairs joined together with an arm at either end. The joy of these pieces is that they are very simple but delicate and well proportioned. When they have behind them more than a hundred years of being sat in, this obviously adds to their charm. Though comfortable, they were intended for upright conversation rather than for slouching in, and the addition of a few cushions in French provincial prints may not come amiss.

Monumental proportions

Upholstered furniture is usually on quite a large scale, with a solid base, perhaps like a chaise longue, and with elegant covers, possibly striped. Ancient, generously proportioned chairs may be covered in heavy tapestry fabric, velvet or leather. Whether simple or lavish in their design, what this upholstered furniture will undoubtedly be is monumental.

THE GRAND AND THE SPLENDID

This extremely fine inlaid chest of drawers with ornate
metal trim and marble top is very French in feeling, and it
looks completely at home on the faded tiles of the floor.
Wall colours are the pastels of old plaster.

A RELAXING SUN ROOM

This room seems almost cluttered compared with the disciplined
austerity of many French provincial homes. Large panes of glass give
uninterrupted views of a shrubby garden. The vista can be viewed
from the comfort of a striped chaise longue with plenty of cushions
and a furry rug for cool evenings.

COUNTRY SOPHISTICATION

This room—essentially country in feeling, with its brick floor and geometric
beams—has been rather carefully furnished for entertaining. Comfortable sofas and chairs
are arrayed 'conversationally'. There is an elegant chest of drawers and
the odd small table and stool. A large chimneypiece reaches down over
an open fireplace where toes can be toasted in winter.

visitors may spend the night as uncomfortably as pre-
sumably Napoleon himself did.

There may be an extraordinarily ornate and 'heavy'
occasional table against the wall, holding an arrangement
of lupins or roses. The living room is seldom without a
bookcase or cupboards, locally built, and perhaps some
intricate panelling which might be mirrored. You will
probably find much antique linen and lace, not fussily
spread over every surface in the Victorian manner, but
perhaps over the back of a settee, or on cushions.

Another way of thinking, probably best suited to the
south of France and other warm climates, is to use plenty of
wicker and bamboo—in the form of small tables, a variety
of chairs with or without arms, and wall-hung shelves.
This gives a lighter look, and the furniture can be easily
carried in and out of doors as occasion demands. It can be
made more comfortable with the use of cushions, which are
usually in pale colours and cotton fabrics, perhaps lace,
embroidered or with small floral prints.

Texture is important. Wood, willow, cane, bamboo,
cotton, linen and wool fit well in a room where the walls
are bare of fussy decoration and the floor bare of carpet.

Cooking and Eating

Cooking and eating are two of the supreme pleasures of living in France—simple pleasures sharpened by the simplicity of the surroundings in which they are enjoyed. The French place a great deal of importance on food. The preparation, cooking and eating of it is of passionate interest to everyone—it's not a duty but an enjoyment.

Imagine an ordinary French cafe—it is a model of unpretentiousness. A plain plate-glass window, a wooden bar with bottles of coloured liqueurs in front of a mirror, *vin ordinaire* in a stoppered bottle beneath the counter, and a gleaming espresso machine above. You sit at a small marble-topped table on a bentwood chair and your food is brought on a white plate; you drink out of a tumbler. There is nothing to distract you from the excellence of the food, and as each dish is eaten separately the flavours do not compete even with one another. After all, it is the food that you have come to enjoy, not *la patronne's* taste in furnishings, and it is in the food that the skill and artistry of the establishment reside.

The same principle holds true in the French home. The art of living comes first and the kitchen is a workshop devoted to the creation of pleasure. Here the French love of functional design can be appreciated to its fullest. The enamelled coffeepot, the copper saucepans, the wooden plate rack, the wire vegetable basket, the razor-sharp knives and the wooden chopping block are all simple and

PRIDE OF PLACE
The table is the uncontested centrepiece in this magnificent dining room. The colours and furnishings are harmoniously combined so that nothing detracts from the room's function—the pleasure of eating.

functional—the design of these objects has been pared down until they have become no more than an expression of their purpose. Classical kitchen tools survive the test of time because they are enduringly useful as well as being made to last. A gadget that trims irregularities off runner beans may take your fancy, but it will soon find its way to the back of the kitchen drawer. A sharp well-balanced knife, on the other hand, is something no cook will ever want to be without.

Distinctive style of cabinet making

Since the 13th century, cabinet makers in rural France, especially Provence, have been distinguished from those of the rest of the country by the particular attention they have paid to the furniture of the kitchen and dining room.

A characteristic style of cabinet making developed that had nothing to do with the fads and fashions of the capital or the dictates of the court. It was determined by the needs of the practical householder, by the materials available locally and by the skill of the country craftsman. French provincial furniture has no pretensions to grandeur, but by being at the same time charming and solid-looking, it manages to embody both the warm spirit of the country folk and their imagination and gaiety. The combination of graceful curved lines and beautifully carved old wood with the precise function of many of the pieces is unique.

The golden age of French provincial cabinet making came to an end at the close of the 19th century, when the carving lost its freshness and immediacy and became tortured and writhing. After the turn of the century the

COOL CERAMICS
Well-worn tiles act as a splashback to a very basic tap, splashing into a shallow stone sink. A large platter of local earthenware covers the plumbing.

PRACTICAL BUT PLEASING
The French can put together practical solutions which please the eye almost by accident. Beneath these two heavy utensils the wall has been tiled with little thought to pattern matching. The result is nonetheless attractive.

CLASSICALLY SIMPLE

Everything is designed with cooking and eating in mind in this very large kitchen. The enormous flagstones are easy to clean and cool to walk on; the spectacular collection of copper pans makes for versatile cooking for numbers great or small.

demand for hand-made pieces waned as cheap mass-produced furniture became widely available. But at its height, cabinet making was a highly prized skill and one that people were prepared to pay well for. A good piece of furniture was designed to last for centuries and made a worthwhile investment. Prosperous families were able to commission several pieces, and even those who were less well-off could claim ownership of at least one treasured piece—often an *armoire*—which could be handed down to the next generation.

Furniture formed an important part of a bride's dowry, and symbols played a large part in the decoration of the furniture. A pair of turtledoves, hearts, myrtle leaves and eglantines signified married love, then there was wheat for fertility and prosperity, and vine leaves for long life. Olive branches, acanthus leaves, grapes, pomegranates, farm

A SPECIAL ATMOSPHERE

This picture epitomizes the French acknowledgement of eating as one of
the important aspects of life, and the preference for eating outside when
possible. The window shutters on to this space are flung wide open,
revealing a small lamp made out of a bottle. A vine has been trained up the
window and beyond it can just be seen some dark-framed paintings.

tools, musical instruments, urns and pine cones are other popular motifs.

Although the degree of ornamentation varied from region to region, the furniture features the same solid shapes, often with the curved *chapeau de gendarme* top which gives cupboards an air at once jaunty and majestic, and vigorously carved mouldings.

A celebration of natural materials

All the drawers and doors of French provincial furniture are ornamented with very attractive polished metal trim. This includes beautifully wrought hinges, locks and handles as well as purely ornamental 'finger plate' panels on doors. Delicate and lacy, it provides further opportunity for the craftsman to display his skill.

Walnut was a favourite wood of the French provincial carpenter and the trees were once abundant, though sadly this is no longer so. Walnut was prized for its golden colour that mellows with age as well as for its firmness, which makes it respond well under the carpenter's tools. Less frequently used though nevertheless popular woods were olive, mulberry, cherry, chestnut and pear, which was stained to resemble ebony.

Buffets and dining tables

In the dining room the *buffet* or sideboard is the most important piece of furniture apart from the dining table. A country *buffet* can be a very simple unornamented piece with double doors and a plain top, or it can be a tour de force of scrollwork standing on feet the designs of which were named after animals familiar to country people—*corne de belier* (ram's horn), *escargot* (snail) or *pied de biche* (doe's foot). The more elaborate ones have two tiers. In the *buffet à glissants* the upper tier holds only one row of dishes, but the *buffet à deux corps* (double *buffet*) has a slightly recessed upper part which is twice as high as the base—it's a relative

A TEMPTING VISTA
With pale blue walls and doors outlined in a darker blue, this vestibule holds a dark, impressive-looking chest with brass handles. The contrast created by the pale blue of the walls gives an added warmth to the dining room which can be seen through the open door.

PRIMITIVE GRANDEUR
This is a very rural scene: the kind of home you would find in a remote mountain village. Strength and simplicity are the keynotes. The copper pans and the important-looking table and sturdy chairs highlight the emphasis on good country food.

of the dresser. A further *buffet*, the *buffet crédence*, is often topped with a slab of marble. In the corner of the dining room you may see a triangular corner cabinet.

French provincial dining tables are not particularly remarkable except for the good wood of which they are made and their dimensions—large ones are long enough to seat a dozen people. But the chairs on which the diners sit are quite distinctive. Often made of willow, they are delicate, with straight spindle legs and three backslats that may look identical at first glance but turn out to be just slightly different from one another on close inspection. This is a French speciality that is always pleasing to the eye, the aberration being the best part of the design.

The chairs may be painted, most likely in light silvery blue or green with a subtle matt finish that looks slightly faded, and perhaps embellished with garlands or flower sprigs. To reproduce this effect you can use a matt or silk finish wood paint or even just undercoat, which leaves the wood with a faintly powdery, flower-petal texture. Gloss is too aggressive for this sort of work. The seats of these chairs are invariably of rush, though you could add a French provincial print cushion and tie it to the chair back with tapes.

On dining room and kitchen walls were small *etagères*, racks or storage units, designed to hold, variously, crockery, glasses and cutlery. Plate and glass racks were sometimes made with graceful spindles and might be backless to emphasize a dainty effect or with a wooden back for strength if made to hold heavier pieces. When hung over a tiled surface or by the sink, *etagères* can serve as drainage as well as storage units. Placed elsewhere, the back of the *etagère* (like the inside of an *armoire*) can be covered in French provincial print for extra warmth and interest. Modern completely plain versions of *etagères* are now being made for people who want to look at their crockery as well as store it conveniently to hand.

White china

On the whole the style of china most favoured in large French country houses is basically white and rather dig-nified. The plates are generously large, and the bowls, in a simple shape which can be cupped in the hand, are often used for drinking breakfast coffee. Ovenproof white china is common in the form of flan and soufflé dishes, gravy boats, and so on. Table china may also be in a one-colour transfer pattern on a white background. The French seem to be fond of angular shapes, such as the heavy, thick white or green stacking cups of the kind used in cafés but there are also octagonal cups and plates in more delicate china. A soup tureen is considered important though few house-holds would baulk at serving soup straight out of the pan.

Both eating and cooking utensils are bought in local ironmongers or in vast warehouses hidden away in the country, which aim to sell mainly to the trade but where you can go in and buy as few as five plates if you wish.

Modern ironmongers' shops tend to stock rather second-rate china with unnecessary floral transfer decorations. It's all stacked up on shelves and among the dross you can often find a set of traditional salt-glazed coffee mugs, basic brown earthenware casseroles or plain white china. Pounce on it when you see it, because there's no guarantee that this china will necessarily be stocked again in that particular shop.

Cheerful hand-crafted pottery

In the south, eating ware may be jollier and more informal, veering over towards the Mediterranean. Hand-moulded plates and platters and hand-thrown jugs and bowls of red clay are glazed with bright iridescent enamels—greens, blues and vivid yellows. Or they are finished in creamy white and hand-painted with delicate sprigs of flowers in blue, green and pink. The red clay seems to glow through the glaze, giving the pottery warmth and depth. Despite its robust appearance the glaze is quite brittle and chips easily, but to have a speck of terracotta showing through here and there does not detract from the appearance of a much-used plate or bowl.

There is a liveliness about hand-crafted pottery that makes it a delight to use. The shapes are homely, chunky and wholesome—it is pottery that is meant, primarily, for

AN OLD DAIRY RETAINS ITS FUNCTION

The dairy of an old French provincial farmhouse is still the best place for storing
bowls and jugs and other kitchen items such as jars of flour. The brick walls
have been painted white; the oblong quarry tiles are cleaned with a damp mop. Having
a rickety-looking but serviceable shelf or two is very French—somehow they manage to
look charming rather than scruffy. A row of metal hooks holds clean, white aprons and cloths.

BASIC HYGIENE
This small sink and tap are about as basic as you
can get. It has been given a style of its own by
the bold yellow and terracotta tiles placed
diagonally on the wall and lining the sink.

UNDERGROUND DINING ROOM
This large, spacious cellar dining room gets its
light from the ceiling. On hot days, this
space is cool but cheered by splashes of
sunlight. On cool evenings or in wintertime,
the open fire and neat pile of logs
will keep it warm and cozy. The refectory-type
table, upright chairs and long blanket chest
give this room a formal feeling.

everyday. But it is also good to look at, which is one of the
reasons it is stored on open shelves and in racks rather than
out of sight in a cupboard.

Modern French potters have much to offer the collector.
The rural craftsman's veneration for natural materials and
the French pleasure in using ordinary objects that are well-
designed and good to handle as well as to look at are very
apparent in the pottery, and a set (preferably not a matching set) of French provincial crockery can bring that
pleasure into any home.

The red clay of the south is put to another important
use: making tiles. In any Provençal home most of the floors
will be tiled. Natural or glazed tiles are cheaper there than
wood and particularly practical in kitchens and dining

A COOL CORNER

Rays of sun shine through leaded windowpanes to brighten a cool corner. Thick stone walls conserve the cool atmosphere. A slab of polished wood forms the windowsill, and traditional blue and white pictorial tiles act as a splashback.

A BASIC EXTENSION

In this very basic extension the walls are built of the same rough planks as the cupboards, and the roof beams are left open to view. The French doors are large and well-built and, although the furniture is far from perfectly finished, the whole place has a cared-for look.

FINE KITCHEN FURNITURE

This enormous dresser may have been built to fit this
particular space but it is not built-in—like most
French provincial furniture, it is free-standing.
Many large provincial farmhouses have one or two pieces of
furniture of very good quality, which might equally
be found in a chateau. This one will probably stand more
or less on its own. Who needs more?

rooms because they are so easy to keep clean. In the long
hot summers they remain deliciously cool; in the winters
they retain the heat of the fire. The commonest tiles are
plain red and hexagonal, square or rectangular, but all
shapes, sizes and colours are available and there is nothing
to stop you using an imaginative combination of sunny
colours. Rich reds and pinks and oranges, golden yellows
and brilliant blues and greens mixed at random on a floor
or on a small area of wall will seem to give off warmth by
their very lusciousness even in a cooler climate.

The heart of the kitchen

The kitchen hearth in an old French provincial farmhouse
is an enormous alcove big enough to walk in and seat

CONVENIENCE AND CHARM

This tiny piece of wall says much about
French provincial style. The interesting spoons
are hung on nails simply hammered into
the wall in a convenient position.

PROVINCIAL AT HEART

Here is French provincial being dragged into the 20th
century. The floor is tiled but in parquet, not ceramics. The
cupboards are built-in, but by a local carpenter, to the
design of the cook, and some wall units are doorless.

several cooks. In the walls around the fire are niches for condiments and pots and pans. Originally a huge spit stood over the flames. When a family moved house they proclaimed ownership of their new home by hanging up the cooking pot hook in the hearth. This alcove in the kitchen is the ideal place for a range—it might be an old cast-iron model or a new stainless steel one designed for the professional chef. Efficient cooking facilities are the first essential of a French kitchen, though it has to be said that a superb meal can be cooked on a single-burner camping stove, and the best that money can buy is no good unless you know how to use it.

In a French provincial farmhouse the food will be served up in the pan in which it has been cooked straight from the stove on to the table. Of solid wood and sturdily built, the kitchen table is where the family generally eats. It may have a tiled top that can be wiped clean—if the tiles are old and cracked and mismatched, that is part of their charm. Or the table may be covered in oilcloth, which is equally quick and easy to wipe clean.

Essential equipment

The *batterie de cuisine* is the first thing a sensible French bride will concern herself with. And first among essentials is a good range of kitchen knives. No French kitchen will ever be seen with a blunt knife. There should never be fewer than three well-balanced knives, the most important probably being a 25 cm (10 inch) chef's knife. The knives should preferably be of carbon rather than stainless steel; carbon knives can be honed much sharper than stainless steel. They can be cleaned with steel wool.

No self-respecting kitchen would be without a 'Mouli' (you can't make potato 'vermicelli' with a kitchen mixer), or a wire egg whisk. There will also be an enormous wooden chopping board. Other essentials are a pestle and mortar, a salad shaker, a heavy enamelled *cocotte* for braising, earthenware lidded casseroles, a *marmite* (the traditional French stockpot) which may be of earthenware or the more modern cylindrical aluminium pot, gratin dishes—large oval earthenware dishes, about 5 cm (2 inches) deep—and a fish kettle. There should also be a range of heavy saucepans, a double saucepan for sauces, and a good heavy aluminium or enamelled cast-iron frying pan.

Practical considerations

Earthenware is used a lot—for good reasons. It is slow to conduct heat, which makes it excellent for storing fresh vegetables and for keeping milk cool, as well as for carrying cooked dishes straight from the oven to the table, since it is also slow to cool down when hot.

Much of the equipment is what might be considered elsewhere as catering equipment: no-nonsense, down-to-earth, practical stainless steel, rather than pretty-pretty floral-finished aluminium.

Enormous meat platters are provided with grooves for the juices to run into. Glass jars with dried herbs, bay leaves, fruit in brandy, or herbs in oil or vinegar line the shelves. Glass bottling jars with clip-on lids and orange rubber seals make good storage jars. You can often buy paté or bottled fruit in these and they can be kept and used afterwards.

Wine may be decanted into simple glass carafes or poured from the bottle. For informal meals, it may be drunk out of rather basic long, thin tumblers. Although many continentals don't know what a kettle is, they all have at least one coffeepot. It may be a filter, a Cafetière or a percolator, or a jug used with or without filter papers.

The importance of food

In France the whole business of food is of paramount importance. Everything must be fresh when prepared, so

FORM FOLLOWS FUNCTION

This is a classic example of utility and ingenuity meeting to make a satisfying space. The walls were once painted yellow. The large shelf and the panelled doors were built to last, but not to be over-zealously cleaned and polished. The equipment is old-fashioned, practical and good-looking, but new equipment (such as the chip pan) is unhesitatingly added, if it is *really* useful.

what is not grown in the garden or on the farm is bought every day and bread perhaps twice a day. Since much of the day is spent planning, shopping for, preparing and eating meals, a feeling of leisure accompanies the process. There is no question of getting things done in a hurry, or of cooking 'convenience foods'. All is to be enjoyed.

After the daily visit to the market one end of the kitchen table will be piled with fresh produce. Vegetables enjoyed in country areas include garlic, tomatoes, Swiss chard, courgettes, peppers, fennel (both root and leaf), flat plate-like lettuces with curly leaves, green beans and lots of parsley. Cooking may be done with maize oil or sunflower oil, but salad dressings are always made with olive oil.

Regional characteristics

As France is a large country, the climate and what is grown in each region have an important influence on the arrangement and running of a country household. Thus in Normandy and other parts of northern France, where the climate is wetter than in the south, fires are lit more frequently, *pots-au-feu* and casseroles are provided for meals oftener than salads and there will be an abundance of cooking pots such as casseroles and *daubes*, each with their own function for different types of stew.

In the Bordeaux area, a traditional crop is plums for making prunes, and many a household will have wooden racks in the attic, the same sort of shape as snowshoes, for

MORE CLASSIC EQUIPMENT

This *batterie de cuisine* has proved itself through long use, and will not be renewed until it breaks. Ladles and long-handled spoons hang on a metal rail; garlic crushers, flour measures and suchlike tuck behind it. Old and valued knives have a special wooden rack of their own.

DEEP SHADE

The darkness of this stone-flagged floor is
deliberate: it is easier to work in on hot
days and helps to reduce glare from the sun.
The windows open right back to let in
as much fresh air as possible and
are shaded by white-lined curtains.

drying the plums. Here, too, tobacco is grown, and an airy, light space is used for hanging the large leaves to dry. Such spaces are ideal for storing fruit, vegetables and home-made preserves, drying herbs and stringing onions.

In the wine-growing areas, many households buy their wine from the local co-operative, bringing home five litres (about one gallon) at a time in large plastic containers. These containers are a common sight in kitchens, as are a medley of wine and brandy bottles into which local farmers decant their own home-made wine. This is often pretty rough, the red a sort of purple colour, the rosé deep red, and the white a very dark yellow.

During the vendage the farmer's wife will provide sumptuous meals for the helpers. In the evening particu-larly, such a meal consists of six or seven courses including soup, charcuterie and roast guinea fowl, all interspersed with several vegetable dishes. The meal will be followed by fruit and cheese carried over from the traditional marble-topped double *buffet* where knives, glasses and so on are also kept ready for use. All is liberally washed down with last year's vintage.

The basket of free-range eggs, the freshly killed chicken waiting to be plucked, the locally made goat's cheese and the leafy bunch of newly pulled carrots—this is what the French provincial kitchen is all about. Every implement and arrangement in the room is dedicated to the moment when the family sits down to savour each morsel of a long, leisurely meal.

TERRACOTTA POTS

Terracotta storage and cooking jars are so typical of French provincial life that it is sad to think that these pots are fast disappearing from the countryside as French cooks turn to cast iron and stainless steel. Old terracotta pots are part of the country's heritage. While they are no longer suitable to be used for the purpose for which they were first made, they make evocative antiques in a country setting.

Food is of vital importance to any French person, and these earthenware pots are essential in the French farmhouse for cooking hearty peasant dishes — country cassoulets, choux farçis, daubes and civets lose something of their flavour and charm if cooked in an ordinary metal saucepan.

The name cassoulet comes from cassol d'Issel, the original clay cooking utensil from the little town of Issel near Castelnaudray. The dish itself is a slow-cooking stew of haricot beans, goose flesh, sausage and bacon which is layered in the pot and left to cook in a very slow oven until the beans are ready.

Confit d'oie is another classic French dish which relies on these tall, deep cooking pots. Layers of goose or duck flesh are preserved

222

in their own fat—thus sealed, they can be stored for a long time. Preserved goose forms the basis of many regional dishes in the southwestern corner of France.

These terracotta pots were created out of a natural abundance of clay. No one region can lay claim to the pots we have photographed—so many small French towns and villages produce their own pottery that it's hard to distinguish between them. Typical are the mustard-yellow or emerald-green glazes. The oil and wine jars with a spout and carrying arm would have

had lids, whereas the cooking pots with carrying handles on either side would have been sealed with a thick crust of bread or fat.

Originally made for use in an old clay oven, terracotta retains its heat and spreads it evenly across its cooking surface. Nowadays, earthenware can be put on top of the gas or electric stove, provided a heat-proof mat or fireclay simmering mat is placed underneath. The most important point in caring for terracotta is to avoid a sudden change of temperature—pouring cold water into a hot casserole will simply crack it.

FROM LEFT TO RIGHT

Collection of rustic mid 19th century cooking pots and oil and water well jugs.

Sleeping and Bathing

In France the most private apartments of the house, the main bedroom and bathroom, are often joined by an interconnecting door and complementary décor. This convenient arrangement obviates the need for walking down draughty corridors in the middle of the night and creates an intimate atmosphere otherwise associated with a luxurious hotel suite.

The voluptuous functionalism of a French bathroom is intensified in country houses, where creeper-framed windows and even French doors are thrown open to nature and the sun floods in to envelop the bather in warmth.

French provincial bathrooms are usually large uncluttered rooms where the focus of attention is the bath, the toilet, the bidet and the washbasin. Even in a small room, sparseness of decoration will emphasize function. As ever, the proportions of the room are respected. The eye is not distracted by other furniture or by details of decoration, nor is any attempt made to transform the bathroom into something softer by blurring its functions and dressing it up as a sitting room or a boudoir. There is no particular attempt to hide the plumbing. Soft furnishings—cushioned chairs, elaborate drapes, thick-pile carpets—are usually missing. Comfort resides instead in the commodious design of the bathroom fittings themselves.

Take the bidet, for instance. Designed for personal hygiene and comfort, the bidet is regarded as essential to

BATHING IN GRAND STYLE

As with other French provincial rooms, the bathroom is on a gracious scale and so is the bath. This room is 'furnished' rather than 'equipped' and its huge marble bathtub is an experience in itself. The tap is a splendid old-fashioned object.

VIRGINAL WHITE

Simplicity is the keynote in this all-white bedroom. You must be very single-minded to keep linen as beautifully laundered as this, and the room requires little else in the way of decoration. Snowy scallops, ruches and white satin stitching hold sway.

A BATHROOM FOR CHILDREN

The French take their ablutions seriously. This room, designed specially for children, has two free-standing basins, with a mirror each, a low chair and a sheepskin rug for the feet. The globe lamps are a little too near the water to comply with safety standards in some countries.

FLAIR FOR THE UTILITARIAN

This is a modern view of an old style. There is nothing here that is not
practical. The bare boards are sanded and sealed, and the door is also sealed.
The roughly finished walls are painted nearly-white; one wall-hung basin,
with sculptural plumbing, is fed by an all-white tap. The only other furniture
is one free-standing towel rail and a shelf on sturdy modern brackets.

civilized life in all French homes. Washbasins, too, are
designed to be used. Generously proportioned, they are
shallow and broad with taps set well back so that you do
not knock yourself while washing and can sluice the water
over your face in the knowledge that the basin is big
enough to catch most of it as it runs off. The ideal basin
should be roomy enough to bathe a baby in, and with
recesses for soap and plugs that are large enough actually to
hold these items.

It has to be said that the French seem to take their bidets,
which are streamlined and beautiful, more seriously than
their toilets. However, this apparent lapse is more than
compensated for by the French baths, for it is on these that
the French really lavish their attention.

Commodious baths

French baths are made to soak in, that is, they are long
enough to accommodate a tall person and deep enough to
hold a good quantity of soothing warm water and
perfumed suds. Because of the importance of its function,
to cleanse and to relax, the bath may be placed in a
prominent position, either in the centre of the room or,
particularly in country bathrooms, facing a panoramic view
which will do as much to restore and revive the bather as
the bath itself. With this aim in view, bathrooms often
occupy a prime site in the French house, rather than being
relegated to a room where there is no window at all or one
that overlooks only a blank wall.

The bathtub may be of cast iron with ball-and-claw feet,

in which case the taps will probably be of shining brass, perhaps lacquered to spare frequent polishing. A shower attachment offers the most convenient means of washing the hair. Such a bath is often given an imaginative paint treatment on the outside and could feature marbling or stencilling in a bright luminous colour such as rose, violet or turquoise.

Stone baths are also very desirable, though hard to come by. Dating from the 19th century, they are absolutely simple in style: smooth oval tubs that appear to be growing out of the floor, a seemingly natural rock formation worn into shape by the bodies of countless bathers.

Plain materials, uncluttered lines

Ceramic bathroom fittings are almost always plain white, though you might find the odd flower-bedecked faïence washbasin. The floor is likely to be made of stone or tiled in terracotta or glazed faïence in a neutral colour, or traditional black-and-white tiles in a simple geometric pattern. The walls could be tiled too, or they might be simply whitewashed or colour-washed in a light colour with a warmish tinge such as cream, honey or rose.

Over the basin there might be a bamboo-framed mirror illuminated by a brass-stalked wall light, and near the bath a wicker chair over which to throw clothes not held by the hooks on the door. A handsome plant, perhaps a large weeping fig in a terracotta urn, echoes the greenery outside the window. There will be no patterned drapes to detract from the view, but shutters to be closed at night or simple muslin curtains on a pole or lace blinds that can be pulled to filter strong sunlight.

Luxurious thick white towels may hang from a brass towel rail on the wall with more towels piled up in a walk-in cupboard or on open shelves. Softness may be there, too, in a bowl of delicate garden flowers among the toiletries on a shelf.

A typically French touch is to create a still life of natural objects in one corner of the room. In a window recess you might find a collection of exotic shells or pieces of coral or driftwood found on the beach. A large bowl of fircones will

GREENERY INSIDE AND OUT

A free-standing bath and basin sit in lonely glory in this bathroom. The bath is placed for maximum enjoyment of the view from the window. An old-fashioned ceramic urn on a pedestal and some tumbling green plants make this a bathroom of simple pleasures.

bring back memories of a country walk. Objects such as these are far more intimate mementos of places visited than any manufactured souvenir could be, and like flowers they bring a fresh outdoor feeling into any house.

Sparse elegance

The sparsely elegant style of the French provincial bathroom adapts well to other countries and climates. To recreate the French feel underfoot while at the same time avoiding a cold floor, choose red and white, or black and white, vinyl tiles and lay them in a diamond pattern with perhaps a small stripe border of narrow tiles around the edge. Paintwork can be stripped, or painted white or cream if the wood is not special. At the window hang a heavy lace curtain from a brass pole. To suggest southern warmth you could colour-wash the walls in pinkish beige or terracotta. Of major importance is to choose a bath and basin in classic style and of generous proportions. Keep other furniture to the minimum—cane, bamboo and wicker will be well suited to the airy feel.

Restrained extravagance

More exotic bathrooms are to be found in the French country homes of the rich, to whom they offer an unparallelled opportunity for restrained extravagance. Given unlimited imagination and a budget to match, a bathroom can become a shrine dedicated to sensual purification rites. A bathroom might, for example, be tiled completely in luminous Italian faïence, either patterned or a mixture of plain colours. Such a bathroom has a stately feel that demands a pair of washbasins and a fitted shower as well as a bath. Though sophisticated, its clean lines, natural materials and functional design make this style very acceptable in a country house.

The bedroom—rustic simplicity

An archetypal French provincial bedroom can be almost monastic in its austerity, yet the overwhelming impression is of vibrancy and warmth. Take a red-tiled floor, whitewashed walls, pale grey paintwork, green shutters opening on to a sunlit balcony, and a huge brass-framed bed with crisp, freshly laundered white sheets and coverlet. Or take a room with a stone floor and roughly plastered walls washed in faded terracotta; the woodwork is bare, the window is shuttered, a heavy walnut bed is covered in a red patterned cloth, and a huge bunch of herbs and a straw hat hang on the wall above it. Or again, take a mellow parquet floor, honey-washed walls and heavy lace curtains. Throw over the bed a vividly patterned hand-printed quilt and put two enormous, square, flower-sprigged pillows at its head.

The essence is simplicity and the focus is on the bed, which because of the bareness of the room appears oversized. The texture of natural materials, the proportions of the room, the mass of the bed and the light streaming in at the window are what you first notice about a French provincial bedroom, and it is these that should be borne in mind when translating the spirit of the room.

As in rooms elsewhere in the French provincial house, the main architectural feature is the fireplace, which is often

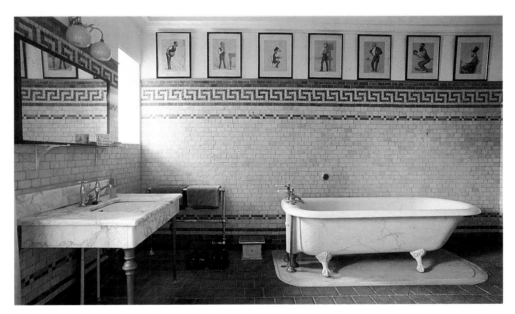

GREEK KEY FRIEZE

Here is a more elaborate variation on the same theme—that bath and basins
are furniture, not 'suites'. The tiles and marble create a functional, cool,
'serious' atmosphere, offset by the cartoons hung above the Greek
key frieze and a few flashes of colour.

PROVINCIAL DRESSING

Many French provincial homes have spacious
bedrooms and dressing rooms. Here, recessed
windows house a collection of dolls and *their*
accessories.

HYGIENIC WHITE

White is the colour for this bathroom. The white of
the tiles, bath and basins is alleviated by a dark row of
tiles above the white ones, dark diamond shapes on
the floor and the pedestal with its vase of flowers.

huge and ornate, making a striking contrast with the
plainness of the rest of the room. Even in a country
bedroom the fireplace can be staggeringly grandiose,
perhaps of carved stone or marble. If you are going to keep
the rest of the room simple, with rustic furniture and an
uncarpeted floor, an elaborate fireplace, perhaps with the
mantelpiece left bare or adorned only with a hand-thrown
pot or a glass of wild flowers, can make a stunning centrepiece.

An old cast-iron fireplace can be set with Art Nouveau
tiles. The gorgeous jades, lime greens and turquoises
favoured in the early years of the century and the sinuous

curves of Art Nouveau designs have the exuberance of
spirit that characterizes French provincial style. If you are
lucky enough to find a large stash of tiles, you could
continue the same theme into the bathroom. Most opulent
of all would be an Art Nouveau fireplace in moulded
faïence embellished with herons fishing or waterlilies or
other flights of fancy. The point is that you can afford to
make a contrast—one grand piece in an otherwise plain
room can look very dramatic, and yet at the same time
surprisingly at home.

Kaleidoscopic prints

Fabrics with true colours and small intricate patterns are
popular in France and are ideally suited to the light fresh-
air feel of a country bedroom. In fact, Provence has become
internationally known for its own glorious printed cottons,
the major manufacturer being the house of Souleiado.
Today Souleiado prints most of its fabrics industrially, but
when the firm was first established over 200 years ago the
cotton was hand-blocked with vegetable dyes from designs
carved in fruit wood. The fruitwood blocks, more than
40,000 of them, with their rich or delicate fruit, floral,
paisley and geometric designs, are carefully preserved and
form the basis of today's operation.

The colours and the kaleidoscopic quality of the designs
reflect the sun on the Provençal countryside—saffron
yellow, faded blue, lapis, mint green and indigo. The
dazzling richness of these fabrics is reminiscent of the
Indian prints introduced into France in the mid-17th
century, which is when the craze for brightly coloured
prints of intricate pattern began. It has raged unabated ever
since. Souleiado prints hang at windows and cover tables,
beds and cushions. The firm began by making *mouchoirs*,
huge kerchiefs. Today its classic and most covetable
product is the *boutis* or quilt.

A French provincial-style bedroom can accommodate as
many of these gorgeous prints as you like—they look
exotic *en masse* and as natural as a summer flowerbed. At the
window, unlined floor-length curtains look clean and fresh
in a dainty rosebud print with a border of full-blown roses.

CLEVER CONVERSION

This stone cellar room has been cleverly converted into a washroom without spoiling the character of the room. Once again, French flair has devised an ingenious layout—the basin is in the windowsill and the lavatory the other side of the 'flying buttress' of the arch. The brick floor needed no changing; the stone walls are painted white and there is a long bench to relax on.

A paisley quilt on the bed could be contrasted with flowery pillows and another quilt of geometric design over a small table that holds a glass bowl of flowers and perhaps an ivory toilet set. Such fabrics glow more richly against a polished wood floor, but if your floorboards are not special, stain them blue, green or pink—stained wood has more depth and sheen than painted boards and gives something of the illusion of reflected southern light.

Fresh and crisp bed linen

The right bed linen is very important: it must both look and feel good. Polyester has no place here. Neither does nylon, with its unpleasant habit of snagging dry skin and its tendency to smother. Sheets and pillowcases must be 100 per cent cotton, washed perfectly white, blown dry in summer breezes or baked on the washing line, and ironed flat and smooth. There is nothing more comforting than slipping into a soft bed between freshly laundered cotton sheets. In summer a thin sheet may be all that is needed; in winter warm honey-coloured woollen blankets create an echo of the sun under a patterned quilt.

Or of course you may prefer a fat, downy duvet like those that plump up the wooden beds of villages high in the Alps and hang from the windows in the morning to

absorb the Alpine air. Linen could be used for the duvet cover, and tapes or ribbons to fasten the opening. Patterned linen covers are sometimes available, and blue-and-white or red-and-white gingham looks particularly crisp and attractive in a French provincial style bedroom. Pillows need not match the other bed linen—in fact, several large, square pillows in different delicate flower prints hold much more charm than a matching set.

Solid furniture, glowing wood

The classic French provincial bed has a carved head-board and low posts at the foot. The impression is of solidity, of a good piece of furniture that will be handed down through the generations. A large cupboard or *armoire*, possibly in walnut, may be the only other imposing piece of furniture in the room. More solid than most wardrobes, the *armoire* was originally designed as an all-

WINDOW VIGNETTE
Sunny windows offer plenty of opportunity
for pretty little views and arrangements.
You wouldn't know you were in a bathroom
at all here, as you gazed through the bars
to the dense, brightly lit greenery beyond.
The dishes on the windowsill hold lavender
and aromatic herbs.

WASHROOM EN SUITE
This charming bedroom has a washroom en suite,
its marble steps and large jug just visible through
the painted door. The free-standing dressing
cabinet is curtained in cream-coloured cotton. The
arched ceiling, metal hanging light and dark
furniture all contribute to a medieval look.

purpose cupboard, to hold food as well as clothes. There may also be a walk-in wardrobe in which clothes can be hung.

Chairs will not be too heavy. Rush seats emphasize the country look, and the delicate wooden backs, arms and legs may show evidence of hand-painting faded in the sun. The dusky blue, silvery green and bleached straw of these chairs form a subtle contrast to a brightly patterned cushion. As elsewhere in the French provincial house, the new and the old exist happily side by side and no attempt is made to smarten up pieces dignified by age.

Special details

Squat, functional night tables at either side of the bed hold mineral water and reading lamps. A writing desk under the window or in an intimate alcove of its own is highly

DRAMATIC PROPORTIONS

Sun streams in through tall windows to cast oblong yellow shapes on to the floor. This is a
grand room, its high ceiling alive with carving and painting. No attempt has been made to 'fill it up'
so its proportions remain to be seen and enjoyed. A huge tapestry hangs above the bed. A large
chest stands at the far end. The decorative tiled floor is highly polished. This room needs nothing more.

polished to a golden sheen. The desk or mantelpiece might be the place for a collection of silver-framed family photographs or antique perfume bottles. Fresh garden flowers in a series of delicate glass vases in different shapes and sizes are another possibility.

Decoration to the walls will be kept simple, whether they are colour-washed, wood panelled or covered in delicate flower-sprigged paper. A couple of original paintings in heavy ornate frames and a personal photograph or two are likely to be found alongside bunches of lavender and dried grasses suspended by a ribbon from a nail in the wall. A large gilt-framed mirror takes the place of a dressing table.

The view from the window as always holds the attention—it seems as much a part of the French provincial room as the interior itself, and calls to mind the glorious light and intense colours of the window pictures of Bonnard and Matisse.

MEDIEVAL ELEGANCE

This bedroom is a mixture of the gracious with the pretty. The dark beams, the draped bedhead and the upholstered chair have the look of a medieval castle, but the painted *armoire* is purely pretty.

Inside meets Outside

There is nothing the French like better than eating outside. When the sun beats down out of an azure sky, the light dances and the heat is a luminous caress, those lucky enough to live in the country have spilled out into the open. Not so much avid for the scorching midday sun as grateful to get out of it, they are lunching on terraces and verandas, under parasols and plane trees.

Country life in rural France in summer is led as much outside as in, the doors and windows are thrown open and now and then a gentle breeze lifts a gauzy curtain and sends a waft of apricots and lavender billowing into the deserted room.

The French provincial country house in summer is cool, still and fragrant, a refuge from the dizzying assault on the senses that is the outside world: the intoxicating light, vibrant shimmering colours, fierce heat, heady perfume of fruit and flowers, the clatter and din of people and animals going about their business. If the garden with its dappled shade, the balcony with its opportunities for calling to friends and idly watching the world go by, the pool with its glinting blue water constantly seduce you outside into the heat and light and noise, then a cool, airy room offers a welcome and refreshing retreat. The clean lines, classical proportions, neutral colours are an antidote to the tumult of summer.

Van Gogh wrote of living in Arles: 'My house here is

A GREEN AND SHADY SPOT

Courtyards and terraces feature a great deal in both French provincial and Mediterranean styles. But the French provincial version is greener and lusher, with more trees and less of the shrieking red of exotic flowers and the uncompromising white found in the more southerly climates.

A SUN-DRENCHED TERRACE

Here is a terrace in the south of France,
with its pink tiles, its oak supports
and the wisteria hanging in great violet tassels.
Inside, the home is cool and dark, but
out here on the tiled floor, one can
sit in white-painted chairs and sip kir.

MAKING A SPLASH

Majolica tiles are an
efficient splashback to
this stone water
fountain—a pretty object
to catch the attention in a
courtyard.

A LONG AND SHADY BOWER

This long terrace has been shaded over,
making a sort of avenue of spiky shapes and
a protection against the mid-day sun.
At the far end is a gingham-covered table with
some traditional local cane chairs.

grotesques and clenched fists are popular subjects for knockers. Indoors, delicate window catches and door fittings are often of brass.

Splashes of bright colour

Full sun on a window is an invitation to dress it with flowers. Delicate blooms will wither in such a hot spot— this is the place for the hardy and prolific geranium, one of the few plants that will thrive in a small pot of rock-hard earth in smouldering heat. Even that will need to be watered twice a day, once in early morning and again in the cool of the evening, when the air is filled with the song of gathering swallows—a pleasant task that can be combined with that of watching the neighbours tending their own window boxes.

A window could be entirely framed by a creeping plant, like brilliant magenta bougainvillea. Though nothing as spectacular as bougainvillea will flourish in a cooler climate, a grapevine will grow quickly to cover a sheltered south-facing wall and can be trained over a terrace pergola for a strongly French feel. Alternatively, wisteria trained up a warm wall provides an abundance of soft, trailing, lilac-coloured blooms followed by delicate, feathery leaves and fast-growing tendrils. A peach tree can be grown just as successfully against a wall in a suntrap in temperate climates as it can in hotter countries.

Just as a sunny windowsill or wall seems tailormade for a profusion of blooms, so too a terrace or balcony must be well-stocked with luxuriant plants. An extension of the living area, the terrace is the joy of the French provincial house. In hot climates, shade is an important factor on a terrace, but in cooler places an outside living room should be situated where it will get most sun, least wind. In those places some of the space could well be glassed over to maximize the heat; in hot climates the temperature in a conservatory would be insupportable.

Furniture for outdoor living

Garden furniture has become a passion in France. The fact that it is used almost as much as the furniture indoors means that people are prepared to spend quite a bit of money on it and that they choose with care. As with indoor furniture, priorities are simplicity and elegance of line, suitability to purpose and quality.

Wicker and cane are materials traditionally used for furniture in hot countries and can be crafted into chairs that are both comfortable and beautiful. Tables can be of wicker, wood or iron, topped with a cool marble slab. Gothic-looking iron chairs are tempting to the eye but searing to the skin if left in the sun and in any case not designed for prolonged lounging.

What you will not find on a French terrace is white moulded plastic chairs—they are hot and sticky to sit in and ugly to look at. Plastic slats are even worse, leaving a sweating pink imprint on the thighs of anyone desperate enough to perch on them.

Neither will you see imitation Victorian cast 'wrought-iron' furniture. Too fussy and cumbersome for French taste, even the originals seem designed rather to be looked at longingly from the house through the drizzle than to be sat on. Cast iron in France is generally reserved for intricate and delicate balcony rails and grilles.

For lounging, colonial chair-beds can be set out in the shade of a veranda, cushions strewn on the floor. The upholstered swinging seat with its own fringed canopy would look extremely out of place next to its austere French provincial cousins. Maybe in cooler climates people feel the need to jolly garden furniture up, to detract from the fact that the sun isn't that hot after all.

In fact, the deep blue of the sky is what many people miss most about the south of France. As a reminder, blue tiles could be used in the floor or walls of the terrace, perhaps in certain patches only, and even using broken tiles or pieces of broken blue and white china. A blue pool, even a very small one, can reflect a great deal more of summer than there may be in the sky.

In the south, rattan blinds are hung horizontally so they can be drawn across a terrace to shield it from the sun. In cooler climates they could be hung vertically in a frame to create shelter from unwelcome breezes.

FILL THE HALL WITH LIGHT
Here is a pretty little sun-drenched hall, furnished
very simply with a banquette and mirrors to give
a sense of width. Pale walls make the most of the light. The faded
green of the window frame, reflected in the mirror, and the battered brown of the door
are in keeping with an instinctive feeling of colour and informality.

Container collection

Plants and flowering shrubs can be grown in any number of containers, provided they are not white moulded plastic 'urns'. Plastic pots of all shapes look totally inappropriate, roll away in the wind and do not hold water as terracotta does, which makes the smaller ones especially unsuitable for outside use. The Versailles box, traditionally for orange trees, square, on small feet and made of wooden slats painted dark green or white, is an elegant formal planter for something permanent such as a bay tree or a standard rose. Otherwise you might find a charming miscellany of terracotta pots of all shapes and sizes jumbled up together, containing a gnarled and blooming forest of brightly coloured geraniums.

Line smaller pots up against a sunny wall—a crowd looks better than two or three—and stand a couple of large

COOL AND GLISTENING

If only every hall could boast a fountain.
But you need space, and sunlight to catch the droplets
and make them glisten. All around, everything must be
cool, shiny, pale and clean.

prize specimens in prominent positions. Otherwise restrict the decoration of your terrace to a minimum.

What you will see sometimes on a Provençal terrace is a gigantic terracotta or stoneware 'Ali Baba' jar, such as might be used for olives or wine. A useful object made of natural material, a simple satisfying shape of classical proportions, such a pot is a perfect thing to focus on drowsily through your eyelashes as you bask in the sun. It

also makes a startling decoration in a simply furnished room.

Another delightful sight on a French terrace may well be a flock of white doves. A feature of French provincial architecture not to be ignored is the dovecot. Pigeons used to be bred for the table and the manure from the dovecot was used on the fields. A dovecot could house up to 3000 doves, and some of them are architectural masterpieces,

A MAGICAL CORNER

Here in a little wild corner under the shadow of tiled eaves in the
south of France, crickets chirp, beetles run, butterflies land and exotic
flies hover. French cafe chairs painted yellow are set around a little table
covered with a blue tablecloth and all is ready for a bowl of coffee and
some breakfast in the sunshine.

STRENGTH AND GRANDEUR

Curved stone steps lead down from a *trompe-l'oeil* gallery through a cool stone lobby to the hot outdoors. Here the banisters, though metal, are restrained and dignified, as is the whole scene. The strength and grandeur of the place require no other decoration.

UNCLUTTERED QUALITY

Among the most attractive of French provincial houses are the large old farmhouses, whose basic fabric is so elegant and well-made that they don't need to be given a sophisticated finish. This is the entrance to just such a house. The door is sturdy, well-made, even intricate.

like small follies, with the entrances for the birds cut in the shape of hearts or clover leaves. Today doves are kept mainly for the pleasure of looking at them and listening to them. They are extremely easy to breed (in fact, it is more of a problem keeping the numbers down) and a dovecot is a charming addition to any garden.

Eating alfresco

A barbecue is an undoubted asset for anyone who enjoys eating outside. The taste of food cooked over charcoal and eaten in the open air is incomparable. A compact Japanese free-standing barbecue, one simply constructed of brick, or a meat tray with holes punched in the sides, filled with charcoal and covered with a grill rack—the equipment is unimportant compared to the enjoyment of cooking and eating the food.

Make the table setting as simple as possible. A cloth should not be necessary unless to hide the reflected glare

from a white-topped table. Provençal pottery—heavy, chunky glazed earthenware, simply hand-painted—is ideal for outdoor eating because of its liveliness, immediacy and sturdy rustic feel. Heavy handblown glass, greenish, irregular and full of bubbles, gives the impression that it is less fragile than crystal and will contribute to a relaxed occasion. If the weather is very hot, try serving rough red wine as it is drunk outdoors in Spain. It is brought to the table completely frozen and should be poured as it thaws: the hotter the sun, the faster your thirst will be quenched.

Nothing could be better than fruit picked straight off the tree for dessert. Sitting on a balcony in the south of France at night being deafened by the cicadas and watching the twinkling lights of the village in the valley below, one could reach out and pluck a bunch of cherries or a couple of ripe figs from an overhanging bough: in cooler climates, a strawberry pot set on the table would make a delicious finale to the meal.

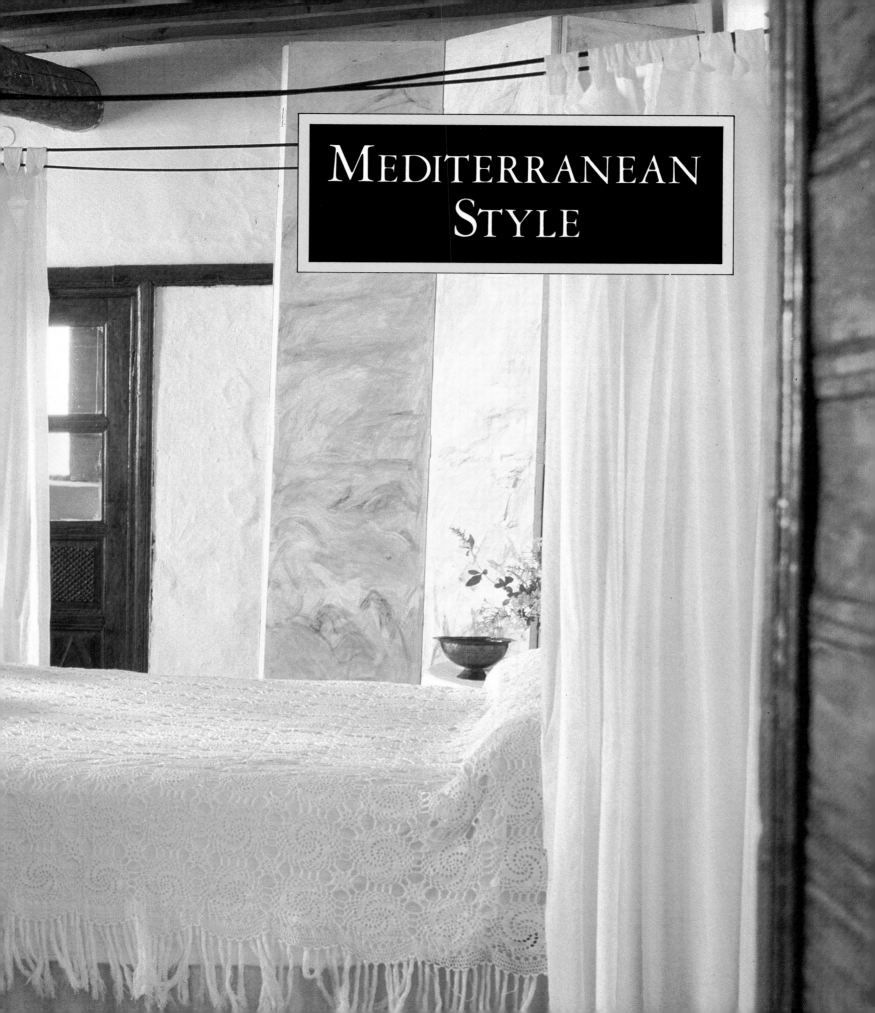

MEDITERRANEAN STYLE

A Mediterranean house belonging to someone who lives and works by the sea has no need for great space or lavish furniture. It must be practical and simple to look after—it's a place to retire to, for rest and good food. There is no demand for large windows; in fact, the windows are deliberately small, to keep out the relentless sun. With its thick, whitewashed walls and sparse furnishings, the cool, cavern-like interior is in total contrast to the heat and colour outside. It may seem hard to transplant this style of home into a dramatically different setting, but there are elements which are very suitable for being recreated anywhere in the world. In particular, the wonderful, uninhibited use of colour, the honest details set off by simple white interiors, and the fitness of purpose of most of the materials and furniture used in the Mediterranean house can be a source of inspiration for any home.

ACHIEVING THE LOOK

The hot Mediterranean climate has produced a way of life which is slow in pace, often hard, but richly satisfying. The houses reflect this in their simplicity and even a kind of roughness at times.

Underfoot

Floors are invariably tiled in some way. This could be rough, unglazed, brick-like paviours or the large square terracotta tiles common in Spain. Stone or marble might be used if it is locally abundant, or cool highly glazed ceramic tiles in a plain colour or an all-over small design. These surfaces are easy to look after, they last practically for ever and they give a welcome feeling of coolness which helps to counteract the heat.

Walls and ceilings

The Mediterranean method of building hasn't changed for centuries: the style is practically ageless and difficult to date.

Inside walls are characteristically roughly finished, but if you are aiming to emulate this, do try to avoid the trowelled effect of too much plaster daubed on too thickly. The roughness should simply be an indication of the lumpiness of the stone underneath and it is hard to cheat at this effect convincingly. Similarly, the wobbly arches and crooked alcoves and niches often found in these buildings are never successfully faked but are best done in, say, a semi-basement or cellar.

Skirting boards and door surrounds are likely to be irrelevant in a Mediterranean house. Doors should be of a

The Mediterranean is a land of bright glare and deep shadow. Gardening is done in large pots, which can be watered. The flaming colours of the flowers show up sharply against the white walls.

Of all areas, the Mediterranean is the one for stone or tiled floors. These are wonderful for bare feet on a hot day. A little wooden chair like this can be picked up and moved indoors or out very easily. Elderly people often sit outside the front door so as to enjoy the life in the village.

simple, vertical-board construction, though somehow they are never very obvious as they are normally left open the whole time. Sometimes a bead curtain is hung to take the place of a door, screening the room while at the same time letting the air through.

Fabrics and window treatments

Fabrics, which have never been used very lavishly in the humbler Mediterranean homes, tend to be quite straightforward and sometimes even naive. Peasant embroidery has been an influence for border pattern motifs and fresh all-over floral designs. Checks and stripes of all kinds would look right in the Mediterranean house. Plain fabrics work well, especially if they are made from thick hand-woven wools, cottons or cotton blends. Avoid rich or silky fabrics and choose instead hard-wearing naturals which will stand up to rough treatment and frequent washing. Colours that look right are bright white, reds and blues.

Windows in the Mediterranean house are always small. Designed to keep out the sun, providing an air inlet rather than a view, they are usually simple and wooden-framed. Shutters are often used either inside or out; they are considered to be part of the window treatment and not simply added as an afterthought or decoration.

A window set into a thick wall makes its own deep recess or sill, which can be tiled or left with the same finish as the wall. These window spaces make marvellous places to store things, to display something special or to show off a plant.

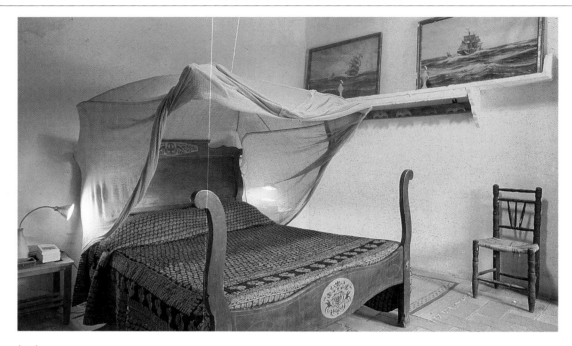

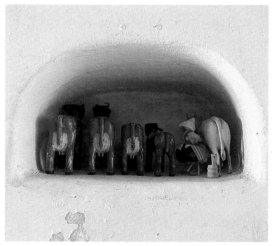

The sparseness of this room is offset by the sunny yellow walls and the surprisingly decorative quality of the wooden bed with its flimsy canopy.

Thick, thick walls allow plenty of room for small carved-out niches and alcoves which can be used for storing things or displaying flowers or collections.

If the window has shutters, curtains are not always necessary in a hot climate, though the movement of air through a light gauzy fabric or rough cotton lace has a beautifully cooling effect on a close sticky day.

Furniture

Mediterranean houses are very sparsely furnished. The furniture you do have should be cool, light and easily portable. Basket chairs and rush-seated chairs are ideal for using at a table and are easy to move from indoors to outdoors when the need arises. Benches can stay outside for meals at an outdoor table and very often make sensible and inexpensive indoor seating for a dining or kitchen table, very much in keeping with the simple Mediterranean look.

Turned or carved wood is commonly used on furniture, very often in dark timber or pale wood which has been stained. It is often quite crude but can be charming used in moderation. Simple board construction is generally used for bigger pieces of furniture, made by local carpenters. Sometimes furniture is painted but there is virtually no decoration. The effect you want is a simple naivety, not clever sophistication.

Mediterranean homes have very little built-in furniture, and storage is best left absolutely simple. Use open shelves where possible, and perhaps a little cupboard or two tucked into an alcove or under stairs. Baskets can contain any overspill—they can stand beside other bits of furniture or in awkward left-over spaces and swallow up all manner

These slightly arched windows are high off the ground so that they let in some sun, but not too much of it. A cushion for seating is placed on the modern white ceramic tiles.

Mediterranean people have an instinctive and uninhibited sense of colour: these colours have no obvious connection with each other, but the white, blue and apricot go well together.

These deep, narrow shelves, set in the thickness of the wall, store pottery used for eating—the most important occupation in most Mediterranean homes. The yellow and green glazed bowls have a Spanish flavour.

of bits and pieces which would otherwise need large pieces of furniture to contain them.

Warmth of the hearth

In the Mediterranean, an open fire is not really a necessity. However, in a cooler climate, an open fire could provide a suitable atmosphere if the right design is selected. Choose either a small, simple wood (or solid-fuel) burning stove, or a straightforward hole-in-the-wall fireplace, without a surround or mantelpiece. Store your logs in a big squashy basket beside the fire or stack them neatly in an alcove or special space near the fireplace. Keep a box of pine cones and bundles of herb twigs to throw on the fire for an instant scent of summer and the sea.

Finishing touches

Most of the objects in the Mediterranean home are there for a purpose—principally eating, drinking, or sleeping—and there shouldn't be a lot of extra fussy details and decoration. There might be special tools for a particular craft or job, an ancient jar used to store a local vintage of olive oil or wine, a hat or two for the fiercest midday heat, a lamp handed down for generations, or an enormous tureen kept for family feasts.

You might find some small olive-wood salad bowls, blue-and-white or yellow-and-green ceramics, or brown half-glazed pots and plates. There could be bunches of herbs in the kitchen, a basket of garlic or peppers and in the window a bottle of homemade vinegar.

Living and Relaxing

The emphasis in the Mediterranean home is likely to be on living and working rather than relaxing. Socializing often takes place outside the home simply because the climate makes it possible and there is a strong tradition of eating out and drinking in cafes, bars and tavernas.

The house plays an important but different role. It is always welcoming in a far more personal and intimate way, with cooling drinks always on offer and little snack meals such as the Spanish *tapas*, olives and bits of seafood ready for guests whatever time they arrive. There is little formality, only a sense of correct hospitality, a warm welcome and honest food and drink.

In the Mediterranean house you would enter the welcome deep shade through the open door straight into the living room. Cool floors and an open window, cold drinks and olives or nibbles would greet you. Everyone might be sitting on primitive wooden chairs ranged around the edge of the living room, with perhaps a table covered with an oilcloth and little else to fill the space—except the food, drink and friendly atmosphere.

In many Mediterranean homes the kitchen may act as the living room. With sun and warmth so plentiful, and so much of people's working lives spent outdoors, leisure time is spent in the cavern-like gloom of the kitchen or under the shade of a trellis or tree in the cooler evening. Larger homes may have a separate room indoors which

MEDITERRANEAN-STYLE LUXURY

A rather sumptuously furnished Mediterranean living room. The cave-like interior, with its thick walls and arches, low ceilings and ancient beams, bare floors and plain whitewashed walls, is very characteristic.

<u>FRAMED WINDOWS</u>
Windows create attractive 'pictures' in Mediterranean houses.
The almost universal whitewashing of interior and exterior walls,
and stained or painted woodwork are very characteristic.
This room looks beautifully cool compared with the glare
of the sun seen through the open doorway.

<u>A VIEW OF THE SEA</u>
If you live near the sea, it makes sense
to be able to enjoy the view. Here an
enormous window looks across the
silver sand to the deep ultramarine
beyond.

would be largely used for entertaining and therefore be furnished with a certain formality.

The walls will be painted white or yellow, often with a dark contrasting colour for the paintwork, such as a very deep blue-green or an egg-yellow. Woven wall hangings in bright colours may serve as decoration on the wall, or perhaps one icon or painting of local fishing boats.

Light will come in through a narrow window, probably hinging inwards in two halves, through which you can glimpse a glare of blue from the sea, or a haze of blue-green olive grove where the hills climb away from the coast.

Since there is no necessity, as in colder climates, to close doors, rooms may open off each other, divided only by a large arch or perhaps a bead or bamboo curtain (or, as often as not, coloured plastic strips these days).

Expanses of floor

Mediterranean living rooms generally have tiled floors. These might range from elegantly simple plain white glossy ceramic tiles to yellow-and-blue, yellow-and-terracotta, or blue-and-white patterned tiles. Sometimes floors are made from large slabs of local stone. A big expanse of hard floor can look rather bland, however, and you might prefer to subtly break up the vista with furniture or rugs. The aim is to make a change of texture, for example by adding a cream long-pile wool rug to a shiny cream tiled floor.

Tiles can be noisy and cold and the click of hard-soled shoes irritating, while in Mediterranean conditions of course they are bliss to pad around on with bare feet or soft espadrilles. You could recreate the feeling of space without actually using ceramic tiles, by laying a plain, pale carpet or one of the sheet or vinyl tile floorings which are available. These would all have the right look but without the drawbacks of the real thing.

Functional seating

A wooden chaise longue or old-fashioned deck chair or a simple settee with some comfortable armchairs or upright chairs of wrought iron or wood are the rule. On Spanish and Italian coasts quite heavy black iron chair and table frames are common, as is leather upholstery, perhaps with white cushions. In France wicker and wood are more common or French cafe-type folding slatted chairs with metal frames. In North African countries (Morocco and Tunisia) you might find hammocks and large floor cushions, and in Greece hand-woven rugs and cushions in cotton or wool.

Basically, in the Mediterranean-style house, seating should be functional without being luxurious. Square

ROUGH BRICKS AND SIMPLE CERAMICS
The simple, modern treatment of this Mediterranean
home creates a feeling of coolness with rough bricks
and black and white tiles, on which sit a plain wooden
rocking chair and an upright wooden settee.

shapes are better than curvaceous ones and look good covered in the checks, stripes or plains suitable for this style. Close upholstery will suit these shapes better than loose upholstery.

A generous piling up of cushions will add any comfort that might be lacking—try big square or oblong cushion shapes. Bolster cushions used either end of a simple wooden day bed would be very much in keeping with the style. Cushions are important for the extra spark of colour they add and for their softening effect on an austere room. Also, in practical terms, in a hot climate they stop you sticking to the furniture.

Sofas are often wooden-framed and low-backed with seat cushions plus loose cushions strewn along the back. Unit seating suits the Mediterranean style well. Units can be pushed back against a wall to make maximum use of the space in a small room, and they have the clean unfussy lines and strict shapes which suit this style of furnishing.

Charm and integrity

Other pieces of furniture in the living rooms should be both useful and delightful to look at. Often real Mediterranean pieces have a clumsy kind of charm but a great integrity. One large cupboard might be used to hold

A MODERN INTERIOR

Dark, sturdy beams; rough-hewn walls, painted
stark white, with windows cut into the stone; slate
floors and lots of colourful woollen hand-woven
wall-hangings are very characteristic of a modern
Mediterranean house. The overall impression is
light and cool.

everything of value in the household and, though it should be roomy, it shouldn't totally dominate a small room. The only other pieces of furniture that might be needed in a living room are one or two low tables for lamps and small bits and pieces, and perhaps an extra stool or some large floor cushions to accommodate an overspill of people.

Plain square ceramic lamp bases with very simple shades or wall lamps on metal brackets are the kinds of lighting to go for. Metal ironwork candelabra would also be suitable, or, if you can find them, hanging lamps made from wood or metal in a pretty twisty shape to take little candle bulbs or, ideally, real candles. Rustic storm lanterns and any kind of authentic oil lamp also have the right feel to them. Search for candlesticks in wood or metal and group several together—they don't have to be matching. Use these to eat by indoors or to light a corner of the room. A tray full of small, squat, cylindrical candles would look lovely lit for a special occasion.

Simple pleasures

Further decoration is probably not necessary, though a bowl of ripe peaches or nectarines, a melon and some loquats on a small table or a wide windowsill look inviting. On the floor, a large earthenware urn or vase filled with lavender or another locally grown shrub, fresh or dried, will also look pleasant and give the room a fresh smell.

Curtains of white cotton or wool may be held back from the window by a piece of string, a ribbon or even a safety pin, or tied in a loose knot during the day. If you prefer, narrowly slatted venetian blinds will help to keep the sun out during the hottest part of the day or allow its rays to slant diagonally in stripes across the floor.

A ROOM FOR VISITORS
A living room conversation corner. In many Mediterranean homes, the living room is mainly for entertaining and has a formal quality appropriate to this. Here, chairs and a small settee are deliberately arranged for conversation, with low tables ready for drinks.

CONCRETE CAVE
Stone and concrete are good materials for hot countries. They can be built into arches and painted white, and their density provides good protection from the heat. The wooden bench catches the sun through the window, while the main blast of heat remains outdoors.

ANTIQUE WINE BOTTLES

Collections of old wine bottles, whether from Mediterranean regions or elsewhere, look very suitable in Mediterranean style homes. In the 16th and 17th centuries bottles were a valuable commodity. Made to order, they were often marked with a gentleman's name or crest and would be used time and time again.

The wine bottles shown here are all made from natural 'bottle' glass. The various shades of green and brown are caused by the impurities in the raw materials, local sands and different oxides creating a regional colouring. Because bottle glass was considered the most basic type, it was also made from the cheapest materials—fine, ornamental glass was made in 'flint' glass houses. The technique has changed little from the times of the Roman Empire when, in the 1st century BC, they were making both free-blown and mould-shaped glass containers.

The wine bottle originated in England, and by the 18th century had become the standard for most European countries. Since these early pieces were confined to table use,

they were known as 'decanter bottles'. The earliest shape was like that of an onion—a squat, bulbous body with a short neck. This gradually became mallet-shaped and then more cylindrical, until by the mid 18th century the shape resembled the bottles of today.

Bottles weren't sealed with flush-fitting corks until the early 19th century. Previously, a few threads of glass encircling the neck of the bottle provided anchorage for the cork to be tied on—hence the 'string rim'.

French wine bottles were either flowerpot-shaped or flattened oval spherical shapes covered in woven rush or wicker. With increasing mechanization during the 19th century, shapes became more standardized and each wine-growing region came to favour a particular style.

Italian wine was sold in locally made pear-shaped bottles encased, like the French, in woven straw but with a woven foot so the bottle could stand upright. Dutch bottles are the most commonly found—vast quantities were exported.

FROM LEFT TO RIGHT

Free-blown cylinder bottle c.1760 *with string rim. Dutch onion-shape bottle* c.1730. *Early 19th century French champagne bottle. English onion-shape wine bottle* c.1700. *Dutch long-neck bottle* c.1780. *Bottle with tooled neck* c.1800 *with personalized seal. Mallet decanter bottle with iridescent surface* c.1735. *Half-size mallet-shape bottle* c.1740.

Cooking and Eating

Food and its preparation and cooking are of fundamental importance to the Mediterranean way of life. Based very largely on garlic, olives, tomatoes and seafood, the result is basic and often sublime. Food fills the days with pungent smells and colours which seem as much a part of the region as the landscape itself. The styles of cooking, secondary ingredients, and other details differ throughout the area, but in every case there is a vivacity and simplicity, together with a reliance on very fresh ingredients, often cooked in uncomplicated ways.

In the Mediterranean countries many meals are eaten out of the house in restaurants and tavernas, but the kitchen at home is still an important place for the preparation of everyday meals. As a room, it is often the centre of the house, and a place to bring visitors. The kitchen is fundamentally a cool, dark cavern away from the sun. It will be furnished with two important pieces of equipment: a large refrigerator/freezer and a gas or electric cooking stove.

Again, a cool, tiled floor would be practical, good-looking and authentic in a Mediterranean-style house. Although the woodwork might be painted blue in the Mediterranean, the walls are always whitewashed. Emulsion or vinyl matt paint would make a practical, modern equivalent.

Kitchen windows rarely need curtains unless the room is

SIMPLICITY OF LIFE

Rough stone walls painted white
and a smooth stone table in its natural state
epitomize the basic simplicity of life in the
Mediterranean. Colourful tableware and
fresh fruit complete the picture.

used often at night to eat in, but if the windows need dressing in some way, plain Roman blinds in the same colour as the walls would look good or very fine slatted blinds or even wooden louvred shutters. Other alternatives are coarse, peasant-style lace panels or soft muslin or cheesecloth.

Back to basics

Nothing is built-in in the Mediterranean kitchen, and the equipment is very basic. The cooker is always free-standing. Work surfaces could be thick slabs of wood, smooth and untreated, or pieces of slate, stone or marble. Another choice might be small-scale tiles set into a wooden-edged surround. These could be plain or with a simple design on them.

But in the main, free-standing furniture is more common: a panelled cupboard, rather like an *armoire* for china and glass; a free-standing table for food preparation; a chest of drawers for linens and cutlery; and hooks in the wall for hanging ladles and other implements. The kitchen is usually fairly sizeable, so these pieces should be enough without the need for 'head-height' cabinets.

Tiles hung on the diagonal look very Mediterranean, and there are many hand-made tiles, plain or decorated, which are beautifully thick and irregular and can make a spectacular splash-back behind a worktop or stove.

Choose a round sink made from ceramic (or similar-looking man-made materials), either very deep or very shallow, with pillar taps. Or put two small rectangular sinks side by side with a mixer tap in dull chrome.

STONE BUILDING BLOCKS
This basic set of shelves and sink-unit has been built from rough stone—like a dry stone wall. An unusual collection of bulbous green hand-blown glass bottles sits happily on its shelves.

<u>MEDITERRANEAN BLUE</u>

This bright blue is very popular along
the Mediterranean coast. It very much
echoes the blue outside and looks so fresh
next to white-painted walls. Figs, limes
and a melon indicate that we are in citrus
grove country.

CAVE-LIKE ARCHES
Arched ceilings give a cool, cavernous feeling to Mediterranean interiors. Here, the essential
white walls are topped by a dusky pink ceiling to give a little
softness. On the well-used, solid circular table lie bowls of produce ready
for the next meal: shallots, tomatoes, strawberries and the end of a baguette.

The simplest equipment

Cooking pots should be made from ceramic, copper, cast iron or enamelled steel. Frying pans and skillets, black and well seasoned, heavy and purposeful, will be used for fast dishes such as omelettes and certain fish recipes. Special pans might be needed for dishes such as *paella* or a Moroccan *tagine*.

Many Mediterranean dishes require much hard work during the preparation stages, with lots of pounding and chopping. A pestle and mortar would be a much-used piece of equipment, along with well-sharpened carbon-steel knives and good, solid chopping boards worn down to a perfect smoothness. There might be hanging wire baskets full of fresh lemons, onions or eggs waiting to be used, crates of tomatoes and always good olive oil to hand to enhance the plainest meal, though nowadays many cooks will use corn oil for cooking and olive oil for salad dressings.

Colourful eating

Often in Mediterranean countries, where people rise early, before the sun gets too hot, breakfast is a perfunctory affair. Midday is time for the siesta, and lunch is an important meal—sometimes the main one, but at least time to stop for a drink and a few bits and pieces to eat.

Once the day has cooled down and people have finished work, then they feel inclined to relax and have a good meal. Eaten outside, it might continue late into the night, with just the sounds of insects and the sea in the distance. An open grill or barbecue set up somewhere sheltered and

THE OLD BREAD OVEN
An old bread oven has been preserved and maintained,
almost like an altar to the past. It has a
white painted front and marine blue ceramic tiles with
a mantelpiece high above it.

permanent would be a perfect way of recreating those lazy meals of sardines grilled over scented vine twigs or rosemary, perfect fresh fruit like peaches, figs, nectarines, melons, and loaves of local bread and homely soft cheeses.

Eat it all from a wooden table covered with a brilliant cotton cloth to clash and contrast with the colourful bowls of salad, grilled peppers, watermelon or saffron rice. Use candles in bottles, small storm lanterns or covered candle holders for night-time meals and plan a campaign against any biting insects that could spoil a perfect alfresco meal.

Because the sun is always there, Mediterranean people are apt to take it for granted and are prepared to eat the midday meal indoors. This may be at a small table in the kitchen, rather like a cafe (which many private kitchens *are*) or in a separate room. In either case, a clean cotton table-cloth will be laid; chairs will be smallish and upright, possibly covered with tie-on cotton cushions.

Forget the niceties of lots of good matching crockery and cutlery. Instead, use one plate for all the savoury courses and put the bread straight on the table. Serve dry foods such as pitta bread in baskets, and the rest in large, shallow serving dishes to show off the colours and textures of the food. Keep all crockery, cutlery and glass on a solid scale so it's tough enough to withstand frequent journeys in and out of doors. Cutlery should be as basic as possible—stainless steel will do, either plain or with vividly coloured handles. Pour wine and drinks into jugs for serving at the table. Provide good-sized napkins in thick woven cottons or simple sunny ginghams. If they don't match, never mind—the food is the important thing.

Sleeping and Bathing

A cool quiet space which is suitable for midday siestas and night-time sleep is important in the Mediterranean climate. The bedroom isn't used much apart from being slept in, and so is very simply furnished. With whitewashed walls and scrubbed floorboards (or tiles if the room is downstairs), it is rather like a small, white cell.

To adapt this look to a home elsewhere, plain white or faintly colour-washed walls are peaceful, with some barrier at the window to diffuse or block out light for daytime naps. Shutters are often used for this, but many people don't like the claustrophobic atmosphere that they create and prefer a softly blowing curtain to filter a small stream of moving air into the room.

The bed can be simple, even austere, with perhaps just a good mattress on a solid wooden base or iron bedstead, or a built-in platform with a mattress on top. Rather than an elaborate bed with headboard and footboard, choose a square shape with few fussy details. This basic bed may be narrow and low, with an iron frame, or larger and more dominating in thick, chunky wood.

Fresh, plain white bed linen would be best, or perhaps a pale or bright summery colour such as sky blue, warm yellow or almond green. Neat crisp stripes or checks would also look good or a plain sheet with a strongly patterned border running right around it. Blankets, a cotton comforter or a thin duvet would be authentic, since these

TAPS STRAIGHT OUT OF THE WALL

The simplicity of this bathroom is fully in keeping with Mediterranean style. The walls are rough and white; the trelliswork cupboard doors are topped with brick, and the most basic of taps sprout straight out of the wall.

KEEPING THE SUN AT BAY
Everything here is conspiring to keep the sun at bay: the thick walls with their
solid wooden shutters; the crisp white cotton bed curtains, to reflect the heat. The delicate
bent shapes of the iron bedstead are like spiders' webs among the gossamer fabrics.

are used in the winter in the Mediterranean. Top the whole lot off with a thickly textured plain bed cover and tuck it all in neatly to produce an almost monastic look.

Other furniture in the Mediterranean bedroom is likely to be sparse. Many clothes are not necessary in a sunny climate, and, in any case, the bed takes up much of the space. A small hanging cupboard built into an alcove or the thickness of a wall or a small wooden cupboard is more usual than a wardrobe. The sun and fresh air are the only beauty treatments most people want, so fussy dressing tables are unnecessary, as is endless storage space.

A jar of flowers picked from the hillside, a hat hanging from the corner of a rush-seated chair and a little painting or religious figure in an alcove on the wall are just a few of the things that might be used as a decoration. For practi-

cality there should perhaps be a painted wrought-iron chair to lay a few clothes on. A small woven or sheepskin rug by the bed would also be typical.

A little ceramic hand basin fixed by brackets to the wall is convenient in a bedroom. Towels can hang over the brackets, and a small white or metal framed mirror can hang over the basin.

A functional bathroom/shower room

The bathroom is a room which, though used frequently, will not be lingered in. Regular showers after salty swims and as a refreshing start to the day are quicker and more efficient than a bath, and are also a good way of cooling down after long exposure to the sun. Although you might find a bathtub in a Mediterranean bathroom, a shower

MOCK-PEASANT LOOK

Here is a tongue-in-cheek 'peasant' interior, created with carefully painted 'rough plaster-work'. The primitive wooden bed has a piece of added decoration on top. The chair and the bedside table, though 'real', fit in very well.

WELL-FURNISHED ROOM

For the Mediterranean this room seems almost overfurnished, but the beams, white paint and bedcover, and the shelf are all typical.

cubicle would be more typical. Ideally, build it as part of the bathroom, with fully tiled solid walls. Or you could even make the whole room the shower, with perhaps a hand basin as well, and the water can drain into a hole in the floor. Wooden duckboards are a necessary item in this kind of arrangement, as is efficient ventilation.

If you choose to have a bathtub, then make it small and white, either free-standing or built-in against a wall, with panelling made from the materials used elsewhere, such as tiles or stone.

Many Mediterranean bathrooms will have been plumbed into already existing rooms quite recently. Existing materials may be perfectly suitable for the floor, since they dry out quickly in the heat. If the room is on the ground floor, it may already have its own stone or tile floor.

Bleached, scrubbed wood of any kind looks right on the bathroom floor, like the pieces of driftwood washed up on the shore that are smooth and almost silver from the action of salt air, water and sun.

A tiny bathroom could be tiled throughout but choose plain white except perhaps for a deep blue line or border. A simple idea such as this demands high-quality workmanship for it to look very good. If tiling throughout is not possible, a roughish plaster finish above the tiles would be an acceptable alternative. Paint it white or yellow ochre.

The details in this kind of bathroom should be functional rather than fussy—not rows of bottles and lotions, but square chunks of olive oil soap, big scratchy brushes and natural sponges. Plain white or brightly coloured towels look right, or even big jolly beach towels.

Inside meets Outside

When the sun shines and the air is warm, who can resist being out in the open? Many day-to-day activities can be done outside. It is a whole lot easier and much more pleasant to sit and top-and-tail a basket of French beans at a table outdoors, watching the world go by, or to chop a handful of fragrant herbs just picked from the garden.

What you need in order to make this possible is a shaded area right up against the house, near a door. It then becomes virtually another room to the house, but one which is open to the sky and sunshine. Many houses in very hot countries are built around a courtyard which is used as an extension to all the rooms in the house. This means that, except when the sun is high in the sky (and everyone goes indoors for siesta) there is always shade somewhere in the courtyard. But a small terrace area is also suitable. It should be paved with brick, stone or tiles, which can be swept easily and make a good flat base for furniture and pots and plants.

A table which can stay outside is the first essential, to hold drinks and glasses. It can be a simple solid-wood table (or even a piece of wood laid on a couple of trestles), perhaps with benches either side. A metal-topped cafe table or something really durable such as a marble top sitting on solid cast-iron legs would also be in keeping. For seating that is appropriate to the Mediterranean style, use little upright wooden kitchen chairs. Avoid reproduction metal

WIDE DOORS INVITE FRESH BREEZES

The wide opening between the interior of this house and its courtyard creates a feeling of coolness. Crumbling stucco, a daubed-on pink interior and the dark green painted doors and window frames are all very Mediterranean.

WIDE EXPANSE OF SHADE

Crazy paving continued right away from the house and covered with a roof of vines gives welcome shade when the sun is at its hottest. It leads out on to an uncovered paved area where lizards can bask in the hot sun. A generous table in the shade invites the household to eat meals there rather than in the cool gloom of indoors.

A LONG, COOL COURTYARD

The walls of more than one building provide the basis for a patio garden filled with plants, pots, comfortably shabby garden chairs and a stone fountain. Concrete slabs provide a suitable material underfoot.

HOMELY RETREAT

Buttresses in the wall provide a division between these two rooms, since doors are not so necessary in a balmy climate. The furnishings create a pleasant, homely atmosphere.

OPEN-PLAN AIRINESS

A seemingly unsupported staircase leads upstairs from the outside door in this
open-plan interior. The space under the stairs has been used as a book-case.
Walls and the side of the staircase have been roughly painted white,
while the concrete floor remains a nondescript dust colour.

FLYING STEPS

Slabs of concrete make the steps of a 'flying' staircase. Quarry tiles support a huge plant pot and lead up a single step to a mysterious painted door in the wall.

A SHADY BOWER

In front of this house is a small, leafy bower overlooking a steep escarpment. A circular table is covered with a lace cloth, ready for a hearty meal.

chairs, which are too fussy and bright for this look. But tiny metal chairs with slats (as used in French cafes), curly wrought-iron chairs or wooden-seated benches with curly metal frames would all be suitable.

Verandas and vines

You may have a long, low house which would look right with a veranda attached to it. Verandas are usually roofed and sometimes partially enclosed, so they provide more shelter than a terrace; but they are a bit limiting as to what you can fit on to them and are not so good for growing plants on as an open part of the garden.

A little paved area for outside living is often slightly screened for privacy. This can be done with pieces of trellis and a few wooden uprights and cross pieces. If you need to create some shade for days which are too bright and sunny, you could make a kind of roof in a similar way. The aim is to grow a few climbing plants which will twine up and cover the structure, making enough shade for blazing afternoons and a little shelter on autumn evenings.

In the Mediterranean, brilliantly coloured shrubs like bougainvillea, oleander and hibiscus are often used to produce protection on the veranda or terrace, but in cooler climates it is difficult to recreate the exotic effect of these plants. However, grapevines make a delicious bower of

shade and you can watch the tiny bunches grow and ripen until it's time to pick them off. They grow rapidly and have lovely leaf shapes in a constant fresh green colour. They lose their leaves in winter, of course, but this gives you the chance to check the woodwork and clean it up.

Whatever you choose, it is best not to grow anything too rampant which will need frequent cutting back. But you could try other climbers such as *Actinidia chinensis*, with large heart-shaped leaves, or the more delicate *Akebia quinata*, which twines gracefully and has dainty cut leaves. You could also grow a summer jasmine for its heavenly scent or the very vigorous evergreen honeysuckle *Lonicera halliana* which also has a beautiful scent in the evening and with luck will attract the hummingbird hawk moth. A terrace may have a rendered wall, painted white with a ceramic tile 'shelf' at the top. This may be nearly a metre (about three feet) tall, and on it you can grow busy lizzies (*Impatiens walleriana*), geraniums and other bright, hot-weather plants.

As well as climbing plants for your outdoor 'room' you should furnish it with pots of purely decorative plants. A glossy-leaved orange or lemon tree could stand outside for the summer along with oleander and lemon verbena. In a cool climate they would probably all need protection in the winter. All your foliage houseplants could stand out on the

COOL BLUES UNDER AN ARCH

An open-plan room has been meticulously
painted in varying shades of blue. Double
doors lead on to a natural wood floor with a
blue woven rug.

terrace each summer and a fig and a peach or apricot would
be fun to grow in a pot. Grow lilies for their fragrance and
fuchsias for colour.

Vivid colours, simple flowers

With their artless style and hot colours, geraniums (or,
technically, pelargoniums) are the very essence of the
Mediterranean. Stand them in terracotta pots along a
windowsill, down a flight of steps or marching along both
sides of a pathway. For a very typical look, paint old metal
cans or any other discarded containers in brilliant colours,
especially brightest blue, and fill these with single scarlet
geraniums. Enormous terracotta Ali Baba pots also capture
the Mediterranean flavour.

Look out for the varieties of geranium designed for
growing on balconies or window boxes. These are small
plants which become smothered in flowers by the end of
the season. They need to be planted quite high up so that
their natural cascading habit is fully appreciated. Hanging
baskets should be filled with fuchsias and trailing
geraniums and then hung on a bracket sticking out from
the house, at a height at which they can be seen to
maximum advantage. White daisies in pots add a fresh
coolness to an overheated garden, and all white flowers
look spectacular at night.

Outdoor details

Evidence of the nearness of the seashore will be obvious
inside and outside the Mediterranean house. Collections of
fishing nets and floats may be on display. Large pebbles lie
strewn about or are used as door stops. Discarded mollusc
shells from gourmet meals are used as utensils or stuck on
to wet plaster as a naive kind of patchwork. Ancient
baskets which were originally used for unloading fish at a
quayside finish their life as rickety plant pot containers in a
sunny corner of the terrace. Any old worn-out basket can
be employed as an unusual container, and Mediterranean
housewives from Spain to Greece have made an art of
turning the most mundane containers into flower pots.

Outside the door of the Mediterranean home, there may
be pairs of scuffed and battered espadrilles encrusted with
silvery sand. On the outside of the house are little
decorations which contrast with the painted walls and
colourful shutters, such as hanging plant pots with yet
more geraniums or an intricate little wire or wooden bird
cage, which once held tiny brown song birds and brightly
coloured finches. Even the garden walls may have
decoration, in the form of a row of tiles set into the
concrete or stone. In the street or courtyard, a small chair
frequently provides a place for an elderly person to enjoy
the evening coolness and nod to neighbours.

COUNTRY
GARDENS

The most important feature of a country garden is the larger setting of the countryside itself, the rural backdrop, which the garden can visually 'borrow' as its own. Standards for informal country gardens are quite relaxed: mildly overgrown or dishevelled plants simply add to the charm. The presence of full sunlight is also implied in a country garden, compared to the often shaded urban plot (woodland gardens being the exception). One expects plants to grow luxuriantly in a country garden, and, provided they are chosen with care, they usually oblige. On the other hand, weather—strong winds and fierce temperatures—can be more extreme and, hence, more of a challenge. But whatever the size, locality, style or aspirations of a successful country garden, it provides an ongoing source of pleasure, for the owner/gardener, guests and passers-by alike.

COTTAGE GARDENS

The mention of cottage gardens conjures up far more than an image of a particular garden style or selection of flowers. Cottage gardens symbolize all that is lovely, uncomplicated and romantic about rural living. A cottager's lot in life was, in fact, harsh, but the idealized, sentimental version of rural life is very seductive, and many people long for a cottage garden of their own, a verdant private retreat from the 20th century.

The basic approach

A cottage garden depends for its charm on simplicity, modesty, thriftiness and a human, rather than grand, scale. Tidiness and close, enduring links with the past are also essential: old-fashioned plants, old-fashioned materials and old-fashioned features. A true cottage garden is never contrived or ruled by passing fads, whether the frenetic bedding-out schemes of Victorian times or the contemporary penchant for fiercely coloured hybrid tea roses. Space is valuable and used economically; trees support climbing plants as well as providing fruit, and vegetables and flowers cohabit. Economy, as much as necessity, is the mother of invention, and so a discarded terracotta chimney pot or white-painted tyre becomes a home for plants in the cottage garden.

Though the archetype is English, with a backdrop of a thatched, timbered cottage and the soft English countryside beyond, cottage gardens can be created in other landscapes and complement other architectural styles. It is easier to do in temperate climates than in hot ones, because traditional cottage garden plants need a period of winter dormancy. Many parts of Europe, North America, Australia and New Zealand, however, have ideal climates for traditional annuals, perennials, bulbs and woody plants.

The framework

A cottage garden is deliberately set apart from the larger agricultural landscape or wilderness. (To the city dweller, sweeping countryside views are delectable; to the true countryman, who spends his working life confronting nature, such views hold no charm.) Hedges of beech, hawthorn, holly or privet define the boundaries. Yew, rowan and holly trees often grow by the house, and though

SUNNY SUMMER COLOUR

Petunias, nicotianas, African marigolds,
rudbeckias, coreopsis, hydrangeas and
calendulas, planted informally—almost
willy-nilly—fill a modest cottage
garden with stunning but unsophisticated colour.

GLORIOUS CHAOS

Typical of many cottage gardens, this one combines
vegetables and flowers in an exuberant free-for-all.
Runner beans (originally grown for their flowers,
only later for their food value) provide a backdrop
for petunias, marguerites and annual hollyhocks.

PRIDE AND JOY

The proud owners and creators of this archetypal
cottage garden, shown in early summer. Hybrid tea,
floribunda and climbing roses rub shoulders with delphiniums,
lupins and wild, self-sown foxgloves. The mature trees
in the background complete the picture.

HOLLYHOCKS

Classic cottage-garden flowers,
hollyhocks can be treated as short-lived
perennials, hardy biennials or
half-hardy annuals. Colours range from
white and cream to pink, yellow, rose,
red and purple; and there are single and
double, or 'powder-puff' forms.

PAINTERLY APPROACH

Tiny strokes of colour weave their way
through a soothing backdrop of greenery.
Knapweed, or centaurea, *Geranium* 'Johnson's Blue'
and forget-me-nots provide a range of blues.
Oriental poppies, *Geranium* 'Wargrave Pink'
and roses add red, orange and pale pink.

RUSTIC CHARM

A rustic wooden pergola echoes the shape of
the white-painted wooden porch, and supports a pair
of climbing roses. The lawn path is delightful, but suitable only
for the lightest use. Honesty, here in
transition from purple flower to silvery
seedpod, is a classic cottage-garden plant.

<u>BOX AND BLOSSOM</u>
Tiny, scaled-down topiary balls stand sentry
either side of a white-painted cottage door. A medley of
climbing roses, including the pink 'Cecile Brunner',
are allowed to roam freely, while hydrangeas
will provide late summer and autumn colour.

they provide vertical interest and visually anchor the house to the landscape, their original purpose was more basic: to ward off evil spirits. The reason for fruit trees is obvious, and their combination of usefulness and beauty is a recurring cottage garden theme.

The path from the front door of the house to the lane divides the garden and often creates a pleasant symmetry. Herbs or flower beds lining the path reinforce the basic geometric layout. Behind these orderly beds might be rows of vegetables and fruit bushes—cottagers were nothing if not self-sufficient—or a mixture of flowers and ornamental shrubs. Climbers clothe the house walls, and clamber up and over rustic pergolas or arches.

Garden features are often scaled-down snippets from grander landscapes of the past: perhaps a single topiary bird, carved out of yew or box, and reminiscent of Elizabethan times; or a seat under an arbour harking back to medieval monastery gardens. Beekeeping is a traditional cottage-garden pursuit, and hives become modest little focal points within a setting of greenery. (White-painted wooden beehives can house garden tools instead of bees, thus earning a place in a modern cottage garden.)

A MODEST ENTRANCE

Lack of pretentiousness is a hallmark of
the cottage garden. Here, slightly weedy
gravel meanders up to the front door.
A half beer barrel makes a home for pansies,
and a few odd bricks edge a tiny bed.

GENTEEL DECAY

A weather-beaten wall forms a pleasing
backdrop for climbing roses.
The pink, white and green colour theme
is more subdued than in other cottage gardens,
but the overgrown quality is a classic cottage hallmark.

A SECRET HIDEAWAY

Half-hidden under a mass of roses and
clematis, a white-painted latticework
summer house has room enough for two.
An old brick garden wall offers shelter and
support for a range of climbers and shrubs.

<u>UP THE GARDEN PATH</u>
Here, as in many cottage gardens,
the formal symmetry of a central path
is neutralized by informal planting
allowed to overhang
and overlay the hard surfacing.

The plants

Hardiness is the main requisite of cottage garden plants, but within that category there is a wealth of possibilities. Wild flowers are always cherished in cottage gardens: foxglove, columbine, lily-of-the-valley, primrose, bluebell, cowslip, sweet violet, snowdrop and daisy. In return, winter aconite, evening primrose, greater periwinkle and barrenwort are just some of the plants that have escaped from the English cottage garden and now grow wild, and each country has its own equivalents.

There is, paradoxically, also a place for carefully bred, but never flamboyant, cultivars: sweetly scented and charmingly named garden pinks; richly and variously coloured violas; subtly patterned auriculas; and double sweet Williams and polyanthus. Imported plants slowly make their way into cottage gardens on a modest scale, as seeds, offsets and cuttings or 'slips' are traded among friends. Cottage garden sunflowers, Madonna lilies, crown imperials, tulips and clematis share this foreign origin.

New plants, however, never replace old favourites, and cottage gardens are havens for rare species grubbed up from wealthier, more 'fashionable' estates.

Herbs grown for medicinal, culinary or cosmetic use include sweet bay, lavender, rosemary, sage, thyme and rue; the many mints and members of the umbellifer family: chervil, parsley, angelica and lovage. Herbaceous perennials, though, form the backbone of a cottage garden: delphiniums, paeonies, Michaelmas daisies, stocks, lupins, iris, lady's mantle, everlasting pea, hollyhocks, campanulas.

Fragrance comes from a profusion of sources: old-fashioned Bourbon, China, cabbage and damask roses; lilac, honeysuckle, mock orange, and the modest looking mignonette. Self-seeded, slightly unruly forget-me-not, pot marigold, love-in-a-mist, feverfew and honesty are accommodated within the orderly, comfortable garden framework. Though the cottage garden is at its best in early summer, there is always something in flower, more by happy accident than design.

FORMAL COUNTRY GARDENS

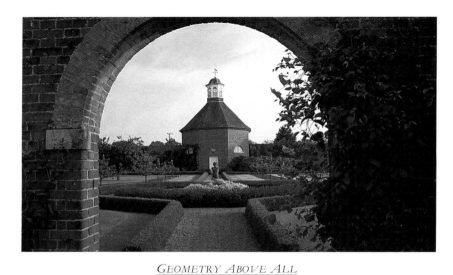

GEOMETRY ABOVE ALL
Imposing formal geometry upon
random nature is the key
to formal gardening.
Even plants lose their individuality
to create a geometric pattern.

Formal country gardens existed in ancient civilizations and, in one variation or another, have been developed to give pleasure ever since. Whether based on historic example or frankly modern, and in whichever culture or climate they occur, formal country gardens have in common a geometric layout and an obvious imposition of human will on both landscape and plants. (The great 18th century English parkland landscapes, as laid out by Capability Brown and others, are just as artificial, but they idealize nature, which is more subtle then conquering it.)

Formal country gardens can be any size, though they are often more successful on a small scale than a mammoth

one, which can make those using it feel uncomfortably dwarfed. And, although often associated with traditional formal architecture, formal gardens can also complement modern country houses, with their equally clear geometry. Lastly, formal country gardens often contain a wealth of detail, as contrast and relief to the potentially boring geometry.

To many people, formal gardens are the ultimate in pleasure gardening. Grand royal or civic examples, such as Versailles, are designed purposefully to be breathtaking, with their majestic scale and intimations of endless wealth and power. Even smaller formal gardens, such as the tidy gardens of Williamsburg, Virginia, with every flower in place, are more reminiscent of a jeweller's art than of physically grappling with nature. Yet in spite of their aspirations and lofty commitment to perfection, formal gardens have humble origins.

In ancient Egypt, the irrigation system of straight canals created square or rectangular parcels of land, and similar subdivisions within them. Wherever water was carried by hand from a well, gardens were usually circular, with paths leading radially from the central source of water. And many medieval gardens were made within the walls of ancient ruins, which also provided roughly geometric boundaries and internal subdivisions.

Today, economic pressures create a new pragmatism, and rural development land is usually subdivided geometrically, to get the maximum number of houses on a site. Though square or rectangular gardens needn't be formal, an outer shape often suggests an inner structure: paths running parallel to boundaries, and from front door to garden gate may well intersect to dictate right-angled beds.

The basic approach

A formal garden is meant to impress when viewed from the main windows of the house, and from within the garden itself. It should also be a worthy setting for the house, which is usually the keystone of the garden's layout. Symmetry often plays a part: in the overall plan, in smaller areas or single beds. And although there may be seats, formal country gardens are traditionally meant to be seen more than lived in—no children's climbing frames, clothes lines or barbecues can be cheerfully accommodated!

Rough terrain is less suitable for a formal layout than flat land, on which an uninterrupted pattern can be set out. Level changes in one direction, however, allow balustraded terraces and steps, themselves great elements of formal progression. The Renaissance Italians were masters of carving formality out of steep hillsides, using phenomenal earthworks, massive retaining walls, grand staircases and water cascades.

The geometry in a formal garden may be markedly three-dimensional: avenues of trees; pleached *allées*, or

THE GRAND MANNER

Formal stone steps and balustrades, in the Italian manner, have an imposing presence. The effect is softened, however, by the presence of lawn daisies, aubrieta and even the odd dandelion.

FORMALITY WITH A VIEW

The rugged distant mountains form an extraordinary contrast to this formal terrace, with its decorative tiles, statues, and plants used as carpet bedding and arrow-straight edging.

KNOT GARDEN

Lavender in flower and clipped dwarf
box create a long-lasting display, as
aromatic as it is beautiful.

TULIPS ON PARADE

Tulips, tightly packed and colour
separated, add a note of formality
to this otherwise relaxed scheme.

GREEN ON GREEN

Flowers are all but excluded from this
magnificent topiary garden, which transforms
lawn and yew hedging into pure geometry.
The wisteria in the foreground and distant
forest trees provide a softening touch.

FOUNTAINS AND FORMALITY

Immense topiary pyramids of yew add
grandeur to the formal stone pool and
fountain. Water's sound, movement
and reflective qualities make it
a natural focal point.

walkways; huge hedges creating room-like enclosures; mazes; and larger-than-life topiary of realistic or mythological creatures. On a smaller, more human scale, there are parterres and knot gardens, with their tidily clipped hedges and edgings; and colourful formal bedding-out schemes, beloved by the Victorians, and, more latterly, by City Parks Departments.

Flat geometry is created by straight or tightly curved paths criss-crossing the garden, usually in a hierarchy of widths and ending in focal points, whether fountains, statues, obelisks, gazebos, distant vistas or the entrance of the house itself. Though lawns can be a major part of formal gardens today, they are a relatively recent feature, dependent as they were upon grazing sheep (which may not distinguish between grass and ornamental shrubs and flowers), and the lawn mower, a 19th century invention.

Water, like the land, is tamed: into formal canals, pools and fountains. Garden ornaments are used as bits of architecture in the landscape, to lead the eye from one impressive view to the next or to emphasize the grandeur of the house (and by implication, the owner).

The plants

Formality extends to the treatment of plants, which often lose their identity and natural form, for the greater glory of the whole. Those that can be used to create architectural features are most associated with formal gardens: yew, box, eleagnus and holly, for clipping into hedging, or perhaps

IN SUPPORT OF ARCHITECTURE

Formal gardens and formal architecture
are mutually enhancing, the symmetry
of one reinforcing the symmetry of the
other. Here, the only hint of 'raw'
nature is the backdrop of forest trees.

for topiary; lime trees, for pleaching; and dwarf box, cotton lavender, lavender and rosemary for clipping into edging. Even plants not normally associated with formal training can be roped in to do duty: laburnum to form laburnum walks, for example, or wisteria trained, then mercilessly pruned, to form standards. Other plants trained as standards and often displayed in serried ranks of containers include bay and orange trees—status symbols *extraordinaire*, intimating orangeries for overwintering them, and skilled gardeners to keep them alive.

Colour, like form, is used with military precision. Again, the qualities of an individual flower hold no particular interest and, indeed, coloured pebbles, sand, brick dust and ground porcelain were often used to supply colour in parterres and knot gardens, in place of flowers. Today, annual and tender perennial bedding plants provide brightness, and formal rose beds offer a more permanent alternative. Even the humble vegetable can be formalized. The *potager* garden, now finding favour again, contains fruit, vegetables and herbs set out in ornamental geometric patterns, to please the eye as much as the palate.

There are no happy accidents of unplanned colour associations in a rigidly formal garden; no self-sown seedlings kindly allowed to reach flowering and fruition in the wrong place; no strays from the wild to turn a blind eye to. On the other hand, there is an enormous feeling of pride, not only in being part of a long historical tradition, but also in having absolute control over nature.

EDWARDIAN COUNTRY GARDENS

<u>*LARGESSE AND LUXURY*</u>
In Edwardian times, land and labour were
relatively inexpensive, and vast expanses
of neatly clipped lawn and perfectly kept
flower borders were de rigueur, for both
suburban and country houses.

Although the Edwardian era, spanning from 1901 to 1910, was brief, it yielded one of the most delightful garden styles. At their best, Edwardian gardens combine, within a formal layout, the modest charm of a cottage garden, a romantic love of nature and an honest respect for plants and people. Edwardian gardens, like all gardens, reflect the aspirations and lifestyles of the time. And Edwardian life, for the middle classes anyway, was elegant and comfortable, though not wantonly opulent. Money murmured, not shouted, and a garden was there to be enjoyed as well as admired.

For some people, the Edwardian garden is nostalgic, representing a time when land and garden labour, both of which an Edwardian garden demands, were cheap and freely available. For other people whose main acquaintance with the period is through nostalgic books, it is a pleasant daydream or distant goal. And though the period is named after an English king and its greatest exponents were English gardeners—Gertrude Jekyll and William Robinson—similar gardens can be found throughout the Western world, dating roughly from that time or lovingly created since. (Miss Jekyll herself designed gardens as far afield as America and France, using vernacular plants and building materials.)

CONTROLLED WILDERNESS

Within a usually formal layout, there was
room for a 'wild' garden. Here, foxgloves,
poppies, euphorbias and daisies mingle
happily with one another.

WISTERIA WALKWAY

Iron framework pergolas, whether trained
with laburnum, fruit trees or, as here,
wisteria, add a touch of romance to the
Edwardian garden scene.

THE SPRING GARDEN

Seasonal gardens were a frequent feature
in Edwardian times. Here ferns, wild alliums
and trilliums combine with the fresh green
of unfolding leaves to create a perfect scene.

TOUCHES OF FORMALITY

Grand formality, austere and imposing,
was generally reduced to a more human
scale. Here, a stone urn nestles among
the greenery of a little woodland glen.

The basic approach

An Edwardian country garden usually has a clearly defined
layout, dividing the garden into separate but interconnecting areas, each with a specific purpose, theme or focal
point. The high hedges and walls which mark out the
garden boundaries and the 'rooms' within also give the
garden a coherence and comfortably human scale, as well as
providing neutral backdrops for various floral displays.

The Edwardian garden is a setting for its house, the
various axes of which generally determine the garden's
main paths and, hence, the layout. (Many Edwardian
houses and gardens are asymmetrical, with symmetrical

'mini-gardens' set in the larger scheme.) But the garden
also has a life and character of its own. While strictly formal
gardens steamroll over any individuality or natural quirk of
a site, such as a dell or spinney, Edwardian gardens incorporate, or even enlarge, them to best advantage.

This juxtaposition of formal geometry and informal
features gives the Edwardian garden its special character. A
formal rectangular pool, surrounded by topiary and potted
lilies, may reflect the facade of an Edwardian house; elsewhere in the garden, hidden from general view, a small
stream may flow through banks of planted primulas. Both
are equally important. Enough land to separate one feature

A CELEBRATION OF SPRING
Camellias, a flowering cherry and
the very last of the daffodils
create a pleasant spring garden,
enjoyed perhaps one month of the year,
and visited again in a year's time.

THE ALL-WHITE GARDEN
White tulips and spiraea, set against
a background of greenery, form a tiny,
'colour-coded' garden. Silver and grey
gardens, blue gardens, pink and red gardens,
and yellow gardens were equally popular.

from another is also vital; small gardens that include such a multitude of focal points in one space are frenzied, not Edwardian!

The hard landscaping takes its style and combination of materials—generally local stone, wood and bricks—directly from the house. There is a terrace, on which tea can be served and from which the garden can be viewed; and networks of retaining walls and free-standing walls, steps, paths and minor terraces. There are also innumerable little garden buildings such as summer houses, lodges, gazebos, boat houses and shelters. The craftsmanship is excellent, but sturdy and rural rather than classical: dry stone walls and pleasant brick, tile or stone copings, rather than rusticated stonework and balustrades. There is a touching attention to detail: the brick patterns in a path, the decorative inclusion of a millstone in paving, a viewing hole cut through a garden wall. And Edwardian garden furniture, much of which is reproduced today, is as comfortable as it is attractive.

The living picture

For many Edwardians, creating a garden was a skill akin to creating a painting. Though there are no 'picturesque' follies or other instant ruins dotted around for moody contemplation, the Edwardian garden does contain a series of pleasant, 'living' pictures. Again, land was plentiful enough to allow for a winter garden, a spring garden and, as its zenith, a fabulous herbaceous border in summer. Various beds, borders, walkways, pools and pergolas are planted so that there is something at its best at any time of year. And there are beckoning views: a doorway cut through a garden wall may line up exactly with a second and third doorway cut through parallel, distant garden walls. There is always something more to see and somewhere else to go.

The plants

Hardy plants—trees, shrubs, perennials, biennials, annuals and bulbs—form the basis of an Edwardian garden, partly as a reaction to the tender bedding-out schemes that so captivated Victorian gardeners. Edwardian gardens are generally not collectors' or botanists' gardens, with rare plants grown regardless of their visual merit or capricious needs. They are gardeners' gardens, reflecting the fact that the owner often designed the garden and worked enthusiastically alongside the gardener. Plants are chosen and arranged to frame views, to create attractive scenes and places to sit, and to provide drifts of colour and scent.

Edwardian colour schemes are also a reaction against their Victorian predecessors, who strove exclusively for

HEDGING ONE'S BETS
Tall yew, hornbeam, beech,
box or holly hedging was often used to divide the
Edwardian garden into separate 'rooms'.
It also provided backdrops for flower beds and
focal points, such as this charming statue.

ever purer and more strident floral hues. Pale colours, whites, grey and silver foliage, and masses of cooling greenery are used with the same controlled enthusiasm as reds, purples, magentas and stinging yellows. (The single-colour bed, such as the white garden or grey and silver garden, is an endearing Edwardian feature, much used today.) Treating foliage as a positive asset—hosta, fern, yucca, euphorbia and bergenia, for example—is another lovely legacy from the Edwardians.

Plants soften the appearance of the architecture and hard landscaping, overspilling pavings, self-seeding in dry stone walls or tumbling over terraces. Roses—old, new and wild—climb and ramble or stand to attention in formal beds. They are trained over arches, up pergolas and poles and along rope or chain loops, to form living swags.

Walled kitchen gardens contain espaliered and fan-trained fruit trees, and tender peaches, nectarines and grapes in separate greenhouses. (Heating was as cheap as land and labour.) Vegetables filled neat beds, and a right-angled path system gave easy access and an excuse for flower borders each side.

Perfect velvet lawns form the foreground in many Edwardian garden pictures, but are for relaxation and use: for garden parties, for games of tennis and croquet, and for children's picnics. These gentle pastimes, in turn, add their own colour and particular nuances to the Edwardian scene.

FAIR WEATHER
COUNTRY GARDENS

<u>*HEAT AND LIGHT*</u>
Ancient olive trees, cypress, and
sun-loving silver-leaved plants
form the bulk of this fair weather garden.
Dimorphothecas, or African daisies,
add bright splashes of orange.

The absence of hard frost is perhaps the most important climatic factor in a garden. Though urban gardens in cold climates may be frost-free because of shelter and latent heat retained in pavements, walls and buildings, shade is a frequent side effect. Country gardens, with their open spaces, can respond more dramatically to an unending supply of relative warmth and sunlight.

This can be seen not only in the plants grown, but in the layout, the furnishings—a frost-free country garden really is an extension of the house—the treatment of water, and the relationship with the larger landscape beyond. Whether a frost-free country garden is in the Mediterranean,

southern or west-coast America, the Antipodes or those few parts of Britain favoured by the Gulf Stream, it shares with others maximum utilization of a genial climate, while keeping its own cultural identity.

The basic approach

The transition from house to garden is often more generous and less abrupt than in cooler climates: the wide verandas and porches of the pre-Civil War American South; the loggias of Italy; and the endless plate-glass windows, sliding doors, big wooden decks and terraces of California. (This California style, a complete fusion of

ORCHARD GARDEN WITH A TWIST
Instead of apple trees, olive trees surmount
a carpet of wild spring flowers,
including bright-blue borage.
A backdrop of rosemary in flower
completes the sun-filled scene.

architecture and landscape architecture, is now an international vernacular for modern homes in hot climates, and examples can be found all over the world.)

Perhaps the one exception is country gardens in extremely hot, arid places. Here, tiny slits of doors and shuttered windows keep the heat and fierce sun out.

A certain informal dustiness is part of the language of the Mediterranean country garden; sun-baked earth offers somewhere to park a car, play *boule*, or set up a table and chairs and sit drinking *pastis*. It is also a sensible admission that there is no point fighting the greater dustiness at large.

The English frost-free garden usually retains its politeness, lawns, and traditional tidy layout. It is a green and pleasant place, with the choice of plants often the only indication of the favourable climate.

Fair weather gardens are lived in, as well as viewed from indoors. Frequent cooking, dining and entertaining outdoors are taken for granted. Easy access to the kitchen is as important as access from the living room; and there is

always hard, level surfacing, whether stone, concrete, wood, brick, glazed tiles, baked earth or gravel. Night illumination, ranging from sophisticated built-in spotlights to old-fashioned 'fairy-light' candles, is the *sine qua non* of summer evening drinks parties.

Sun and shade

Shade becomes a valuable asset, the equivalent of a sunny, sheltered spot in a cool garden. When not provided by trees, it is created: gazebos and summer houses in Britain; the eccentric grottos of Italy; and, universally, leafy bowers, covered walkways and verandas. More transient shade comes from awnings and umbrellas, which can respond in a moment to changes of weather.

Colour seen in bright sunlight can be more intense than that in overcast skies, without appearing inappropriate or jarring. As well as colour contributed by flowers, such as bougainvillea in all its hues, there is the colour from hard landscape elements. The turquoise-blue swimming pool

PAINTING WITH PLANTS

Drifts of soft colour, reminiscent of
Monet's paintings of water lilies, fill
this hot, sunny bank. Veronica, punctuated
with lilies, creates a sinuous curve
through artemisia and various herbs.

ON THE TERRACE

Terracotta pots filled with lemon trees,
a sun-faded facade hung with wisteria,
and shuttered windows embody the essence
of fair weather gardens, and fair weather
entertaining out-of-doors.

VIEWS FROM THE GARDEN

Whether a sun-baked distant hillside or
soft green fields, the benefits of such a
backdrop permeate a country garden.
Here, rosemary in flower and a gnarled olive tree
add foreground interest.

POTTED PLEASURES

Evergreen oleander, almost as attractive out
of flower as in, fills classical terracotta
pots in a sunny courtyard.
The heat reflected off the walls and cobbled paving
ensures a good crop of flowers later on.

that looks depressing in cool, grey climates, for example, becomes genuinely inviting in a hot one. Even white is more intense under a hot, clear sky. It loses any trace of greyness and assumes the brilliance of light itself, whether in white rock roses or white-rendered buildings.

The plants

Palm trees, used as low-growing ground cover or lofty spires, instantly indicate the absence of hard frost. There are also silvery olives, eucalyptus, cork oak, ilex, cypress and sweet bay, and a wealth of flowering trees.

Hot, dry climates favour succulents—each one, a self-serving water tank for 'personal' use in drought. The aloes, yuccas and cacti grow to enormous proportions and flower here. On a smaller scale are the charming little mesembryanthemums and hottentot figs, with their bright, daisy-like flowers that open only in full sun, and the ever-present geraniums (technically pelargoniums).

Scent is perhaps no more powerful than that in an English rose garden in high summer, but it has a heady, exotic quality. Oleander, orange and lemon trees, mimosa, French lavender, jasmine, *Pittosporum tobira* and, in the evening, the penetrating scent of datura, or angel's trumpet, provide flowers and fragrance in equal measure. In Mediterranean climates, the rich and slightly pungent scent of maquis often underlies the sweeter scent of garden plants.

Spring can be as colourful as, or more colourful than, summer. There are species of spring-flowering iris, crocus, narcissus, anemone, hyacinth, allium, scilla, grape hyacinth and tulip that grow wild in warm climates. In some gardens, native plants are welcome; in more sophisticated ones, they are excluded in favour of cultivars. In any case, cultivated plants often make their way eventually into the native flora. Pomegranate, for example, is now naturalized in walls, hedges and rocky spots throughout the Mediterranean, as the fuchsia is in the soft, mild Irish climate.

Water

Water is treated in several ways in fair weather gardens, but always with respect; the hotter and drier the climate, the more respect is accorded to it. As well as the ubiquitous swimming pool—a sign that one has found favour with Mammon as well as the weather—small stone wells and fountains can dominate a whole garden, with their soft sounds and refreshing intimations of coolness. Likewise, formal water courses, channels and bubbling fountains, such as those found in Spanish Islamic gardens, recirculate a tiny amount of water again and again, deriving from it maximum effect and satisfaction.

WOODLAND, WATER AND MEADOW GARDENS

SYMPHONY IN GREEN
Bamboo, ferns, wild grasses, weeds
and forest trees make an idyllic
composition, complete without a
single flower. Though seemingly wild,
such a garden needs careful management.

Trees, water and rough grass can be incorporated into any garden. In urban and suburban surroundings, such elements tend to be used formally, even preciously, simply because space is at a premium. (Informal water-features in city gardens somehow never ring true, and small areas of rough grass almost always look scruffy.)

Country woodland, water and meadow gardens, with their generous scale, invite a more informal approach. The main elements can be natural, fortuitous features, such as a stream running through a water meadow, or a stand of mature oak, centuries old. They can also be contrived, such as a clump of quick-growing birch planted specifically to shelter spring flowers, or an artificial pond or water course. With careful siting, design, and choice of plants, these 'man-made' gardens can be made to look natural, and in this, the countryside setting inevitably helps, as does the passage of time.

Woodland, water and meadow gardens are sometimes referred to as wild gardens. This enchanting bit of poetic licence implies that they are allowed to run wild. In fact, successful woodland, water and meadow gardens are highly managed. The plants cultivated are hardy and largely self-sufficient, however exotic their origin, but controlling bramble and bracken in woodland gardens,

A combination of cultivated and wild plants
intermingle, creating a romantic setting
for this classical folly. Variegated
dead nettle, polygonum and valerian
fight it out in the foreground.

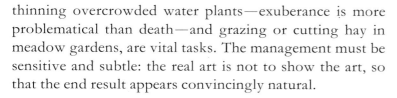

PEACEFUL GROVE

In this grove of trees is a placid stretch
of water. A charming small pavilion
with white-painted columns and a
filigree dome stands unobtrusively on
an island in the middle.

thinning overcrowded water plants—exuberance is more problematical than death—and grazing or cutting hay in meadow gardens, are vital tasks. The management must be sensitive and subtle: the real art is not to show the art, so that the end result appears convincingly natural.

Woodland garden

The best woodland gardens are created in dappled light. They are orchestrated so that each plant gets the light it needs at the right time, and one display follows another in pleasant succession. Deciduous trees, such as oak, birch and hazel, are leafless when winter- and spring-flowering plants are most active. In turn, these become dormant when the trees' own leaves unfurl. The autumn leaf fall is a natural mulch, protecting the plants beneath in winter, and providing an ongoing supply of nutrients.

Some plants, such as ivy-leaved cyclamen and lily of the valley, actually prefer rough woodland to a nurtured garden. Others, such as shrubby honeysuckle and winter heliotrope, have deliciously scented flowers but are otherwise unruly-looking or rampant: ideal qualities for a 'wild' garden.

The choice of plants varies according to locale, but traditional temperate-climate favourites include snowdrop and winter aconite, followed by primrose, alpine anemone and bluebell. Clearings between trees are as important as trees, and in sheltered clearings, such exotic beauties as Himalayan blue poppy and the giant lily, *Cardiocrinum giganteum*, thrive, as well as the humbler foxglove, fern and Solomon's seal. Shrubs and climbers have a role to play: laurel and rhododendron provide evergreen foliage and low-level shelter; honeysuckle, daphne and azaleas provide fragrance. Woodland garden plants should grow in clumps and drifts, the smaller plants in tens and hundreds. If happy, they naturalize, increasing their numbers, and your pleasure, of their own accord.

Water garden

Though formal, sterile water features have a place in grand schemes, the partnership of plants and water makes informal country water gardens particularly enchanting. Light is the third partner, essential both for plants and reflections. Whether a lake, stream, pond, ornamental pool or drainage ditch, water has enormous potential, and even a bog can provide a home for treasures.

Many native water plants have the charm of cultivars, and are worth cultivating. (Given time, they tend to appear, without any help from a gardener, in suitably wet

A WEALTH OF GREENERY

Curtains of mahonia in the foreground add
drama to the trio of religious statues,
hidden in a woodland glen. The wide range
of leaf shape, size, texture and tone
creates a rich tapestry of green.

THE PIPES OF PAN

Half-concealed by foliage, a joyous statue
of Pan adds an element of surprise to this
woodland scene. The pink pelargoniums in
the foreground are an equally unexpected,
and equally pleasant, touch.

ON THE ROCKS

A background of trees and an informal,
laissez-faire approach to plants
intermingling results in an unusually
relaxed and natural-looking rock garden,
devoid of all suburban overtones.

LADY OF THE WATER

Water and waterlilies are almost
inseparable, in the mind of a gardener. Here,
a pure-white form displays an innocent beauty
perhaps missing from more stridently
coloured varieties.

MEADOW GARDEN

High on a hillside, rough meadow grass and
lawn daisies embody the best of both worlds:
nature controlled but controlled gently, so
that the beauty and modest charm of native
plants can be appreciated to the fullest.

places!) In Britain, for example, there is marsh marigold;
sweet flag; yellow iris; water forget-me-not; water violet;
water mint; flowering rush; and yellow and white water
lilies. Other countries and climates have equally attractive
equivalents.

If space allows, traditional waterside trees, such as
willow and alder, can be grown, as well as bamboos and
coloured-barked dogwoods, which are doubly dramatic
when reflected in water. There are exotic hostas, primulas,
astilbes, gunneras and waterlily hybrids for the con-
noisseur.

The wildlife of a country water garden can be as
enchanting as the plants: dragonflies, toads, frogs, newts,
fish and water fowl. Garden birds often stop by for a bath
and wild mammals may put in a fleeting appearance.

In an artificial water garden, any hint of plastic or
fibreglass must be concealed. Turf might meet water in a
gentle overlap, or overhanging paving stones hide the
transition. Plants such as creeping Jenny, equally happy in
soil and water, make ideal camouflage. Lastly, somewhere
comfortable and dry to sit nearby lets you enjoy the fruits
of your labour, if only for a few minutes in passing.

Meadow garden

The approach is similar to that of a woodland garden, but
rough turf replaces trees and shrubs, and full sunlight
replaces light shade. In both, sequential drifts of colour are
the ultimate aim. Throwing handfuls of bulbs on the
ground, and planting them where they rest, is one trick;
scattering pebbles, and planting perennials where each
falls, is another. Bulbs might include fritillary, spring and
summer snowflake, daffodil, poet's narcissus, and autumn-
flowering colchicum. Perennials might include camassia,
cranesbill and cowslip. Broadcast seed of wild poppy,
chamomile and buttercup inevitably germinates and grows
in the most suitable place. The aim is not to cosset difficult
plants, but to match plants, whether wild or cultivated,
with the particular environment, so they grow and
multiply with minimum help.

Half-way between woodland and meadow is the orchard
garden, which combines rough grass with widely spaced
fruit trees, and perhaps, offers the best of both worlds.
Clematis and roses are trained up the trees, which
themselves flower and fruit in season, and low-growing
flowers form a pretty carpet right through the year.

INDEX

The publishers would like to thank the
following photographers and picture libraries
for supplying photographs and material
for use in this book:

Arcaid
Brigitte Baert
Peter Baistow
Tim Beddow
Guy Bouchet
Linda Burgess
Camera Press
Edifice/Darley
Edifice/Lewis
Esto Photographic
EWA Library
Michael Freeman
Christine Hanscomb
Robert Harding
Pat Hunt
Tim Imrie
Simon McBride
Maison Marie Claire
Bill Mason
Chris Mead
Michael Boys Syndication
Tania Midgeley
Derry Moore
The National Magazine Company Ltd.
Clay Perry
Ianthe Ruthven
S & O Matthews
Christian Sarramon
Michael Skott
Jessica Strang
Ron Sutherland
John Vaughan
Weldon Trannies
Jeremy Whitaker
Tim Woodcock
The World of Interiors